INTERNATIONAL
BUSINESS
COMMUNICATION

D1416276

INTERNATIONAL
BUSINESS
COMMUNICATION

David A. Victor
Eastern Michigan University

HD
2755.5
.V53
1992

■ HarperCollins*Publishers*

CACO254

INDIANA-
PURDUE
LIBRARY
WITHDRAWN
NOV 12 1999
FORT WAYNE

Sponsoring Editor: Melissa A. Rosati
Project Editors: Shuli Traub/Brigitte Pelner
Design Supervisors: Dorothy Bungert/Molly Heron
Cover Design: Circa 86, Inc./Brian Molloy
Production Manager/Assistant: Willie Lane/Sunaina Sehwani
Compositor: Digitype, Inc.
Printer and Binder: R. R. Donnelley & Sons Company
Cover Printer: The Lehigh Press, Inc.

For permission to use copyrighted material, grateful
acknowledgment is made to the copyright holders on pp. 265–
266, which are hereby made part of this copyright page.

International Business Communication
Copyright © 1992 by HarperCollins Publishers Inc.

All rights reserved. Printed in the United States of America. No
part of this book may be used or reproduced in any manner
whatsoever without written permission, except in the case of brief
quotations embodied in critical articles and reviews. For
information address HarperCollins Publishers Inc., 10 East 53rd
Street, New York, NY 10022.

Library of Congress Cataloging-in-Publication Data

Victor, David A., 1956–
      International business communication / David A. Victor.
          p.   cm.
      Includes bibliographical references and index.
      ISBN 0-673-46091-6
      1. International business enterprises — Communication systems.
2. International business enterprises — Social aspects.
3. Intercultural communication.   I. Title.
HD2755.5.V53   1992
658.4′5--dc20   91-25753
                                                                        CIP

7 8 9 10-DOC-01 00 99 98

For Cindy and Megan

Contents

Preface

International Business Communication sets forth a comprehensive system for conducting business communication across cultures. The premise of this book is that students and practitioners need an approach to international business communication that enables them to ask the right questions in a multicultural environment. *International Business Communication* provides a framework for formulating such questions when assessing the role cultural differences play in any international business interaction.

Business communication is no longer limited by national boundaries. Because we live in an increasingly integrated world economy, circumstances in one nation bear directly on business decisions made in another. Indeed, almost no other area of business has grown as rapidly as global trade. Most of the world's large corporations conduct a sizable portion of their business abroad. Even when businesses choose not to compete outside their home base of operations, they find that their competitors come from abroad or that their employees have immigrated from other parts of the world. As a result, more businesses need familiarity with the people and practices of other countries than ever before.

The ability to compete in the world economy is arguably the single greatest challenge facing business at the end of the twentieth century. No business, regardless of national base, is exempt. Globalization is as much an issue in Detroit as in Bombay, in Frankfurt as in Tokyo. Few things, in turn, are more important in conducting business on a global scale than skill in communication, because few other areas of business practice depend so much on an understanding of the cultural heritage of the participants. Communication and culture are inextricably intertwined. Indeed, culture itself is one form of communication, as

Chapter 1 describes. Consequently, the study of cultural differences and similarities so essential to international business success is largely inseparable from the study of international business communication.

This book's central premise is that business students and practitioners can learn the skills needed to conduct international business communication in any culture. Admittedly, teaching people skills and concepts for communicating effectively in the global workplace is difficult. Global business communication demands flexibility and personal judgment. Still, the LESCANT model described in this book encourages the individual to assess the specific needs of any international (or domestic multicultural) business interaction, by isolating and evaluating those aspects of culture most likely to affect communication in a specifically business setting. These aspects, each discussed in a separate chapter, are language, environment and technology, social organization, contexting, authority conception, nonverbal communication, and temporal conception.

While it would be impossible in a single course or a single book to provide all the information needed on any foreign culture to conduct effective business communication, this book provides a framework for asking the right questions for a starting point. In this respect, this book is unique. It is the first work of its sort devoted wholly to international business communication.

It is no coincidence that internationalism and business communication are two of the four major areas of development that the American Assembly of Collegiate Schools of Business (AACSB) has targeted for attention during the 1990s (the other two are entrepreneurism and ethics). The need for both international training and for strong communication skills is essential, and considerable thanks are due to Robert Crane, assistant director of international affairs for the AACSB, whose advice and suggestions have proven very helpful in the focus and direction of this book.

I would also like to acknowledge and thank those who have added their perspectives and special insights to this book. The strengths of this book are shared by each of them; the errors and oversights are mine alone. My thanks for their guidance go to Joseph A. Alutto, dean of the Ohio State University College of Business; Jack R. Borsting, dean of the University of Southern California School of Business Administration, and Robert G. Hawkins, dean of the Rensselaer Polytechnic Institute School of Management. All three met with me at the AACSB Conference on Internationalization in Miami during the nascent stages of the book and contributed greatly to its formulation.

Examples of international business situations were also shared with me by the late George Morris (formerly vice president of labor relations for General Motors) and my good friend Stefan Umstätter (sales and marketing training administrator for Germany, BMW). I would also like to thank my father, I. W. Victor, whose insights and

examples—taken from his experiences over the years as a leader of the
General Electric Aircraft Engine Group's work with such cultures as
the French, the Swedish, the Japanese, the British, and, most recently,
the Soviets—have added a fuller and more personal understanding of
the role of business communication in international joint ventures.
Thanks are due to both Robert S. Corredera (currently retired to South
Carolina, and formerly vice president of international operations for
Hoover Universal—now Johnson Controls—and executive-in-residence
at the Eastern Michigan University College of Business) and to Herbert
W. Hildebrandt of the University of Michigan for bringing to my
attention the importance of intercultural communication in a business
setting in the beginning years of my research. Both of these men—
through their words and their examples—encouraged me to pursue the
topic more thoroughly, for which I remain grateful.

My appreciation also goes to Tom Glynn-Jones (St. Andrew's
House, England, and formerly of British Petroleum), Chad Hilton
(University of Alabama), Mohan Limaye (Colorado State University),
and Gary Shaw (College of William and Mary) for their insightful
readings and lengthy discussions on the manuscript. For help with
several idiosyncratic expressions in French, I thank J. Sanford Dugan in
the Department of French at Eastern Michigan University. Similar
thanks go to John Schmale for help with German idioms. The funding
of research assistance from Ray Schaub and Geoff Voght of the Eastern
Michigan University World College, and conference travel support
from both the World College and Ray Hill, management department
head at Eastern Michigan University, have aided in making this a
stronger book. My thanks also to Stewart L. Tubbs, dean of the Eastern
Michigan University College of Business, for his support.

I am also grateful to my reviewers for all their helpful comments,
criticisms, and enthusiasm. I would like to thank: Tom Glynn-Jones, St.
Andrews House, Surrey, England; Judy F. West, University of
Tennessee at Chattanooga; Mohan Limaye, Colorado State University;
Chadwick B. Hilton, University of Alabama at Tuscaloosa; Janet
Howard, Brigham Young University; John P. Fleming, New Hampshire
College; and Gary Shaw, College of William and Mary.

Additionally, much credit belongs to the outstanding research
provided by the Eastern Michigan University Department of
Management graduate assistants, especially Wendy Chan, Amy Kahn,
Kathy McCabe, Rajeev Nath, Susan Simmerman, Kelli Stewart, and
Paul Young. Thanks also to Karen Carter for checking citations and to
Julie Schutte for typing and especially her work on the indexes.

Much of the success of this book rests with the fine editors with
whom I have had the pleasure to work—first with Vikki Barrett at
Scott, Foresman and, following Scott, Foresman's merger into
HarperCollins, with Melissa Rosati, Shuli Traub, Brigitte Pelner, and
Maureen O'Neill. My thanks for their patience, guidance, and assistance.

Rose Butterworth, the nanny of my daughter, has allowed me the freedom and flexibility to devote myself to writing this book. For this I am deeply grateful.

Finally, my deepest thanks go to Cindy Rhodes Victor, my wife. Her assistance in putting the manuscript together, her careful scrutiny of the content of each chapter, her invaluable editing, her insight and suggestions, and her encouragement have, more than any other contribution, made this book a reality.

David A. Victor

List of Figures and Tables

INTERNATIONAL
BUSINESS
COMMUNICATION

Chapter
1

Conducting International Business Communication

*T*he way in which people communicate in a business setting varies from culture to culture. Such variation occurs at all levels of culture, whether from one corporate culture to another or one region of a country to another. These differences, however, usually are most marked among nations. Most rules of business communication, therefore, apply to one's domestic business environment; intercultural business communication requires knowledge and skills that differ from those within a culture.

Nevertheless, the basic objectives and principles of business communication are the same whether conducted domestically or internationally. The concern of business communication in all cultures is the transference, in the workplace, of one participant's message to another to facilitate standard business functions.

Poor international business communication can create major difficulties. Indeed, in a survey by David Ricks and Michael Czinkota, U.S. firms ranked communication as number 1 out of 33 major international problem areas (1979, p. 99).

What *does* change in an intercultural setting is the manner in which business communication is performed. The basic tenets understood to be effective in transferring ideas and messages in the workplace in one culture may prove entirely ineffective or even counterproductive in another culture. This book describes the behavioral factors and processes that are most likely to change in an intercultural setting.

1

THE DIRECT PLAN APPROACH: AN EXAMPLE OF CULTURE-BOUND BUSINESS COMMUNICATION

To illustrate how cultural expectations limit the way in which business communication takes place, it is worthwhile to provide an example: the so-called *direct plan* approach, based on a primary method of business communication taught in U.S. colleges and reinforced in U.S. businesses.

In the direct plan approach, key information is placed at the beginning of a message. The objective is to get straight to the point. In the United States, the direct plan approach is considered both a courtesy (for not wasting the other person's time) and a necessity (since information at the end of a business message may never be read). The technique is, however, a poor means of business communication for the majority of businesspeople outside the United States. For example, in India and in many other nations, bargaining is typical in business negotiations. One is usually expected to refuse the first offer one receives. The U.S. business-person's penchant for placing key information up front may lead their Indian counterparts in negotiations to believe that such information represents only a starting point from which to bargain.

Differences regarding the direct plan approach go beyond simple negotiations. On an interpersonal level, the use of this approach in business communication is frequently seen as brusque or rude. In Spain and a number of other countries, for instance, the U.S. direct plan approach is less likely to demonstrate a courtesy for not wasting another's time than to suggest that U.S. businesspeople dislike their Spanish counterparts so much that they wish to make any communication as short as possible. It is not that the Spanish needlessly lengthen business communication, but rather that, unlike U.S. businesspeople, they emphasize getting to know those with whom they conduct business.

Despite the differences demonstrated in this example, people are unlikely to be sensitive to the nature or extent to which business communication in one national setting is ineffective in another until an obvious blunder or rift occurs. Even if one gains experience in dealing with businesspeople from one culture, that experience remains limited in use. A French executive's knowledge of Italian business practices will probably not prove valuable in Japan, Mexico, or the United States. The rules of business communication shift with each country.

A CULTURE-GENERAL APPROACH TO INTERNATIONAL BUSINESS

Communication

Although it is impossible to know all the variations in business communication in all countries, businesspeople can prepare themselves for those experiences they are most likely to face when conducting business in another culture. In any international business exchange, it is advisable to learn as much about the other culture as possible. This book, however, does not attempt to provide a thorough analysis of the practices of any particular culture. Aside from a few culture-specific illustrations, it is intended as a guide for conducting business communication in all cultures. In other words, this book takes a culture-general approach.

A culture-general approach may, at first, seem to contradict the objectives of the book. That is, since no two cultures communicate in exactly the same way, it may not seem possible to discuss international business communication in any but the most culture-specific terms. To some extent, this is correct. The best way for people from two countries to conduct business is to examine the differences and similarities between their nations. Thus the only way for an Italian to prepare for negotiations with a Korean is to study the dynamics of Italian–Korean business communication. The difficulty here is that relatively little information exists on Italian–Korean interactions. The Italian must seek out the information on a primary research basis and learn by experience. Such an approach could lead to ineffective or even failed business efforts. Even if the Italian understood Italian–Korean business practices well, it is unlikely that his or her international dealings would remain limited to Korea.

In a global economy, therefore, it is necessary to have knowledge of a wide range of countries. Moreover, expertise in international communication and negotiation is essential for many businesspeople, not just those who go abroad. Employees of multinational corporations—even if they never leave their home countries— must deal with staff members who belong to different cultures and work in different countries.

This book focuses on the interaction between businesspeople of different cultures. No distinction is made regarding the corporate framework within which the business communication takes place. Several researchers have studied the special modifications of business communication among members within a multinational corporation (MNC), as distinct from other cross-cultural business interactions (Hildebrandt, 1973; Hulbert and Brandt, 1980; Doz and Prahalad, 1981; Mendenhall and Oddou, 1985; Bartlett and Ghosal, 1986; Varner, 1990). Admittedly, the MNC influences cultural behavior. Corporate culture acts at times as a buffer to other cultures or superimposes the culture of the home country headquarters on its employees abroad. Still, much of what this book discusses is appropriate in any cross-cultural business communication. Moreover, because of cultural heterogeneity within a nation, even people working in a wholly domestic company will probably find cultural diversity among their coworkers. The number of possible cultures involved in commercial transactions presents a dilemma for the international businessperson: to conduct business abroad effectively, business communicators must learn the specifics about a bevy of diverse cultures. This book furnishes at least a partial answer to this dilemma by providing a culture-general framework within which the business practitioner or student can learn to ask the right questions regarding culture-specific situations.

The underlying philosophy of this book is that most people in business have the problem-solving capabilities to manage cultural factors affecting workplace communication once they are given the appropriate means for interpreting them. This book, therefore, does not provide a list of answers to culture-specific questions. Instead, the reader is encouraged to ask questions aimed at obtaining enough understanding of another culture so that he or she can secure the right answers.

While this book offers examples to illustrate the way in which certain factors affect business communication across cultures, it is not intended to provide a catalogue of "do's and taboos" in international business communication. Such catalogues are at best superficial, and more likely than not, are dangerous; moreover, they tend to stereotype those from other cultures. For example, people in the United States are characterized as friendly because they are quick to use first names in business settings. Similarly, the "secret" to dealing with Arabs is reduced to never handing them documents with your left hand. If a traveler conducts business in the Netherlands, the advice is reduced to the need to be punctual.

It is not that such statements are false; rather, it is because they contain some truth that they are misleading and dangerous. Such collections of trivia are fun for the tourist or traveler abroad. However, cataloguing cultures by selected truisms has been shown to impede cross-cultural competence (McCaffrey, 1986; Beamer, 1990). When behavioral traits are isolated, as Linda Beamer notes, "communication with members of the culture is limited to the dictates of the stereotypes" (pp. 3–4).

INTERNATIONAL BUSINESS COMMUNICATION AS ETHNOGRAPHY

By asking the right questions to determine factors most likely to shift across cultures, businesspeople can observe differences and similarities and draw their own conclusions regarding the best way to accommodate cultural factors affecting business communication. In this respect, the techniques described in this book are arguably a form of ethnography. According to James Clifford, ethnography

> decodes and recodes, telling the grounds of collective order and diversity, inclusion and exclusion. It describes the processes of innovation and structuration, and is itself part of these processes. (1986, pp. 2–3)

An ethnographic approach is well suited to international business communication, which is itself concerned with order, diversity, innovation, and organizational structure. Ethnography provides a system of analysis that allows its user to overcome stereotyping by understanding the logic of the way people communicate as a function of their cultures.

For example, instead of labeling U.S. businesspeople as friendly because they move quickly to a first-name basis, readers of this book might examine the use of titles and social organization to decide precisely how much more (or less) friendly someone in the United States actually is than someone in another culture, or how much this perceived friendliness is an illusion deriving from differences in business communication.

Similarly, by closely watching the nonverbal behavior of those from another country, one can learn to ask the right questions about what certain gestures mean from one cultural environment to the next. One can judge a culture-specific nonverbal cue within the context of all nonverbal communication in that culture. Thus an individual will be less likely to run the risk of believing that the secret to conducting business in a foreign culture is to arrive at a meeting ten minutes early or to avoid a gift of yellow roses.

Finally, by remaining sensitive to differences in the way time is perceived in communicating messages, one can find out in advance of a meeting how punctuality is defined and viewed in a culture. Such sensitivity serves not only as a means of communication in its own right (whether one shows up at the right time or not) but also as an indicator of the way in which dozens of other factors related to time operate within that culture.

The ethnographic method is reductionist. The methodology laid out in this book centers, as we have indicated, on providing businesspeople with a framework for asking appropriate questions. This approach, which, in effect, acts as a *toolkit* for cross-cultural business communication, borrows from Michel Foucault's concept of ethnography:

> The notion of theory as a toolkit means (i) The theory to be constructed is not a system by an instrument, a logic of the specificity of power relations and the struggles around them; (ii) That this investigation can only be carried out step by step on the basis of reflection. (1980, p. 145)

Admittedly, Foucault, as a French anthropologist interested primarily in postcolonial ethnography, never intended the toolkit approach for use in international business communication. Moreover, ethnographers are essentially concerned with recording information about the cultures they observe. By contrast, the businessperson seeks to interpret the behavior of the people in a culture to achieve a specific end—conducting more effective transactions. Still, the use of ethnographic study for pragmatic goals is far from unprecedented. Ethnographers have conducted field studies in a host of areas with pragmatic rather than merely theoretical applications. Those examined ranged from truckers (Agar, 1985) to laboratory scientists (Latour and Woolgar, 1979). Some studies have even dealt with the ethnography of labor relations (Willis, 1981; Marcus, 1986). Cross-cultural business communication, then, can be seen as a natural extension of ethnography used as a tool in the international workplace.

THE MEANING OF CULTURE

We have frequently used the word *culture* without defining the term. The word is not easy to define. To begin with, it is unlikely that in an integrated world economy, such a thing as a pure culture, free of outside influences, exists. As James Clifford has noted, the fact that we live and act in an "ambiguous, multivocal world makes it increasingly hard to conceive of human diversity as inscribed in bounded independent cultures" (1988, p. 23).

In the early 1950s, Alfred Kroeber and Clyde Kluckhohn collected over 300 definitions of *culture* in use in their classic work, *Culture: A Critical Review of Concepts and Definitions* (1954). The number of definitions devised by researchers since then has only grown larger. Kluckhohn's own definition is useful here: "the total way of life of a people, the social legacy the individual acquires from his group" (1964, p. 24).

More recently, Glen Fisher (1988) compared an individual's acquisition of culturally determined ways of thinking and behaving to programming a computer. Fisher calls this mental programming a *mindset*, or the "differing patterns of perceiving and reasoning" (p. 2). In Fisher's conception, the programming process begins at birth:

> the infant mind is somewhat like a blank tape, waiting to be filled, and culture plays a large part in the recording process [since] . . . culture is a pretested design, a store of knowledge and an entire system of coping skills that has been crafted by humans who have gone before, a design that has been socially created, tested and shared, and one that can be transmitted to the child. It is this design, which persists even as individuals come and go, that makes all the difference for humans. So culture is learned behavior, although the learning is often out of awareness. It is shared behavior, which is important because it systemizes the way people do things, thus avoiding confusion and allowing cooperation so that groups of people can accomplish what no single individual could do alone. And it is behavior that is imposed by sanctions, rewards and punishments for those who are part of the group. (1988, pp. 45–46)

The implications of Fisher's concept of culture as mindset are threefold. First, culture is not innate but learned. In other words, no culture is inherently natural or normal. As a result, what is right in one culture is not necessarily right in another culture. In cross-cultural matters, behavior is not inherently right or wrong, only different.

Second, culture functions within the context of the group to which it belongs. To use the Dutch researcher Geert Hofstede's often quoted definition, culture is the "collective programming of the mind" (1984, p. 21). Since culture is a collective phenomenon, individual facets of culturally determined behavior can be understood only within the framework of the culture as a whole. Thus many variables remain constant within the context of a single culture but are subject to change from one culture to the next.

Finally, culture is inseparably tied to communication. The way we communicate results from the programming of our cultural mindset. Nevertheless, as John Condon and Fathi Yousef have noted, while "we cannot separate culture from communication . . . it is possible to distinguish between cultural patterns of communication and truly intercultural or cross-cultural communication" (1985, pp. 34–35). Those variables affected by cultural mindsets are recognizable. How we use those variables, however, is linked to the way we communicate within our own culture.

DOMESTIC CULTURAL DIVERSITY: IMMIGRATION AND GUEST WORKERS

A person's culture shapes a host of business communication factors in the workplace. The way we treat one another, negotiate, manage conflict, give or follow orders, and treat customers, for example, all depend on cultural factors.

Culture would not matter in business communication if we were able to conduct all our negotiations and transactions within a single culture. Increasingly, though, we live in an integrated world economy. Even those firms that choose not to trade in other countries face domestic competition from abroad in all but the most protected home markets. It is highly unusual for businesspeople even in the United States, the world's largest domestic economy, to survive long without interacting with competitors from abroad or competing in foreign markets.

Another aspect of the integrated world economy is the influx of immigrants into the domestic workplace. In the United States, large-scale immigration from non-European nations has significantly influenced the ethnic balance of the workforce. Because of immigration to the United Kingdom from its former territories in the West Indies, Africa, and South Asia, large numbers of British citizens are not ethnically English, Scottish, or Welsh. Likewise, the widespread immigration of people to the Netherlands from its former colonies in Indonesia and Suriname has resulted in large numbers of citizens who are not ethnically Dutch.

In some nations, this imported labor force is either discouraged or flatly prohibited from true immigration. The guest workers, as they are called, in effect represent an international presence within the heart of many countries' domestic economy. Although they are not allowed to become citizens of the country to which they have come, they nevertheless may be integrated into all levels of the economic structure of the countries in which they work. This situation is at its most extreme in the five smallest Persian Gulf states (Kuwait, Qatar, Bahrain, the United Arab Emirates, and Oman), where "approximately two-thirds of the labor force is imported" (Weiner, 1986, p. 52). Indeed, by the mid-1980s, ethnic Qataris comprised less than 38 percent of the total population living there in 1986. Similar situations—though not as marked—exist in Saudi Arabia and other major oil-producing states in the Middle East.

The importance of guest workers is by no means limited to the Middle East. Even excluding day migrants and refugees, the number of nonimmigrant foreigners is sizable in most West European countries. In Austria and Belgium, guest workers make up roughly 7 percent of the total work force; in France and Germany, 9 percent; and in Switzerland, the figure has on occasion risen to as high as 24 percent. Similarly, large numbers of guest or migrant workers are employed in Sweden, Denmark, Norway, and Luxembourg. In all of these countries, they are used primarily to fill the low-prestige and low-paying jobs that the native populations are unwilling to take. As a result, the economic separation of these workers reinforces their cultural isolation from the host population. The countries involved—both the host countries and the home countries of the guest workers themselves—encourage the workers to maintain their cultural identity precisely to maintain their status as guest workers rather than as citizens who identify with the host country.

In countries with both high immigration and large numbers of guest workers, the makeup of the work force is multicultural. The domestic work environment is essentially international in composition. In such settings, managers must be able to supervise a culturally diverse work force; cross-cultural business communication may prove vital in dealing with one's employees even if one neither faces competition nor conducts trade abroad.

INTERNATIONAL BUSINESS OPPORTUNITY

The study of international business communication presumes a recognition of the importance of conducting international business in the first place. International business itself is not a new subject. The Pax Romana of the ancient Roman Empire and the Hanseatic League of the northern European port cities in the Middle Ages are two well-known institutions whose central functions included the facilitation of international trade.

Yet in few periods of history has international trade and global business achieved such prominence so rapidly as it has in our own age. Perhaps no other area of business has grown so much in importance in the last half of the twentieth century. During the 1990s, major corporations will depend more on business conducted outside their home countries than inside their national borders. This has, of course, long been true of corporate giants in countries with relatively small domestic markets. Greater reliance on foreign than domestic markets was necessary to the success of such powerful global companies as Switzerland's F. Hoffman-La Roche and Nestlé, Norway's Norsk Data, Ireland's Jefferson Smurfit, the Netherlands' Philips and Akzo, and Luxembourg's ARBED.

Yet even in countries with huge domestic markets, companies have grown to depend heavily on business conducted abroad. Indeed, even companies based in the United States (the world's largest domestic market) are coming to rely substantially on business conducted abroad. While the very size of the U.S. economy has tended to insulate it from a global approach to business, by 1990 a number of leading U.S. companies received more than 50 percent of their sales from abroad. These included, among others, Gillette (65 percent), Colgate (65 percent), IBM (59 percent), NCR (59 percent), Coca-Cola (54 percent), Digital Equipment (54 percent), Dow Chemical (54 percent), Xerox (54 percent), Caterpillar (53 percent), and Hewlett-Packard (53 percent) (Moskowitz, Levering, and Katz, 1990, p. 575). Nor do these figures necessarily reflect the widespread influence of foreign competition in the domestic market or foreign-based subsidiaries of U.S. corporations.

Increase in international trade far exceeds either the gross domestic product or the industrial production in any single major industrialized country. Rates of growth in international trade increased from a mere $136 billion (U.S.) in 1960 to approximately $5 trillion (U.S.) at the beginning of the 1990s. Similarly, foreign private investment has grown faster than any major industrialized nation's gross domestic product or industrial production.

While the spurt in international trade has led to problems resulting from cultural differences (international business communication included), it has also provided great opportunities. Varied cultural perspectives facilitate a synergistic approach to management and product design, in which the integration of ideas results in a stronger system or end product than the combined individual strengths of the participants. Foreign markets represent ways to slow down market saturation. Because suppliers are more numerous, products and services—selected from the world market rather than from a regional or national market—can be tailored to individual needs. Moribund products can be resurrected by entering new markets abroad. And consumers can benefit from a wider range of products available to them.

TWO COMPETING TRENDS

Interestingly, two contradictory trends simultaneously affect international business communication in this rapidly growing global economy: homogenization of consumer needs and intensification of cultural heterogeneity.

The first trend applies to the universalization of consumer buying habits. One of the initial observers of this trend was Kenichi Ohmae, managing director of the consulting giant McKinsey & Company's Tokyo office. Ohmae noted what he termed "an emergence of the Triadians, or the residents of Japan, America and the European Community . . . whose academic backgrounds, income levels (both discretionary and nondiscretionary), life-style, use of leisure time, and aspirations are similar" (1985, pp. xvi–xvii). Within the Triad, Ohmae asserts, "consumer products have become fairly homogenous." This, Ohmae writes, results in greater similarity among major consumer groups across national borders within the Triad than among different demographic groups within a country. For instance, teenagers in the United States, Belgium, and Japan all are much more likely to prefer fast food, blue jeans, and rock music than are elderly consumers in those three countries: "In other words, within the Triad countries, the generation gap — the vertical difference between age groups — is more pronounced than the difference of tastes across the national borders" (p. 23).

Ohmae's observations among the Triad are not isolated. Indeed, the global success of such products as Italian Gucci handbags, U.S. Coca-Cola, and Japanese Walkman radios derives in large part from the globalization of consumer preferences.

David Whitwam, president of Whirlpool Corporation, the U.S. home appliance manufacturer, has said: "We really do see consumers in the major industrial countries coming more and more together . . . [including] the clothes they wear, the entertainment they have, and in many cases the food they enjoy" (Schiller and Kapstein, 1987, p. 91). Whitwam's comments, when examined in relation to his industry, are illuminating. On the one hand, consumer preferences across the Triad powers have moved throughout the 1980s and into the 1990s toward the so-called Eurostyle home appliance. Eurostyle, or the European look, consists of clean, integrated designs that fit flush into kitchen cabinets. As a result, U.S. manufacturers such as Whirlpool or General Electric and Japanese manufacturers such as Matsushita Electric are as likely to follow a European look as Sweden's Electrolux (the world's largest home appliance manufacturer), Germany's Bosch-Siemens, or the Netherlands' Philips.

Yet for all the similarities of consumer preference in home appliances, enormous differences occur in the actual appliances each culture uses. The average U.S. refrigerator, for example, literally does not fit in the average Japanese kitchen. Moreover, the Japanese use of paper-thin walls makes the typical U.S. or European refrigerator motor intolerably noisy. Conversely, there would not be enough room for the traditional U.S. Thanksgiving turkey in a typical Japanese oven. Moreover, despite the preference for Eurostyling, consumers in the United States have continued to buy top-loading washing machines, rejecting the front-loading design used almost exclusively in the European market.

This contradiction of preferences in the home appliance industry illustrates the second trend in international business communication. Even as whole segments within the global market become more alike, certain elements of national and cultural characteristics become more pronounced.

This second trend was clearly identified by Marcio Moreira, the Brazilian-born chief creative officer of the International Division of McCann Erickson Advertising Agency (which, with 150 offices in 71 countries, is the most extensive global operation of any agency network in the world).

Moreira has noted that "the cultures — the people themselves — are retrenching into the comfort of their cultural identities" (1990, p. 17). While Moreira referred only to advertising and marketing, his observations are equally valid in all aspects of business communication. In the face of rapid globalization in many areas (e.g., consumer preferences), people tend to revert in other areas (e.g., communication preferences) to the cultural patterns with which they are most comfortable. Moreira explains:

> The feeling is let's see what this first phase and the absence of trade barriers is going to feel like. For now, I'm going to be as French or as Spanish as I can be. It's a very natural defense mechanism, except that some of us weren't counting on it. (p. 17).

Thus, as the world becomes more globalized in one sense, the people become more parochial in ways most likely to affect marketing and business communication across borders.

The trend toward economic globalization and national-cultural parochialism will most probably occur where supranational trade organizations begin to affect the workplace and the marketplace. For instance, the tensions between francophone and anglophone Canadians that led to the rejection of the Meech Lake accord in 1990 (accommodating Quebec's unique status) may have been exacerbated — though not caused — by the increasing dominance of anglophone cultural institutions following Canada's free trade agreement with the United States. More pointedly, differences among the European Common Market nations have led to increased cultural boundaries even as the trade barriers among the member nations fell. As Moreira notes:

> The British have never been more British, the French never more French, the Italians never more Italian. As the idea of a unified Europe comes to fruition, the various nationalities' sense of cultural identity becomes heightened and people just retrench. (p. 17)

Similarly, speaking of Japan, Akiyuki Konishi, former editor in chief of *Mainichi Shinbun* (Japan's third largest newspaper), has observed a growing sense of cultural identity among the Japanese, even as they play an ever-larger role in the world economy. Konishi has said:

> You can't be really international without being national; if you are not national you can't contribute anything to the world. In this sense we can contribute the good part of Japanese tradition. (Konishi, Kondo, and Ogata, 1990, p. 51)

The results of these trends for business communication as a field are twofold. First, as global demands for products grow and international trade barriers decrease, the need for businesspeople to communicate with their counterparts from other cultures increases. At the same time, as pressures for global conformity in such areas as consumer preference mount with the expanded volume of international trade, cultural differences will intensify as a defense mechanism. Since the area over which people have the most individual control is their manner of communication, business communication in an integrated world economy will reflect an increase in cross-cultural differences in direct proportion to the decrease in other international barriers.

THE SIGNIFICANCE OF THE TERMS *INTERNATIONAL* AND *CROSS-CULTURAL*

At this point, it is important to indicate that what we have discussed refers in equal measure to cross-cultural and to international business communication. We have used the term *international* as synonymous with *cross-cultural* in this book, even though the two terms are not identical in meaning. *International* means "between or among nation-states." *Cross-cultural* means "between or among cultural groups." We have elected to use these two terms interchangeably precisely because the term *international business communication* occurs more frequently in business practice and in business communication courses than the less well-known term *cross-cultural*. Thus in this book, the term *international business communication* refers to business communication between two or more cultures. If this were a book on communication in general rather than specifically on business communication, more of a distinction might prove necessary. In any event, readers interested in pursuing the role culture plays in business situations should be aware of the distinction.

This is not to deny that the nation-state plays a major part in determining the culture of the groups residing within its borders. Identification with the state is often a significant component of a culture, and a nation tends to promote an "image of the state that is fostered and projected by its institutions, symbols, propaganda, and the like" (Conner, 1986, p. 20). The name of a country often projects a particular culture as its dominant one (e.g., Poland as the land of the Poles, or Thailand as the land of the Thais), while the national anthem may also underscore the primacy of a culture. Political policies often limit foreign influence or place severe restrictions on immigration to maintain the position of the majority culture. Finally, the nation-state influences perception of national culture by creating and reinforcing an official history through a host of techniques —from the books it allows to be taught in the schools, to the national monuments it erects.

As we have discussed earlier, however, several factors within a country determine what the state promotes as the national culture. For example, the number of immigrants and guest workers (and their children) affects the cultural composition of a country. For this reason, the term *cross-cultural* is more appropriate than the term *international*. This book is in no way suggesting that, for example, a British citizen born in Pakistan is any less British than an ethnic Scot born in Edinburgh. Yet, in cultural terms, the Pakistani-Briton is likely to hold a quite different *weltans-chaung* from the equally British Scot. It is this cross-cultural difference —even within the confines of a single nation—to which we refer as *international*.

Finally, the borders of nations are frequently not clearly delineated along cultural lines. This fact has less to do with patterns of immigration or inflows of guest workers than with the fact that political boundaries do not necessarily reflect cultural boundaries.

For example, immigrant and guest workers aside, Canada is comprised of two distinct cultures—francophone and anglophone. Similarly, Belgium's sharply divided population, made up of Flemish-speaking people in the north and the French-speaking Walloons of the south, is reflected in the writer Jules Destrée's famous comment to King Albert: "Sire, there are no Belgians; you reign over two people" (Lyon, 1971, p. 61). Nigerians divide sharply into Ibos, Yorubas, and Hausas, as well as dozens of smaller groups. Switzerland officially recognizes four main linguistic groups within its borders: German, French, Italian, and Romansch. Over 700 languages are spoken within India's borders, while the government officially recognizes 15 of these (each with its own associated cultural group) as regional languages: Assamese, Bengali, Gujarati, Hindi, Kannada, Kashmiri, Malayalam, Marathi, Oriya (the language of Orissa), Punjabi, Sanskrit, Sindhi, Tamil, Telugu, and Urdu.

Moreover, a nation's cultural divisions are not necessarily tied to linguistic divisions. The cultural differences between north and south Italians or north and south Germans are prominent despite a shared nationality and language. Nor do the differences have to rest on geographical separation within a country. Thus in the Netherlands throughout the 1950s and well into the 1960s, the social and political divisions between Catholics and Protestants resulted in the *verzuiling* (literally "columnization") of Dutch society. While Catholics, Protestants, and nonchurch members in the Netherlands spoke the same language, looked alike, and were dispersed throughout the country (with only some dominance of Protestantism in the north and Catholicism in the southeast), *verzuiling* was so strict that each of the three groups read only its own newspapers, listened to its own radio stations, and bought from its own merchants, to the point that the design of municipal buildings and staffs of hospitals were selected by religious affiliation. While *verzuiling* has subsided in current Dutch society, it represents the sort of nonlinguistic, nongeographic division possible among groups of nearly equal power in one nation.

These represent only a few examples of cultural division within the nation-state. Indeed, as one expert has noted, "The political borders of states have been superimposed upon the ethnic map with cavalier disregard for ethnic homelands" (Conner, 1986, p. 20).

In short, we should be careful to keep these distinctions in mind when using the term *international*. If the more specific notion of cross-cultural is understood within the term *international*, we can use the two terms interchangeably to accommodate terminology commonly used in business.

ORGANIZATION OF THIS BOOK

The remainder of this book is divided into eight chapters (the last one is a brief concluding chapter). Each of the seven chapters addresses a major variable likely to shift across cultures in a way that would affect business communication and suggests practical methods for accommodating or capitalizing on these differences. The seven variables are

- Language — Chapter 2
- Environment and Technology — Chapter 3
- Social Organization — Chapter 4
- Contexting — Chapter 5
- Authority Conception — Chapter 6
- Nonverbal Behavior — Chapter 7
- Temporal Conception — Chapter 8
- Conclusion — Chapter 9

Taken together, the first letters of the seven variables form the acronym LESCANT. While the word LESCANT has no actual meaning, it is an easy mnemonic device for referring to these seven items. The LESCANT variables are not all-inclusive, but they do encompass a broad enough scope of reference to provide an insight into the business communication practices of other cultures.

As discussed earlier, the objective of this book is to enable readers to ask the right questions in assessing international business communication. The LESCANT elements constitute the broad rubrics under which these questions can be listed. The chapters provide the means for framing the questions themselves.

Finally, no amount of reading can entirely prepare an individual to conduct international business communication effectively. No one should consider himself or herself wholly competent in international business communication from reading this book or taking a training program or college course on the subject. Actual experience is needed. This book represents a first step, to develop or enhance readers' knowledge and skills while they gain that experience.

Chapter
2

Issues of Language in International Business Communication

*P*erhaps no other element of international business is so often noted as a barrier to effective communication across cultures than differences in language. As we discussed in Chapter 1, language is neither the only nor even the most important communication impediment in cross-cultural encounters. Nevertheless, it remains the most obvious difference that international business communicators are likely to face.

Language is so significant an obstacle in international as well as domestic cross-cultural business dealings precisely because it is so fundamental. Unless the two parties understand a common language, communication is essentially impossible without a translator or interpreter. Without a shared language, direct communication is at best filtered through a third party and at worst altogether impossible.

Although the inability to understand what one party communicates in a foreign language is the most fundamental problem that differences in language pose, lack of a shared language presents many less obvious pitfalls as well. Because these other difficulties are more subtle, they may be more invidious than straightforward incomprehensibility. While a myriad of minor problems may occur when crossing linguistic lines, four of these are most likely to affect business.

First, language, as we will discuss below, shapes the reality of its speaker. Certain phrases and turns of thought depend on the many associations linked to a specific language and to the culture intertwined with it. As a result, the subtle nuances of a language are often lost in translation, even when the speaker of the second language is fluent.

Second, the use of a language may carry social implications of belonging to a common group that for many cultures establishes the trust necessary for long-term business relationships. This trust is often delayed or never available to the businesspeople who do not speak the language and who are viewed with suspicion as outsiders or, at the least, as not committed to the home market of the native speaker.

Third, the degree of fluency among speakers of any foreign language varies, even among the best of translators and interpreters. But unless the speaker of the second language makes frequent grammatical errors, any lack of comprehension on his or her part may go unrecognized. It is easy, therefore, for native speakers to assume erroneously that anyone speaking their language fully understands the conversation.

Finally, cultural attachment to variants or dialects of a language often communicate messages of which the person who learns the language as a second tongue is unaware. Even though the words exchanged are understandable to both parties, the underlying sociolinguistic implications conveyed by the accent used or the choice of words may communicate unintended messages.

This chapter addresses each of these four issues and their influence on business in the form of cross-cultural miscommunication and pseudoconflict. It also discusses the special problems associated with English, both because it is the most common language of international business and because we assume that it is a language shared by all readers of this book. Finally, the chapter concludes by suggesting ways in which to overcome language as a barrier to business communication.

LANGUAGE, CULTURE, AND THOUGHT PROCESSING

Background

The Academie Française has conservatively estimated a total of 2,796 languages currently spoken on the planet. The figure excludes an additional 7,000 to 8,000 dialects of those languages.

Each language, as we will discuss below, helps to form its own cultural group. Admittedly, language alone is not the sole determinant of culture or national identity. The United States, Ireland, and Australia, for example, have a common language but operate from quite different cultural perspectives. Still, it is difficult to overestimate the power of language in shaping a culture. Even when speakers of different languages are of the same nationality, they tend to differ in their culture. This is evident, as we noted in Chapter 1, in the rift that exists between francophone and anglophone Canadians or Flemish and Walloon Belgians.

Because language is so powerful a shaper of culture, the effective business communicator needs to consider all differences in language. It is not necessary or even possible to learn all 2,796 languages and their thousands of dialects. Most of the world's languages are spoken by so few people or are so unlikely to affect international business transactions that their importance is negligible, although never absent entirely. For example, Australia's approximately 50,000 aborigines speak among them over 200 different languages. Similarly, over 700 tongues are spoken in sub-Saharan Africa, many by only a handful of speakers. While it is conceivable that one may need these languages for conducting business, their usefulness in business is limited.

Indeed, of the world's thousands of languages, only 101 have more than 1 million speakers. Table 2.1 lists the top 14 by number of speakers; all have at least 50 million speakers. These figures, however, do not take into account the number of people who speak these languages as a second tongue. Thus English, with approximately 300 million native speakers, is used by an estimated 200 million more as a second language.

As Charles Berlitz has observed:

> Since most of the world's population either speaks or is familiar with one of [these] fourteen languages . . . or with one of three other widely spoken languages—Dutch, Greek, Swahili—with a language in either the Scandinavian, Turkic, or the Slavic group, it is possible for an individual with the time and inclination to be able to communicate with the great majority of the inhabitants of this planet by learning to speak those 20 languages. (1982, pp. 6–7)

The international business communicator does not have to go as far as Berlitz suggests. While the speaker of these 20 languages would without question have a substantial advantage over his or her more tongue-tied counterparts, it is possible (although arguably more difficult) to be effective in the international arena without knowing even one foreign lan-

Table 2.1   RANKING OF LANGUAGES BY NUMBER OF NATIVE SPEAKERS

Rank	Language
1	Chinese
2	English
3	Hindustani*
4	Russian
5	Spanish
6	Japanese
7	German
8	Indonesian
9	Portuguese
10	French
11	Arabic
12	Bengali
13	Malay
14	Italian

*Hindustani is the term for the combined spoken version of Urdu and Hindi, which differ primarily only in their written form.

Source: Berlitz, 1982.

guage. It is important to stress, however, that the cultural sensitivity that usually accompanies the acquisition of a foreign language is much more difficult to attain without such training and, as a result, the monolingual businessperson is frequently at a disadvantage to his or her bilingual or multilingual competitors.

Still, the monolingual businessperson who is aware of the way in which language influences culture can even have an advantage over the bilingual businessperson who has somehow never learned this lesson. Language, intimately intertwined as it is with culture, shapes the thought processes of those who speak it fluently. Awareness of the way in which this phenomenon occurs is the first step in understanding how linguistic differences influence business communication.

Linguistic Equivalence

Many people, able to appreciate an idea, a joke, or an interesting turn of phrase in one language, find it impossible to convey its meaning in another language. "I guess this loses something in translation" is a common expression in the United States. Ideas do lose quite a bit in translation, because no languages are so alike that every term or phrase can be rendered word for word in another tongue.

At best, a translation provides an *equivalence*, not an exact reproduction of meaning. This holds true for all words, even the most concrete of expressions. For example, the word *nose* in French is *nez*. On the surface, they are identical in meaning, but the words have different connotations in the two languages. For instance, the common English expression to be *nosy* or to *nose about*, meaning to be inquisitive, has an equivalent in French: *fouiner* or *fureter*. Because these words have animal associations —the first is linked to the marten and the latter to the ferret—both imply in French an animal slyness or stealth definitively not suggested by the English *nosiness*. One French expression comes close to the English —*se fourrer son nez partout*, or "to thrust one's nose into everything"— but this phrase is much less common and to some extent carries the sense of searching about with one's nose like an animal. Thus the word *nez* elicits much less of the sense of uninvited inquisitiveness than its English equivalent.

The word *nez* does suggest the expression *rire au nez de quelqu'un*, "to laugh at someone's nose," or to show one's amused scorn. In English, this phrase, if translated literally, means only that someone has a funny-looking nose. The equivalent expression in English is *to laugh in someone's face*. In turn, the French word for *face (visage)* has no association with the notion of ridicule.

Often a phrase has no direct translation at all. The English expression *to pull strings*, frequently used in the workplace, conjures up the image of puppetry as a means of getting things done. When one pulls the strings of a marionette, it moves as the strings move. The closest French expression, also common in the workplace, is *avoir du piston*, "to have control of the plunger." This phrase brings to mind the plunger or piston of a syringe. When one pulls the plunger, the syringe fills as directed. Although the two phrases mean roughly the same thing—that is, to take an action to accomplish something—the English expression is somewhat disdainful or at least playful, whereas the French phrase is almost clinical and imbues a sense of precision absent in its English counterpart.

Likewise in English we talk of someone being a *glutton for work*, linking the process of overworking with that of overeating. Again, the French have only a rough equivalent: *bourreau de travail*, "one stuffed with work." Since the French word *bourreau*, is also the word for executioner, however, the expression carries connotations of being killed or killing oneself with work that the word *glutton* does not.

Another associative factor affecting the use of language is the occurrence of homonyms. In English, for example, *fair* and *fare* have no common meaning and yet because of their identical pronunciation, one word may lead the speaker's thought to the other. In French, the words *sceau* (seal, as on a ring), *sot* (fool), and *seau* (bucket) all sound alike, making possible the French insult *Vous êtes un sot en trois lettres*," or "You are a fool spelled with three letters," a clarification for the fool who might think he or she has been called a ring seal or a bucket.

The web of nonequivalent associations goes on and on and is, of course, not limited to differences between English and French. No two languages carry the same associations. Each language, in turn, determines the likely associations of one thought to the next.

Linguistic Determinism

To the extent that one language can more accurately describe one notion than another, that language influences the way in which its speakers communicate what they know. This phenomenon is known as *linguistic determinism*. Linguistic determinism is the assertion that one's view of reality stems largely from the language one uses.

Because the theory of linguistic determinism is so important for understanding the role of language in cross-cultural business communication, it is worthwhile to examine the origins of the theory. In the first part of the twentieth century, several experts put forth the proposition that language shapes reality. First among these theorists was the eminent ethnologist Franz Boas. In his studies of Native American communities, Boas established the link between language and behavior. He suggested that unconscious linguistic forms influence the way people behave and think. As early as 1911 he concluded that "the peculiar characteristics of languages are clearly reflected in the views and customs of the peoples of the world" (Boas, 1974, p. 31).

Boas's observations were extended by several researchers. George Herbert Mead asserted that language is a symbolic system inextricably intertwined with the society that uses it. "Language," Mead wrote, "is the means whereby individuals can indicate to one another what their responses to objects will be, and hence what the meanings of objects are" (1934, p. 114). Language reflects the cultural assumptions and associations of those who speak it.

The two most important figures in the area of linguistic determinism are Edward Sapir and Benjamin Lee Whorf. In fact, the concept of linguistic determinism is often called the Sapir-Whorf hypothesis.

Sapir, in his groundbreaking definition, said that "language is a guide to 'social reality'. . . . Human beings do not live in the objective world alone, nor alone in the world of social activity as ordinarily understood, but are at the mercy of the particular language which has become the medium of expression for their society." For Sapir,

> the 'real world' is to a large extent unconsciously built on the language habits of the group. No two languages are ever sufficiently similar to be considered as representing the same social reality. The worlds in which different societies live are distinct worlds, not merely the same world with different labels attached. (in Mandelbaum, 1949, p. 162)

In short, languages share at best equivalencies in translation but can never fully impart to nonspeakers the social reality inherent in their use.

Benjamin Lee Whorf carried this even further:

> The linguistic system . . . of each language is not merely a reproducing instrument for voicing ideas but rather is itself the shaper of ideas, the program and guide for the individual's mental activity, for his anyalysis of impressions, for his synthesis of his mental stock in trade. . . . (Whorf, 1952, p. 5)

The classic example of this is that Inuit, the language of the Eskimo people, has no word for *snow*, although it has dozens of words for *types* of snow for which most European and Asian languages have no equivalent. Thus, while unable easily to communicate the notion of *snow* itself, the Eskimo can differentiate and communicate powdery snow, slushy snow, granular snow, crusty snow, and many other varieties of snow.

Whorf's assertion has enormous implications for the cross-cultural business communicator. The tools for expressing oneself exist in one's language and — like the lack of an Inuit word for *snow* — direct the way in which the speakers of that language analyze and understand the world around them. As Whorf wrote, "the phenomena of a language are to its own speakers largely of a background character and so are outside the critical consciousness and control of the speaker" (p. 4). To the extent that the words and structure of a language differ from those of another language, their variations create barriers to business communication precisely because the language seems to be the only logical way to view or communicate underlying ideas.

Some Practical Examples of Linguistic Determinism

Perhaps the best way to illustrate how language influences thought in business communication is to provide examples of terms that are unique to their language. Such examples, wholly untranslatable and yet commonplace within their language, demonstrate linguistic determinism in the extreme, since they reflect unique aspects of the societies that speak each language.

The following five words by no means represent an exhaustive list of such untranslatable words. Instead, they have been selected from among the thousands of such words as illustrative of the relationship between language and thought as well as for their frequency of use, particularly in *business* communication.

1. *Fucha* (Polish). *Fucha*, to use Howard Rheingold's translation, is "the act of using company time and company resources (machines, supplies, services) to complete a job for yourself or someone else" (1988, p. 105). *Fucha* has connotations of holding two or more jobs at the same time, as well as of intentionally bungling a task. Its unique meaning, however, is the notion of work-time or work-supply theft, but without negative overtones. Such a notion in English has highly negative implications, although the practice is common enough in English-speaking countries. Indeed, many employees feel it is their right to take home company notepads or pencils for personal use, although such dishonesty constitutes petty theft. Similarly, the corporate accountant who at tax time works on others' income tax returns during company time is practicing *fucha*, but in an unsavory way not associated with the Polish word. To a large extent, the absence of negative connotations of *fucha* directly reflects Polish cultural and political realities. In the United States or Germany, *fucha* suggests petty greed because prospective employees are relatively free to accept or reject a job in which they would use *fucha*. By contrast, in Poland, economic freedom until very recently was kept to a minimum, and job conditions were mandated by a state-controlled employer. Practicing *fucha* in Poland, then, could be seen as a political statement as much as a means to supplement a wage over which the employee had no control.

2. *Ringiseido* (Japanese). The Japanese process of decision making by consensus, discussed later in this book, has no formal equivalent outside of Japan. The Japanese cultural values of group coordination, face-saving, and the avoidance of open conflict have led to the managerial practice of discussing a project with all the people who will be involved. As each person looks over a proposal, he or she places a stamp of approval to the document or makes appropriate suggestions to change the proposal. The document goes from person to person in a *ring* up and down the organizational hierarchy until full consensus is reached. The word *ring* in *ringiseido* is taken from the English word, since the notion was first developed in the United States but was so culturally foreign that it could not take root. In Japan, with its emphasis on *nemawashi* (literally "root binding"),

the informal establishment of consensus through personal interaction, *ringiseido*, flourished.

3. *Papierkrieg* (German). The Orbis-Verlag *Wörterbuch Deutsch-Englisch* defines *Papierkrieg* simply as "red tape." The word, however, actually means "paper war" and carries a unique message that is much stronger than mere red tape. While this term suggests bureaucratic form-filling and time-wasting procedures, just as *Papierkrieg* does, the existence of red tape is a neutral if annoying side product of work in large organizations. *Papierkrieg*, by contrast, implies that the paperwork is deliberate — is, in a sense, a "war," or *krieg*, against the recipient. *Papierkrieg*, unlike red tape, is a weapon used by the organization to keep a complaint or a lawsuit unfiled. In return, motivated complainers or plaintiffs consciously go to battle in the paper war — that is, the *Papierkrieg* waged against them. As we will discuss later, most German-speaking cultures are low context — they place great emphasis on the written word (contracts, instructions, and so forth). The development of a word like *Papierkrieg* both reflects and reinforces this cultural attribute.

4. *Bulmus* (Hebrew). Until the founding of Israel, in 1948, Hebrew was, for centuries, essentially a holy language used for prayers but not for common speech. As a result, many of its words echo religious meanings taken from Judaism. One of these is *bulmus*, which the Israeli writer Amos Elon defines as "a ravenous hunger, a faintness resulting from a prolonged fasting, an exaggerated eagerness, a fit, a mania" (1972, p. 291). Jewish religious writings indicate that a person who is seized by *bulmus* on a fast day (such as Yom Kippur) is to be given food and is not allowed to complete the fast. Yet the word has, as with so many ancient Hebrew terms brought into everyday use in Israel, taken on a meaning for the business communicator. It is the profoundest of deep-seated crazes. A marketer's dream would be for a *bulmus* among the public for his or her product. Elon, for example, talks of "an Israeli *bulmus* for archaeology" (p. 291). Because of the peculiarity of Hebrew's revival, *bulmus* reflects the mix of secular concepts superimposed on religious concepts characteristic of modern Hebrew and allows for a depth of emotional attachment normally reserved in other languages for describing spiritual rather than day-to-day ideas.

5. *Animateur* (French). *Cassell's French-English Dictionary* defines *animateur* as a "quickener" or "animator," but the word has much greater scope than these rough English translations suggest. An *animateur* is "a person who can communicate difficult concepts to general audiences" or "a writer who can present complex scientific or technological information in an easily understandable form" (Rheingold, 1988, pp. 190–91). In short, all effective business communicators are *animateurs*. French has a significant number of abstract terms and such terms may more easily be grasped in French than in such languages as English and Dutch, with their emphasis on concrete terminology. If that is true, *animateur* may rein-

force this cultural trait by providing a word for individuals who can convey in clear terms the abstract ideas of the language.

It is important to keep in mind that an expression need not be unique to a language to influence thought. As we have seen, associative values of words, as well as the frequency of any given expression within the language, is a more common and probably more influential manifestation of linguistic determinism. The businessperson should remain flexible to the presence of associations or interpretations in any translations, to avoid cross-cultural impediments to communication stemming from the relationship of language to thought.

LANGUAGE AND CULTURAL ATTACHMENT

Barriers other than simple accuracy of communication exist when dealing with speakers of different languages. Even in situations in which excellent interpreters or translators are employed or in which all parties speak the chosen language with fluency, the social implications of the language used still remain a factor. Thus even where language differences pose no problem in comprehension, the selection of one language over another may create goodwill or resentment independently of any message actually spoken or written.

Cultural attachment to language most often manifests itself, at least in business communication, in three variations: linguistic ethnocentrism, insider-outsider relationships, and alliances in linguistically determined group dynamics. We'll examine each one in detail.

Linguistic Ethnocentrism

All people are subject to some degree of *ethnocentrism*, or the belief that their own culture is better than other cultures. To some extent, linguistic ethnocentrism, or the belief in the superiority of one's native language to other tongues, is less delimiting than many other forms of ethnocentrism. The reason is that in many cases, the language spoken by the members of a particular society is not confined to that culture alone.

For example, while Spain, Bolivia, and Mexico differ culturally, they all share Spanish as their native tongue. A Bolivian's linguistic ethnocentrism therefore would not apply to a Spaniard or a Mexican. Indeed, the belief in the superiority of Spanish may actually persuade the Bolivian to look beyond the country's borders to other Spanish-speaking cultures. Linguistic ethnocentrism in this case may have a broadening rather than a narrowing effect.

Some cultures demonstrate a stronger attachment to their language than do others. Although it is dangerous to stereotype any group precisely because exceptions exist in all cultures, still, for historical, social, political, or even religious reasons, the members of certain cultures are more likely to take linguistic ethnocentrism more seriously than others.

Historical Reasons   Speakers of languages that have long histories and are associated with nations that have always been or once were major world powers or highly influential civilizations tend to embrace linguistic ethnocentrism. Thus, Greeks, though comparatively few in number, are likely to manifest linguistic ethnocentrism because of the antiquity of their language and its importance in the ancient Greek city-states that constituted the foundations of Western civilization. In some countries that were once governed by colonial powers — Dutch, English, French, Portuguese, Spanish — linguistic ethnocentrism may result from cultural ties to the former rulers.

Social Reasons   Linguistic ethnocentrism may arise for a host of social reasons. Languages spoken in nations of great military strength may gain influence because of their association with military might. For example, the widespread belief among Germans in the superiority of (among other things) German as a language before and during World War II was reinforced by Germany's undaunted power. The popularity of Russian or English as a second language in those countries in which large numbers of Soviet or U.S. troops are stationed reflects the recognition of ethnocentrism on the part of the Soviet Union and the United States. Another social factor in linguistic ethnocentrism is the number of speakers or the number of cultures using a language. Among societies that speak French or Spanish, for example, the global currency of those languages may encourage linguistic ethnocentrism primarily because they are so widespread.

Finally, economic power can also produce linguistic ethnocentrism. For example, the widespread — if erroneous — belief, in the United States, that English is the only language needed for international business is based in large part on the commercial and industrial primacy of the United States (and to a lesser extent on the economic influence of the other English-speaking nations as well).

Political Reasons   The very use of some languages conveys nationalistic or political significance. For example, the use of Basque in Spain — particularly by a non-Basque — is likely to symbolize support for Basque separatism. Even in independent nations, the use of the national language may make a political point. Thus in Ireland the use of Gaelic represents support of Irish nationalism (for all but the few thousand native speakers in Ireland's western fringes).

Religious Reasons   Some languages may inspire linguistic ethnocentrism among their speakers for religious reasons. Arabic, Hebrew, Greek, Armenian, and Russian, among others, are both spoken by a culture and used as the holy language of specific religions. To the extent that Muslims,

Jews, and adherents to the Greek Orthodox, Armenian Catholic, Armenian Apostolic, and Russian Orthodox faiths believe that the languages of their rites and liturgy are divinely blessed or holy, they may feel a linguistic ethnocentrism toward their respective languages in their secular use.

Multiple Factors   Linguistic ethnocentrism need not occur for any specific reason. The mere fact that people grow up speaking a language and therefore are most comfortable with it may lead them to conclude that it is the best language. Indeed, it is safe to assume that speakers of a particular language who have had little exposure to other cultures will feel an ethnocentric bias toward their native language. It is also safe to assume that, because all languages have unique strengths and peculiarities, even the most unbiased people in a setting in which languages are compared feel a degree of favoritism toward their own language.

At times, too, the four factors we have discussed—historical, social, political, and religious—can come to bear simultaneously. This point is clearly illustrated in the case of Arabic:

> There are few societies in which language plays as important a role as it does in the Arab society. It is, therefore, important for the business executive to develop a good understanding of the place Arabic occupies in the life of its speakers. . . . The importance of Arabic rests not only in the hundreds of millions of people who speak it, but also in the vital historical role it has played in the Arabic-Muslim society. In addition to being ancillary to Islam, Arabic has constituted the medium of cultural and national revival in the Arabic-speaking countries. (Almaney and Alwan, 1982, p. 77)

The use of Arabic by a non-Arab, then, may indicate a recognition of what the native Arabic speaker is likely to believe—that is, the innate superiority of the language. As another observer has written, "While most Westerners feel an affection for their native language, the pride and love which Arabs feel for Arabic is much more intense. The Arabic language is one of their greatest cultural treasures and achievements" (Nydell, 1987, p. 101).

Thus for non-Arabs to speak Arabic in a business situation would be advantageous even if their Arab counterpart were fluent in their own language. Its use would make the non-Arab appear enlightened in recognizing the religious and cultural importance of the language, would indicate an awareness of the history of the Arab peoples, and would imply an appreciation for the growing importance of the Arab world in geopolitical affairs.

Insider-Outsider Relationships

To the extent that a language is closely tied to a culture, the use of that language tends to admit entry into that society. The language itself is a window through which the businessperson can participate in the culture and gain the trust of its members.

An often used adage in international business is that you can *buy* in your own language anywhere in the world, but if you want to *sell*, use the language of the locals. To persuade a purchaser, it is almost always best to use the buyer's language, to ensure clarity. Nor should a buyer–seller relationship be considered the only or even the primary reason for using another culture's language. The choice of language affects all aspects of business communication. For example, to the degree that management in a foreign subsidiary can use the primary language of its workforce, its effectiveness in training and motivating that workforce is enhanced.

The reasons for businesspeople to use the language of the culture with which they interact go far beyond mere clarity. The use of a language, for many cultures, symbolizes understanding of or even membership in that culture. This establishes a respect and degree of trust never fully available to the businessperson unable to speak the language.

Because language so strongly affects culture, the use of a language can, as we have seen, act as an admission into that culture. For example, while Brazilian businesspeople may understand a Briton speaking English, they may feel more comfortable and be less reluctant to trust the same Briton if they both speak Portuguese. The Briton's willingness to use Portuguese is likely to communicate the importance that the Brazilian market holds for him or her, even though such a sentiment is never directly stated. Moreover, this feeling may be reinforced because the language abandoned is English. As we will discuss below, English has become the *lingua franca* of business.

Thus the fact that the Briton would use Portuguese communicates a cultural sensitivity that the Brazilian would more likely recognize than if the language abandoned were less widely spoken. By contrast, the Brazilian might well expect a Swede to speak Portuguese when in Brazil precisely because Swedish is spoken by so few people; the Swede could probably not expect the Brazilian to know the Scandinavian language.

Appreciation of a foreigner's use of one's native language is more likely among cultures that themselves constitute a single nation. Every native speaker is assumed to be a part of the same nation-culture, and all speakers of the language as a second tongue would, by inference, reflect a strong interest in the culture.

Table 2.2 lists the most important of those cultures that have dominant languages spoken by only one nation. Such societies are not necessarily homogeneous, however. For instance, in India, Nigeria, Yugoslavia, and the Soviet Union, many languages are limited to one portion of the nation and are not spoken elsewhere.

Another variant in the use of language dominant to a single culture is the case of geographically dispersed peoples who have carried their language with them. Some of these constitute important subcultures within the dominant cultures in which they reside. Thus Armenians speaking Armenian or — especially before World War II — Jews speaking Yiddish

Table 2.2   CULTURES WITH DOMINANT LANGUAGE LIMITED TO ONE NATION

Albania (Albanian)
Bulgaria (Bulgarian)
Denmark (Danish)
Greece (Greek)
Hungary (Hungarian)
Iceland (Icelandic)
Israel (Hebrew)
Italy (Italian)
Japan (Japanese)
Korea (Korean)
Malaysian (Bihasa Malay)
Mongolia (Mongolian)
Netherlands (Dutch)
Norway (Norwegian)
Poland (Polish)
Romania (Romanian)
Sweden (Swedish)
Thailand (Thai)
Turkey (Turkish)

provided a type of international password to distinguish insiders from outsiders.

In any situation in which bilingual business communicators use the language of their foreign counterparts, they should be forewarned that knowing a language without the knowledge of the cultural behavior of a group can be damaging. Because language acts as the shibboleth, or password, between stranger and member of the culture, the use of the language in insider-outsider encounters may lead others to believe that the businessperson fluent in the language is also fluent in the culture. Therefore, errors in behavior that might be excused in a foreigner would no longer be acceptable in the businessperson who speaks the language. As the Australian-born George Fields writes of his own business experience in Japan, "The acquisition of superficial language skills can be a handicap if it leads the student to think he understands the culture" (1983, p. 17).

Alliances in Linguistically Determined Group Dynamics

The language one decides to use may itself have social implications. The use of French in Canada, rather than the more widely spoken English, is a social statement aligning the speaker with the French Canadian community. Canada is not the only nation with more than one official language and in which significant tension along linguistic lines exists. Table 2.3 lists

Table 2.3   NATIONS WITH MORE THAN ONE MAJOR LINGUISTIC GROUP
(Majority language listed first)*

Nation	Languages
Afghanistan	Pashto, Dari Persian
Belgium	Dutch (Flemish), French, German
Bolivia	Spanish, Aymara, Quechua
Botswana	Tswana, English
Burundi	Rundi, French
Cameroon	French, English
Canada	English, French
Chad	Arabic, French
Comoros	Arabic, French
Cyprus	Greek, Turkish
Czechoslovakia	Czech, Slovak
Djibouti	Arabic, French
Finland	Finnish, Swedish
Haiti	Haitian Creole, French
India	Hindi, English
Ireland	Irish, English
Israel	Hebrew, Arabic
Luxembourg	French, German
Madagascar	French, Malagasy
Malawi	Chewa, English
Malta	Maltese, English
New Zealand	English, Maori
Peru	Spanish, Quechua
Philippines	Tagalog (Filipino), English
Rwanda	Rwanda, French
Singapore	Chinese, Malay, Tamil, English
South Africa	Afrikaans, English
Sri Lanka	Sinhalese, Tamil
Switzerland	German, French, Italian
Western Samoa	Samoan, English
Yugoslavia	Serbo-Croation, Slovene, Macedonian

*The table excludes official languages in which the number of speakers of one of the languages is negligible (i.e., Somalia's official languages are Arabic and Somali, although virtually no Somalis speak Arabic as a first language).
Source: *World Data Annual*, Chicago: Encyclopaedia Britannica, 1991.

many of the nations in which more than one official language is used by a large portion of the population.

The term *official language* does not imply that no *other* languages are spoken, either in nations listed in Table 2.3 or in nations that are officially monolinguistic. For example, in Canada a large group of people primarily speak a language that is neither French nor English, the official languages. Algeria does not appear in Table 2.3 because its sole official language is

Arabic, even though Berber-speaking people constitute 17 percent of its population and — due to its colonial history — French is widely spoken as a second language. Indeed, in some cases the official languages may not even be spoken by the majority of the country's population. For example, India's official languages are English and Hindi, spoken by just over 245 million people; however, an additional 556 million speak neither English nor Hindi but one of India's remaining 64 national tongues. Similarly, most Luxembourgers speak the national language, Luxembourgish, while less than 10 percent speak as their first tongue the official languages, French and German (although both French and German are widely understood as second and third languages). In some cases, the official language of a nation may not even represent the major business language of the country. For example, in Malaysia, Chinese is the first language of roughly 30 percent of the population. Moreover, Malaysia's more than 1,600,000 ethnic Chinese dominate the nation's business class. As a result, Chinese is probably the most common business language of Malaysia but is not recognized as an official language in that country.

Consequently, the term "official language" should be understood to mean those languages

> prescribed for day-to-day conduct and publication of a country's official business. Other languages may have local protection, may be permitted in legal action (such as a trial), or may be "national languages," for the protection of which local provisions have been made, but these are not deemed official. (*World Data Annual*, 1991, p. 536)

The international business communicator should be aware, when selecting a language, that tensions of the sort common in Canada are possible in many nations.

DEGREE OF FLUENCY

The degree of fluency of those speaking a foreign language varies. The extent to which the business communicator perceives this variance can have a major impact on the success of international commercial affairs.

In any interaction involving parties with different native languages, the possibility for misunderstanding exists. It is easy to believe mistakenly that what one says or writes has been fully understood by the speaker of a foreign language. The process is often complicated by two factors. First, the receiver of the message, the speaker of language A, may sincerely believe that he or she has understood or correctly translated the message the sender has delivered in language B. Second, the speaker of language A may not wish to lose face by admitting that he or she has not fully understood the message delivered in language B. Therefore, the speaker of language A may pretend to have understood the message without indicating his or her confusion.

In addition, difficulties may arise that are specific to the degree of fluency among speakers. We will discuss three configurations regarding the extent of fluency and describe the way in which they may affect business communication.

No Fluency

The first configuration is that in which neither party speaks the other's language. In such a situation, both parties must rely on an interpreter in face-to-face interactions and a translator in written exchanges. Since translators can be more accurate than interpreters because of the additional time for review, both parties may depend more heavily on translated documents than if they spoke the same language.

In face-to-face interactions, in which the interpreter is directly conveying the message, both parties are likely to focus on that person rather than the speaker and the receiver. It is common even to include the interpreter as part of one's negotiating or training team to translate not only the words spoken but the reactions of the other party. This is a potentially dangerous practice because interpreters are rarely trained in the business issues under discussion. Even when they are drawn from the ranks of the negotiators, the focus on them rather than on all the participants is a mistake that an interpreter's fluency in the language may foster. We will discuss ways best to use an interpreter later in this chapter.

One-Sided Fluency

In many business situations, one side of the communication process has some degree of fluency while the other side has none. This configuration presents several difficulties.

First, side X, with no fluency, may assume that side Y, which speaks side X's language fully, also understands X's culture. For example, a U.S. businesswoman may represent a company in negotiating with a Japanese firm. The Japanese negotiating team with whom she interacts has little knowledge of English. Recognizing that the woman speaks Japanese, the negotiating team is likely to judge her by Japanese standards. When the U.S. businesswoman breaks Japanese gender-linked social expectations and does not behave as they might expect a Japanese woman to behave, she is less likely to be forgiven than a foreigner unable to speak Japanese might be. She would also seem very aggressive in her negotiating style, reflecting a U.S. preference for directness that is generally considered inappropriate or even rude in Japan.

Another difficulty with one-sided fluency is in the assignation of business acumen and general intelligence to the interpreter based on his or her fluency in the language. It is relatively easy for businesspeople who rely on an interpreter to attribute to him or her an understanding of their negotiation strategies, product or service, and other business knowledge. As the expertise of most interpreters is in language skills rather than in business, this is a dangerous assumption.

Two-Sided Fluency

When the two sides appear to be equally fluent in each other's languages, the difficulty arises as to which language both parties should use. The issue of cultural attachment and, to a lesser extent, of ethnocentrism may provide a stumbling block to effective interaction unless the communicator approaches this matter cautiously.

Regardless of the degree of fluency, it is important to remember, as discussed above, that in any interaction involving participants who speak different languages, the possibility for misunderstanding exists. In any of the configurations described or in any variation of them, international business communicators should be aware that they may receive no feedback that what they have said or written may not have been fully understood by the speaker of a foreign language.

ACCENTS, DIALECTS, AND REGIONAL DIFFERENCES

The dialects and accents used among speakers of a language often vary from region to region. How the individual views these differences may color the communication between the two speakers of the language:

> Speakers of one dialect may be set off from speakers of a different dialect by the use of certain pronunciations, words, and grammatical forms. The frequent first reaction of a person who hears an unfamiliar dialect is that the strange sounds and words are a chaotic mess. (Shuy, 1981, p. 485)

Dialects, far from being a "chaotic mess," represent a means for people to identify other members of their geographical group. Such regional variations can exist between national cultures (internationally) or within the same nation (subnationally).

International Regional Variables

International variables consist of those dialects and accents that vary among countries. In most instances these regional variations are readily recognizable. As a result, the listener categorizes the speaker of the foreign dialect as part of the foreign culture.

In some respects, speakers with foreign language accents and speakers with regional dialects can be categorized together. To the extent that many speakers of a second language retain a foreign accent, speakers with regional variations of a common language are treated like other foreigners. For example, an Italian speaker of English as a second language is likely to have a telltale accent that most speakers of English would recognize as Italian. Similarly, a Briton speaking English is likely to be identified as a Briton—by his or her native accent by other Britons and by his or her foreign regional accent by other speakers of English.

One major factor, however, differentiates the Briton's national accent and the Italian's foreign accent. The Briton probably would not attempt to eliminate his or her accent when among speakers of different regional dialects of English (and possibly even take pride in his or her regional accent). For most Britons, the proper way to speak English is both with a British accent and with British figures of speech. An Italian speaking English, by contrast, is likely to be aware that no speaker of English as a native language would consider as proper the use of Italian-accented English combined with Italian constructions and figures of speech. As a result, the Italian might try to make his or her English conform to the dialect used by those with whom he or she interacts.

Regional differences within the same language may also pose problems for the international business communicator: accent comprehension, recognition of usage differences, and stereotyping.

Accent Comprehension

For some listeners, all unfamiliar accents may be difficult to understand —thus regional accents among speakers of the same language may be as much of a stumbling block as foreign accents.

To illustrate, let us refer to our example of the Italian and the Briton in North America. For many North Americans, both the accents may represent problems linked to pronunciation.

People speaking English with strong Italian accents are likely to use open vowel sounds and to add vowel sounds at the end of words ending in consonants. As with any speaker of English as a second language, they may also have difficulty in placing the accent on the appropriate syllable. If these accentual traits affect comprehension, the Italian may try to correct his or her accent.

The Briton's pronunciation would also differ from an American's. The Briton would pronounce several vowels as flat or open that the American would nasalize or pronounce as closed. In many words, British English places the accent on different syllables than the same word rendered with an American accent. And several words would receive entirely different pronunciations. Thus the Briton would pronounce the word *lieutenant* as *lef-ten-ant*, while the American pronounces the same word as *loo-ten-ant*.

If the Briton and American were unfamiliar with these differences, some comprehension difficulty could occur.

In significant contrast to the Italian, however, the British speaker of English is unlikely to modify his or her accent to accommodate the needs of the American. The Italian is aware that his or her use of English is not standard. But both the Briton and the American, even if they have trouble understanding each other, are likely to believe that their pronunciation is the correct version. While people can, to some extent, consciously modify their accents, neither the Briton nor the American would attempt to conform to the accent of the other.

Comprehension differences caused by accents are, on the whole, of relatively little importance. Still, to the extent that they interfere with comprehension or breed resentment and annoyance, they should concern the international business communicator.

Recognition of Usage Differences

Many languages have significant differences in the phrases used or in the variant meanings of shared words. In many cases, a speaker's regional expression has no counterpart in another region, and so the listener simply cannot understand a familiar expression. In British English, an international call is known as a *trunk call*; in the United States it is a *long distance call*. The phrases are likely to be incomprehensible to speakers of the other version of English.

More dangerously, many words and phrases take on identifiable but different meanings from region to region. For this reason the international business communicator should be sensitive to the possibility of misinterpretation. One's first understanding may not reflect what one's foreign counterpart may have actually meant. For example, more than one business deal has been scuttled by the U.S. businessperson's reaction to a Briton's use of the phrase "to table a proposal." In British English when businesspeople wish to act on a proposal immediately, they speak of "tabling the proposal." In U.S. parlance, the same phrase means exactly the opposite — that is, to delay the idea indefinitely.

Regional differences are even more likely to surprise nonnative speakers of a language than native speakers who may have had greater exposure to regional differences. For instance, the English-speaking executives of the U.S.-based Parker Pen Company found in promoting their product in the Spanish-speaking world that wholly innocent words in one region become obscene or racy in another area. Thus in Spain the Spanish word *bola* has the innocent meaning of "ball" (for sports) or "ball point pen," but in some South American Spanish dialects *bola* may mean a coup or revolution; for others, a lie; and for still other speakers, a man's testicles (Ricks, 1983, p. 80). Similarly, the Swedish manufacturer Electrolux used the slogan "Nothing sucks like an Electrolux" to promote its vacuum

Figure 2.1 Electrolux's British advertisement.

cleaners in Great Britain (see Figure 2.1). This slogan proved unusable in the United States, where it means in slang that the vacuum cleaners were of terrible quality while also carrying an obscene overtone.

Stereotyping

Frequently, regional accents, like any intercultural indicator, may suggest prejudices and stereotyped images. Historical interactions between different regions often lead to stereotypes and preconceptions. Such preconceptions should concern the business communicator because they may represent cultural inferences of which he or she is unaware.

Thus Parisian speakers of French may believe that those with accents from the south of France are unbusinesslike, while those from the south of France may find those with Parisian accents pushy or arrogant. Similar tensions exist in the United States between those with Southern and those with Northern accents. Such differences are not insurmountable, as was the case with Joseph Stalin's thick Georgian accent, which was at times a point of ridicule among speakers of standard Russian, and Hitler's orotund Austrian accent, which was considered comical by his critics before his rise to power.

Still, such differences can have major effects on business communication. In the late 1960s, the U.S.-based multinational corporation Raytheon believed it was acting responsibly in sending a team of Italian-speaking experts to Sicily on a salvage operation. The Raytheon team of Italian Americans, however, all had a northern Italian accent. As a result, "Although the team members all spoke Italian, the Sicilians were distrustful of them because all of them had 'mainland' backgrounds" (Ricks, Fu, and Arpan, 1974, p. 58).

SOCIOLINGUISTICS

Sociolinguistics, or the social patterning of language, is an often overlooked issue that the international business communicator should consider. Sociolinguistics involves the way dialects and accents are used to reinforce social roles within the cultural framework of a language.

Not all speakers of a language speak the language in a manner that is considered proper. Class differences may be revealed by phrasing and accent. Such differences are often severe, as was dramatized in the popular musical *My Fair Lady*—in which an upper-class Briton attempts to change the accent of a Cockney woman in order to transform her into a member of his class. The use of certain expressions, though wholly understandable, conveys hidden messages linked to class. Thus the contraction *ain't* for *is not* indicates a lowly station in Great Britain or a lack of education in the United States. Similarly, the title *commendatore* in Italian is often used by those of lower class to show respect for a person without any real title.

Generally speaking, people from lower-class backgrounds exhibit more pronounced regional differences in accent. As Julia Falk observed (in this case regarding the United States), "the speech of people with relatively high incomes and educational backgrounds tends to be quite similar no matter which region of the country they live in" (1981, p. 509).

Sociolinguistic differences can affect international business communication in two ways. First, a business communicator who remains unaware of these hidden messages is at a disadvantage in understanding fully what others in the communication exchange may easily interpret. Second, the business communicator may inadvertently select a translator or interpreter who is unable to adjust to the class level indicated by sociolinguistically determined accents and phrasing. As a result, the business communicator, through the translator or interpreter, may seem to be of a lower class than he or she might wish to appear or, conversely, may seem to be putting on airs by using the accent and phrasing of the upper class in an inappropriate setting.

ENGLISH AND INTERNATIONAL BUSINESS: COMMUNICATING ASSUMPTIONS

It is impossible to examine the role of language in international business communication without discussing the enormous popularity of English as the universal language of business.

Eight of the world's leading trading nations either speak English as a native language or were nations in which English was spoken in a pre-independent colonial period: Australia, anglophone Canada, Great Britain, India, Malaysia, New Zealand, South Africa, and the United States. Together, these eight countries represent well over 25 percent of global imports. The company that cannot sell in English, therefore, faces a major barrier to over a quarter of the world's buying market. By comparison, the next largest linguistic bloc of trading powers — the French-speaking (Belgium, French Canada, France, and Switzerland) — represent only about 15 percent of global imports (McCrum, Cran, and MacNeil, 1986, p. 41).

English is the international language of air traffic. Thus a plane taking off in Portuguese-speaking Brazil and landing in German-speaking Austria uses English as it leaves the ground in South America and touches down in Europe, as well as in any communication that takes place between the two. When the radio replaced signal flags at sea, the language agreed on for transmission was English, even though most sailors do not speak English even as a second language (Weeks, 1982, pp. 39–40).

English is the most popular second language taught in Europe, the Middle East and Africa, Japan, and (recently replacing Russian) in the People's Republic of China. Such multinational Japanese corporations as Nissan and Datsun compose their international memoranda not in the Japanese of the company headquarters but in English. Nor is this limited to Japan. As one observer of European business has noted:

> Spain's Banco de Bilbao demands that all its graduate trainees speak English, and Philips, the Dutch electronics multinational company, conducts all its business in — you guessed it — English. In a management course run by a Dutch-based company, which I attended in London recently, a minority of the participants were native English speakers, but the proceedings were conducted entirely in English. Given the location, this may not be too surprising, but when the same course is held in France or Belgium, English remains the common language among the half a dozen different nationalities attending. (Lennon, 1989, pp. 5–6)

The language of many key industries is dominated by English. This is particularly true in science and technology. As George Steiner has found, "88 percent of scientific and technical literature [is] either published in English initially or translated into English shortly after its appearance in such languages as Russian, German and French" (1975, p. 468).

An extreme example of the role of English as an international language comes from the Italian-based multinational conglomerate IVECO, a heavy truck company. The necessity for English at IVECO has been described as follows:

> Based in Turin, financed by French, German and Italian money, staffed by Europeans for whom English is only an alternative language, [IVECO] none the less conducts all its business in English. Georgio Bertoldi describes a monthly board meeting in which "the vast majority of the people attending

are Italian, or French, or German. But the common language is English. Everybody talks English and the minutes of these meetings are written in English." Peter Raahauge, a Dane, commented that "you wouldn't get a job at a certain level in IVECO if you didn't speak good English." (McCrum, Cran, and MacNeil, 1986, p. 41)

Regardless of its unquestioned importance, however, English ought not to be considered the *only* language of world business. Indeed, the very fact that English *is* the most widely spoken language in commerce represents to its native speakers its most significant handicap. Virtually no other language group believes, as do the English speakers, that its members can effectively compete on a global scale with only their own language. Even among the French-speaking cultures, the next most widely used commercial language, almost all major global competitors use languages other than French. Thus, in a recent survey of French companies conducting business with the United States, all of the respondents indicated that they used English (Victor, 1987). Indeed, Michelin, a bastion of French industry, has been cited as an oddity since it "still issues its annual reports in French only" (Moskowitz, 1987, p. 362).

By contrast, the English-speaking cultures' reliance on English to conduct world business is legion. Kolde (1974) found that most managers in U.S. multinational corporations looked with suspicion on those who spoke a second language. Indeed, a 1979 survey of top U.S.-based international companies found that "NONE . . . had ever hired a person at entry level specifically because of his or her language or area studies background" (Hayden and Koepplin, p. 236).

Nor is such linguistic ethnocentrism limited to the United States. Guy Garvin, in his survey of British exporters, found that less than half of those interviewed "regarded language skills or area expertise important factors in hiring personnel for their export sales offices" (1985, p. 54). The former British ambassador to Tokyo, Sir Hugh Cortazzi, told British businesses on the occasion of his retirement that they should not blame Japanese red tape and import restrictions for their failures in Japan. Instead, he cited the inability of British businesses to speak Japanese as among the most important factors for their lack of success (Garvin, 1985, p. 54).

English speakers' unfamiliarity with other languages places them at a disadvantage despite — or arguably *because* of — the widespread use of their native language. For English speakers in particular, foreign languages represent a trade barrier. To the extent that English speakers cannot communicate in the language of the people whose markets they enter, they may find themselves treated as more foreign than other foreigners who *do* speak the native language. All the language barriers discussed in this chapter, therefore, loom large for monolingual English speakers.

Since English speakers are less likely to understand foreign languages, they are probably not familiar with their foreign markets firsthand. Moreover, they do not usually have access to the magazines, television, films, and other conveyors of popular culture that would acquaint them with the foreign markets they enter. Conversely, since the distribution of English-language magazines, television, films, and so on is common in other countries, companies in English-speaking markets may find that they are competing on an uneven playing field when it comes to cultural familiarity. Non-English-speaking cultures are much more likely to understand the nuances of U.S. or British culture than U.S. or British companies are to understand non-English-speaking cultures. As a result, foreign competitors may enter such English-speaking markets as the United States and Great Britain more successfully than U.S. and British companies are able to enter markets in which English is not the first language.

Another factor to consider is the diminishing economic power of the English-speaking nations. With the growing economic power of such non-English-speaking nations as Japan, South Korea, Singapore, and other Asian nations, as well as the continued strength of the European trading powers, the relative importance of English may dwindle. This is particularly likely if the trend toward the service economy—in the fields of managerial and technological expertise—continues. Service and expertise as commodities requires first-rate communication. Since language barriers constitute an obstruction to communication, the use of a foreign language (i.e., English) to convey the necessary information may become untenable if competitors offer their services and expertise in the native tongue.

To some extent, the monolingualism of the United States has already provided a competitive edge in the export of technological expertise in world markets to bilingual Canadians, since "recent gains have occurred where language has proved the deciding factor" (Garvin, 1985, p. 61). As an official in the Canadian Department of External Affairs has indicated regarding the success of Canada in Algeria and other francophone third world nations: "We offer North American technology and we offer it in French" (Simon, 1984, p. 8).

OVERCOMING LANGUAGE AS A BARRIER TO BUSINESS COMMUNICATION

The premise of this book is that the most effective means for improving international business communication is to increase one's awareness. Recognizing intercultural differences and similarities between one's own culture and the foreign cultures with which one conducts business allows the flexibility and empathy needed in international negotiations. It is for this reason that most of this chapter has focused on matters affected by language.

Still, businesspeople, in addition to increasing their sensitivity to the barriers language poses in international communication, can take five specific steps to reduce the risk of related misunderstanding or pseudoconflict. These steps should not be seen as taking the place of alertness to the possible sources of difficulty described in this chapter until now. Nevertheless, they may help to overcome the roadblocks to business communication that language often creates. The five steps are:

1. adjustment of untranslated communication
2. careful selection of translators and interpreters
3. personal review of translated documents
4. attention to names and key terms
5. back-translation.

Adjustment of Untranslated Communication

Although, as we have discussed, it is almost always preferable to communicate in the foreign language of one's counterpart, it is not always possible to do so. As a result, international business communicators must often decide whether to use their own language or to employ a translator or interpreter. If the other party does not understand the business communicator's language, the answer is simple; a translator or interpreter must be employed. If the other party does understand that language (as is often the case with English), the business communicator is faced with a choice.

In some situations, it is appropriate and less expensive to conduct business in your own language. Ideally, you should decide to use your own language only if you are certain that all the participants are fluent and the material communicated does not involve sensitive issues. Nevertheless, the possibility for misinterpretation increases when information is not communicated in the primary language of all the participants. To reduce the chance of misinterpretation, use language designed for the speaker of a second language.

The following is a checklist for communicating with speakers of a second language.

1. *Avoid idiomatic speech, slang, and colloquialisms.* Idioms, slang, and most informal, colloquial terms usually defy translation. For example, in English we talk about "sitting on the fence," which makes no sense at all in French. The French instead use the expression *ménager la chèvre et le chou,* or "to manage the goat and the cabbage," which has little meaning for English speakers. Similarly, in the United States people often indicate a desire "to touch base" on this or that matter. Such a phrase is meaningless in societies where baseball is not played. A famous example of the failure of idioms to translate involved Pepsi's "Come alive with Pepsi" campaign. The popular English-language advertisement was mistranslated in German as "Come out of the grave" and in Asia as "Bring your ancestors back from the grave" (Ricks, 1983, p. 84).

2. *Speak slowly.* It is difficult even for fluent speakers to think in another language. Talking slowly helps the listener to translate. Doing so is often more problematic than it appears. In some cultures, notably the

United States, the ability to speak and respond quickly is often recognized in the workplace as an indicator of preparedness and intelligence.

3. *Keep vocabulary simple.* When writing or speaking in your own language, try to determine the competency of the other party. Because it is generally safe to assume that people have less competency than they claim to have or even appear to have, it is advisable to choose the simplest possible words. This does not mean that you should use simple concepts. Lack of control of a language does not indicate inability to understand concepts.

4. *Rephrase frequently.* Repeat key ideas in different words. This practice eliminates miscommunication in cases in which the other party mistakenly believes that he or she has understood a phrase or passage. It also provides another opportunity for interpreting what you have said for those who will not admit that they did not understand you.

5. *Use written support.* In face-to-face communication, use written materials to reinforce what you plan to discuss. Since most people's reading knowledge of a foreign language exceeds their spoken knowledge of that language, the written materials help the other party to translate difficult or less familiar phrases.

6. *Become familiar with cognates.* Many languages have cognates, or words that have common roots or are even identical in the two languages. For example, the Italian word for *transaction* is *transazione*, similar to the English word. Using such words when appropriate helps the other party translate.

7. *Be wary of "false" cognates.* Some words sound alike in two or more languages but have different meanings. For example, the Spanish word *confianza* sounds like the English word *confidence*, but the two words do not have precisely the same meaning; the Spanish word carries a much deeper sense of trust, reliance, and unshakability. Recognizing that even those fluent in the language may misinterpret or misuse false cognates, it is helpful to become familiar with the more common ones. This helps you avoid them and understand their use or misuse by the other party.

8. *Summarize.* In oral international business communication, it is advisable to stop frequently to summarize your understanding of the discussion. Summarize both what you meant to say as well as what you believe the other party intended to say. Such a technique helps prevent misinterpretations from building one on top of the other.

Selection and Use of Translators and Interpreters

In most international business communication involving more than one language, a translator or interpreter can prove to be valuable. However, while not all situations require translators or interpreters, there are two instances in which their services are essential: first, when neither party speaks the other's language; second, when the information communicated is highly sensitive or important. If interpreters or translators are to be used, they should be selected carefully. In choosing a language assistant, one should look for three governing characteristics.

1. *Reputability*. Select only reputable translators or interpreters. Examine their credentials, inquire about the types of translation work they have done, and, if possible, ask for references. Avoid using staff members' acquaintances who have limited training (i.e., a few years of the language in college) or people who speak the language but who have no experience as a translator or interpreter (i.e., an immigrant office worker). Instead, choose from established translation services or universities with programs in language for professional purposes. Business translation and interpretation is a difficult skill requiring both extensive practice and the need to stay abreast of current trends in the language. When General Motors entered the Belgian market, it mistranslated its slogan "Body by Fisher" into Flemish as "Corpse by Fisher" (Ricks, 1983, p. 83). While such errors can never be fully eliminated, a reputable translator reduces the chances of similar blunders.

2. *Dialect familiarity*. Determine whether the translator has experience dealing with the regional (and, if possible, sociolinguistic) group with which you are conducting business. As noted earlier, such dialect differences can be serious. Moreover, differences in terminology can be substantial. A well-known U.S. toothpaste producer found this out the hard way. The toothpaste was promoted in Latin America using the European Spanish term for "interesting." The translator apparently was unfamiliar with regional Latin American Spanish, since, as the manufacturer learned, in that dialect of Spanish, "interesting" is a euphemism for "pregnant" (Ricks, 1983, p. 81).

3. *Business terminology expertise*. Most language experts have little or no understanding of business and technological terms and even less familiarity with negotiation strategies. Thus it is important either to find a person well versed in language for professional purposes or to brief the person you use on the likely terminology he or she will encounter while translating. It is also important to resist the temptation to involve the language expert in the business at hand beyond his or her ability to convey thoughts from one language to the other. The language expert can only interpret your words; he or she must not be used to help you think of what you wish to say or write.

In using an interpreter (an oral language expert who provides immediate translation in face-to-face situations), you should take into account unavoidable limitations. First, the person to whom you speak is not the interpreter but your business counterpart. Consequently, your attention and eye contact should be directed to the other party, not the interpreter. Also, interpretation is grueling work; in a negotiation or other high pressure situation you should try to lessen the difficulty of the interpreter's task (and thus reduce the chance for error resulting from fatigue). This can be accomplished by having frequent breaks, keeping responses short or injecting pauses in long responses, and, as noted before, providing clarification of specialized business or technological terms.

Personal Review of Translated Documents

Insist on reviewing personally all translated documents, even when using a translator for a language with which you are entirely unfamiliar. At the least, you may encourage the translator to do his or her best work because of the concern you show. The review should not, however, be wholly symbolic. The following items can benefit from your attention.

1. *Personal names.* Errors in the spelling of your name and the names of the other parties involved are often easier for you to find than for the translator.

2. *Company names.* As with personal names, your greater familiarity with the relevant company names, brands, and trademarks makes you a better proofreader than the translator.

3. *Overall appearance.* Different languages may change the format of a document. Thus, Hebrew and Arabic go from right to left and use lettering systems foreign to the European languages, thus changing much of the written page's appearance. Regardless of the direction of print or nature of the lettering, however, ink smears, whited-out passages, and other evidence of a carelessly prepared manuscript are universal. Neat documents are important in business writing in any language.

4. *Absent diacritical marks.* All reliable translators include appropriate diacritical marks—the squiggles, dashes, and dots that play so important a role as accent marks, umlauts, and the like in French, German, Spanish, and many other languages. While many word processors have diacritical mark options, English-language typewriters have no means for producing these marks. If you know that the language into which your document has been translated uses diacritical marks and they are absent or have been inserted by hand instead of typed, chances are you have chosen an inexperienced translator who used an English-language typewriter. Insist that the translator type all diacritical marks.

5. *Obvious errors.* Few errors in translation are obvious to the person who does not understand the language. For example, in German all nouns begin with capital letters—and thus a parade of uppercase words might look like a clerical error to someone with no knowledge of German. Still, if your name appears uncapitalized, some mistake may have occurred and it is worth asking the translator to explain. Changes in degrees earned, numerals, and dates are other signals that obvious errors may have slipped in. You should also check any numerical conversion that the translator performs to help U.S. documents conform to the metric system; mathematical errors are possible.

Attention to Names and Key Terms

Attention to names and key terms is more useful in reducing tensions than in eliminating actual misunderstanding.

Most people are attached to their names. Therefore, the international business communicator should pronounce the names of his or her foreign associates correctly. This usually means listening carefully and, if possible, practicing in advance. Most people find mispronounced names annoying, but an honest attempt to say a name correctly goes far to improve the matter. Refusing to pronounce a name as too foreign or making a joke about someone's name to relieve your own discomfort in being unable to pronounce it correctly can seriously undercut a business dealing.

Getting names right goes beyond pronunciation. In many Asian languages first names and family names are in a different order from those in most European languages. This may lead to confusion as to which name is the family name. The situation is often exacerbated when well-meaning speakers of European languages give their first name last in Asia and enlightened speakers of Asian languages, in Europe or the Americas, reverse the order of their names.

On the other hand, gender differences in last names may reflect a choice intended to communicate a message. Thus, whether married women adopt the names of their husbands is often a reflection of societal values in the United States. For example, a U.S. woman may choose to keep her maiden name, join her maiden name to her husband's last name (with or without a hyphen), or drop her maiden name and adopt the last name of her husband. Her choice in this matter may (or may not) communicate to those familiar with these options something about her view toward gender roles in society; but to those unaware of these name choices, no message is possible.

Similar difficulties are common for somewhat different reasons in Icelandic. In Iceland, women usually do not change their names after marriage. Children's last names, in turn, are made out of the possessive form of the father's name with the suffix *son* (son) or *dottir* (daughter) added. Consequently, Thor Hermannsson could be the husband of Vigdis Njalsdottir and their children might be named Steingrimur Thorsson and Bryndis Thorsdottir.

In some societies, the popularity of certain names can also be confusing, particularly for a communicator from an English-speaking country, where names are not shared on so common a basis. For example, almost 10 percent of the population, or well over 100 million people, in the People's Republic of China are named Zhang, and over 60 percent of the Chinese have the same 19 surnames (DeMente, 1989, p. 14). The difficulty of keeping people straight based on their names alone is even more pronounced in Korea, where over half the population has one of four names: Kim, Lee, Park, or Choi (DeMente, 1988, p. 29). In such countries, it is imperative to remember the full names and usually the titles and company sections of your business associates.

Indeed, attention to names should not be limited to personal names. Familiarity with the names of the company and products with which you interact is often just as important. Mispronouncing or refusing to pronounce the name of the company is often considered an insult or a sign that you do not find the company important enough to get its name right.

It is also helpful in many cultures for international business communicators to familiarize themselves with a few key terms. Even something as simple as greeting an Arabic business counterpart with "salaam aleihem," or saying "Salud" as you toast a Mexican partner, may prove to be worthwhile. Although such a practice is sometimes useful in itself, its greatest value is symbolic. For many cultures—though by no means is this universal—using even a few phrases of the language may show an appreciation for the society as a whole.

One final point involving names is to determine whether the name of your company or product has undesirable connotations in the language in which you are working. The most famous example is probably General Motors' promotion of the automobile Nova, which in Spanish means "won't go." But General Motors is not alone. Ford's Pinto (Portuguese: "small male appendage"), Colgate's Cue toothpaste (an obscenity in French), and Coca-Cola's Fresca (Mexican Spanish slang: "lesbian") faced the difficulty of having a name with an undesirable connotation, as did the Finnish beer "Koff" and the French pen manufacturer Bich (now Bic) in English-speaking countries.

Back-Translation

The most reliable means to discover translation errors is a system called *back-translation*. Back-translation is a two-step process. In the first step, one translator puts the document into another language. In the second step, a new translator retranslates—back-translates—the document into the original language. The original manuscript is then compared with the back-translated document to determine errors or discrepancies.

Whenever a document is particularly sensitive or important or, in less sensitive or important documents, when time and cost considerations allow, the international business communicator should use back-translation. It is the most effective means for reducing the possibility of mistranslation.

SUMMARY

None of the suggestions provided in the last section can entirely overcome the business communication barriers associated with language described in this chapter. The suggestions may help reduce the most common impediments to effective communication that language imposes.

Still, you should keep in mind the major elements influencing the role of language differences in the workplace.

Each language is a shaper of reality for its speakers, and so no language can ever be translated exactly. At best, a good translator or person fluent in the language can arrive at a rough equivalence of meaning. Because of the importance of cultural attachment to language, you should stay alert to indications of linguistic ethnocentrism, insider-outsider relationships, and alliances associated with linguistically determined group dynamics. You should also make efforts to accommodate difficulties resulting from varying degrees of fluency or even the selection of a language in which to conduct your business dealings. In addition, as an alert international businessperson, you should watch for signs of accent and dialect differences associated with regional or socioeconomic groups that may communicate subtle messages. Finally, if you are fluent in English, as most readers of this book will be, you should remain cognizant of the special characteristics affecting English as an international language. Awareness of the role of language in international business communication provides the most useful tool available.

Issues of Environment and Technology in Business Communication

*A*mong the most substantial elements affecting international business is the role culture plays in determining the nature of the environment in which people live and work. "The environment in which a communication occurs," Marshall Singer has noted, "can be a major factor in determining how effective one can be in intercultural communication" (1987, p. 58).

This chapter is divided into four parts, each dealing with how culturally determined differences in the way people view their environment and technology affect the conditions in which international business communication takes place. First, because the importance of environment is not often recognized in most domestic business communication, the chapter opens with several examples of the way in which environmental factors may affect communication conditions. Next, the chapter describes sources of cultural differences in the work environment: climate, topography, population size and density, and the availability of natural resources. Third, three categories of the culturally based differences in the way people view technology and their consequences for the international businessperson are discussed. Two brief sections examine the positive and negative elements of the three categories and provide guidelines for reducing misunderstandings the cultural differences may create. Finally, the chapter closes with a summary.

DEFINITION AND ILLUSTRATIONS

We may define *environment* as the physical elements—both natural and human-made—that surround a person. These elements influence, on the most fundamental basis, the way each person understands the world around him or her.

Many businesspeople do not recognize environmental factors as culturally subjective. Instead, they tend to view as universal a wide variety of subjects actually shaped by cultural norms and attitudes. Still, the differences from culture to culture in these norms and attitudes directly affect international business communication.

Environmental factors may even include differences in the physical traits of the people living in a society. Japan, for example, refuses to accept clinical data for use in the pharmaceutical industry from abroad. Several companies have interpreted this refusal as evidence of nontariff barriers — in this case, blocking free trade with Japan. This interpretation, in turn, affects the communication practices of these companies, because they view such positions as unfair trade practices. Yet as Sam Maugeri, president of Warner-Lambert Japan has observed, nontariff barriers and political motivations have little to do with the issue. He notes that, with respect to size and metabolic yield of products, the Japanese differ from most North Americans (the home base of Warner-Lambert is in New Jersey). Commenting on the position taken by the Ministry of Health that only Japanese data will be accepted, Maugeri has said, "that's not an unreasonable position in my opinion — especially from a dosage standpoint. Japanese are smaller and you might expect a 10 to 15 percent reduction in dosage right off the bat. Besides, certain products aren't tolerated as well by Orientals as by Westerners; aspirin, for example, has a high incidence of side effects among Japanese" (Christopher, 1986, p. 187).

Differences in the perception of the environment (and the use of technology in that environment) determine how members of a culture view many related business concerns. Such matters include transportation and logistics, health care and sanitation, accident prevention and occupational safety, settlement patterns, and energy cost and availability (Seelye, 1984; Borisoff and Victor, 1989).

A workplace issue of relatively little importance in one culture may be of great significance in another. Indeed, conflicting values may result in ethical dilemmas for international businesses. If one culture, for example, values full employment while placing less importance on the safety of the workplace, it may employ workers under conditions that would be considered unsafe or unsavory in another society. In the United States, relatively greater stress is laid on occupational safety than in many less developed nations. Many such countries culturally (as well as politically) emphasize full employment over safe and healthful working conditions. This raises the ethical question of whether a U.S. company would be wrong to employ workers in those countries under conditions that would be unacceptable in its domestic operations.

Conversely, thousands of guest workers from Turkey and North Africa flooded the cities of Germany and France in the 1960s and 1970s to obtain what to them were high-paying jobs in wholly acceptable conditions. By German or French standards, however, the guest workers lived and worked in appalling conditions for unacceptably low pay. Culturally the Germans and French were used to different environmental standards. Again, an ethical question is raised: Should the French and German employers treat guest workers holding different cultural values the same way they would treat employees from their own cultures, especially *in* their own countries? Several nations with large numbers of guest workers, most notably Sweden, have answered yes. The practice of treating guest workers as fully equal to Swedish citizens in itself represents a cultural trait that differentiates Sweden from France or Germany.

It is natural for individuals who have spent their entire lives in the same country to take for granted many aspects of the physical elements around them. They may be aware, to some extent, of the fact that others within their society may live and work under somewhat different circumstances. Nevertheless, both a rich and a poor person will likely have similar ideals and expectations. Thus, most Europeans or Americans would expect to go home to a bed that is raised from the ground and to eat their meals on a table while seated on a chair. Neither the bed nor the table and chair are universal for all cultures, but they are the norm in Europe and in most of the Americas. This simple and expected life style, however, could be a major factor in the way in which businesspeople negotiate over the issue of *mats*. The assumption would especially affect the product design and advertising of eating and sleeping mats from a culture in which beds, chairs, and tables are foreign. Both Europeans and North and South Americans might remain prime markets for such mats, but only if they were targeted for a purpose suited to their living quarters: sellers might advertise mats for decorating hallways or wiping off shoes more efficiently.

Similarly, people in different professions may be aware of differences in their working quarters. For example, an Australian accountant may think of the workplace as an office with a desk, while an equally Australian chef may think of the workplace as the kitchen in the backroom of a restaurant. Nevertheless, their assumptions are, on the whole, alike. The accountant and chef — as Australians — hold similar views of the physical world surrounding them precisely *because* they are Australian. Their preceptions are alike on a wide variety of subjects, from how crowded to how warm to how well lit their workplace should be. Both accountant and chef would probably expect easy access to electrical outlets, telephones, and other modern devices readily available to most Australians.

Consequently, it might not occur to an Australian, whether an accountant or a chef, who traveled on business to Zaire or the People's Republic of China to specify a work environment with Australian levels of lighting, roominess, temperature, access to electricity or telephones. In turn, the host in Zaire or China might not be aware of the Australian's expectations, either to attempt to provide these facilities or to ease the transition to a different cultural environment.

Environmental factors that affect the workplace differ in three distinct ways from culture to culture:

1. the ecological characteristics and natural resources available
2. the perception of the physical environment
3. the perceived role of technology, or the way in which people manipulate that environment

Because these three elements are likely to vary from culture to culture, the actual environment and technology that exist in one culture cannot usually be replicated in another. The businessperson should be aware of the probability of encountering these differences. In particular, to avoid misunderstanding, the businessperson should be prepared to adapt his or her communication strategy to accommodate such variations.

PHYSICAL CHARACTERISTICS AND NATURAL RESOURCES

To survive, people adapt to the natural world around them and, in doing so, define an integral part of their own culture. While the way in which people adapt to their environment is the defining cultural element here, the natural world is the building block on which the superstructure of adaptive behavior is erected. This behavior, in turn, creates suppositions that affect communication, including business communication.

The five physical elements most likely to influence business communications are

1. climate
2. topography
3. population size
4. population density and space usage
5. the relative availability of natural resources.

Each culture deals with these factors in its own way. Each of these factors has a varying effect on a society, depending on the physical setting of that nation. It is useful to examine each factor separately.

Climate

Some researchers attribute most of a nation's development to such environmental factors as climate. One noted researcher, Andrew Kamarck, has gone so far as to link tropical climate to underdevelopment, citing increased levels of harmful insects, disease, and parasites (Kamarck, 1976). While even Kamarck indicates that it is dangerous to attribute all development to environmental causes, factors like climate do influence a nation's development and cultural mind-set. This is because any environment universally affects the behavior of those who live there. Figure 3.1 shows the major climates of the world.

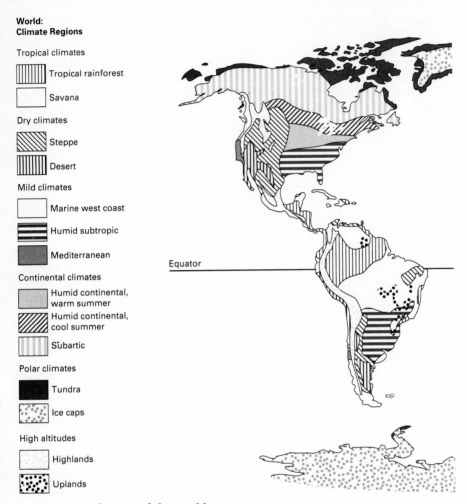

**World:
Climate Regions**

Tropical climates

Tropical rainforest

Savana

Dry climates

Steppe

Desert

Mild climates

Marine west coast

Humid subtropic

Mediterranean

Continental climates

Humid continental, warm summer

Humid continental, cool summer

Subartic

Polar climates

Tundra

Ice caps

High altitudes

Highlands

Uplands

Equator

Figure 3.1 Climates of the world.

Perhaps the most useful way to view climate is less as a molder of perceptions than as a key factor in the way business is conducted. Though not a direct influence on the host country's culture per se, climate nevertheless is something with which residents of a region are familiar, especially if weather or other conditions can be dramatic. For example, one major U.S. food-processing company faced severe production difficulties in Mexico because of a climatic condition (Ewing, 1969). The U.S. company built a pineapple canning facility at the mouth of a river but failed to take into account the flood schedule. The pineapples were grown on a plantation upstream from the facility. The food processor had intended to float the pineapples downstream to the facility, where the fruit would be canned and loaded onto ships. Climatic conditions being what they were, though, the pineapples ripened at the same time that the river reached its yearly flood stage. The current of the flooding river proved too strong to bring the ripe fruit to the cannery. The fruit, consequently, rotted on the barges.

Since the company had no other means of getting the fruit to the factory, it was forced to close. Both the ripening time of the fruit and the flooding schedule of the river were predictable climatic events about which local Mexican experts on agriculture or river conditions could have informed the U.S. food processor if the company's planners had researched the possible effect of climate on their venture.

Even if the Mexicans had referred to flood seasons, however, their meaning would have been foreign to the U.S. businesspeople. In the United States, businesspeople are accustomed to view climate as generally irrelevant, kept in check (with the possible exception of hurricanes or tornadoes) through technological controls. To the Mexicans, at least in this particular situation, the climate was a controlling element to which businesspeople adapted. In both cases, the climate was so much taken for granted that apparently neither the U.S. nor Mexican businesspeople thought to raise the subject.

Topography

Topography too can affect the cultural behavior of those who live in a region. *Topography* can be defined as an area's physical and natural features, such as mountains, bodies of water, and internal distances. In some cases, marked topographical barriers within a country can produce strong domestic cultural differences, of which the person conducting business in that nation should be aware. Thus boundaries formed by the mountains in Switzerland have made each of that country's cantons a distinct cultural entity and have produced four major cultural regions divided along linguistic lines: Romansch in the Grisons, German in the north, Italian in the south, and French in the west (see Figure 3.2). Similar geographic barriers in Spain have contributed to major cultural divisions among those in the geographically cutoff regions of Galicia, Catalonia, and the Basque regions (see Figure 3.3).

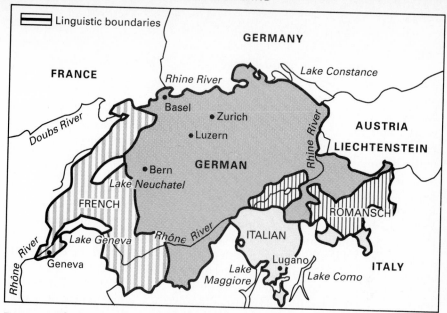

Figure 3.2 The linguistic boundaries of Switzerland.

Figure 3.3 The linguistic boundaries of Spain.

More frequently, topographical features affect a whole nation and help define its culture.

For instance, it has been observed that "the Dutchman was always open to—and appreciative of—foreign influences, precisely because of his close bond with the sea. The geographic position of the Netherlands has more or less compelled the Dutch to take on such an attitude" (Engbersen and Engbersen, 1991, p. 642). The Dutch historian Johan Huizenga (1968) described this sea-influenced cosmopolitanism as a house without windows, open to the breezes of influences from the land (France and Germany) and the sea (Britain), while all the time maintaining the frame of the house as Dutch culture itself. The Netherlands' geographic location, relative small size, and excellent natural harbors have all led the Dutch to look beyond their borders. As a result, environmental issues have shaped the Dutch mentality toward internationalism. This is nowhere more evident than in the area of global trade. From the time of the Netherlands' establishment as a nation in the 1600s, Dutch business has relied heavily on navigation, and from that to world trade. Today, the Netherlands, despite its relative smallness, is a leading power in global trade, acting as a home to a host of global giants, including Philips, Royal Dutch/Shell, Unilever, Heineken, and Akzo.

Similarly, the enormous distances of Canada have led, in part, to the development of that society's culture. "Canadian history," according to one of Canada's leading historians, J. M. S. Careless, "largely records a struggle to build a nation in the face of geographic difficulties" (1965, p. 3). Similarly, Andrew Malcolm has observed that "Canada's awesome geography and its accompanying harsh climates share a palpable power that shapes the life, the work, the thinking, and the values of every soul on its broad landscape" (1986, p. 6). The result is that for Canadians (or other nations of sparse population and great open spaces, such as some regions of the United States) long-distance travel is both commonplace and necessary. By contrast, in smaller nations or those with topographically obstructed regions (such as most nations in Western Europe), mileage is likely to be perceived as a much greater barrier. As a result, a Canadian business executive may think nothing of driving from Toronto to Windsor, a four- to five-hour trip, for an afternoon meeting. By contrast, a Briton traveling from London four hours north to Newcastle might consider the trip a significant obstacle. These conceptions directly affect business communication precisely because the viewpoints seem so fundamental—that is, neither Briton nor Canadian would expect the other's view to differ from his or her own.

The cultural assumptions that topographical features create and that may influence business communication are not necessarily permanent, however. A country's technological infrastructure may alter its topography. Thus the improvement of British motorways has shrunk the time for the same London to Newcastle trip from nine hours to four by enabling motorists to drive safely at faster speeds.

Population Size

Population size is a major factor in the way the members of a society view the world around them. A nation with a small population is fairly limited in the nature of domestic business that it is able to conduct. In fact, its domestic market will be so small, comparatively, that its companies will generally be unable to produce goods solely for the domestic market on a large enough scale to be profitable.

Thus industrialized nations with small populations are often export-driven. Countries such as Sweden or Switzerland, for example, with populations of just over 8.5 million and just over 6.75 million respectively, must look to foreign markets to grow economically. Such major global corporations as Sweden's Electrolux, Saab, and Volvo or Switzerland's pharmaceutical concerns and banks depend primarily on foreign markets to remain profitable. Consequently, the culture in these nations reinforces a tendency to look beyond their own borders. Cultural isolationism is, at least for business, counterproductive, and as a result the culture reinforces cross-cultural sensitivity.

Even countries of relatively large populations face a significant disadvantage when competing with companies from population giants. Firms in the United States or Japan, for example, have the option of selling their services or products exclusively to their own huge domestic markets. Yet businesses even in relatively populous countries like Italy or Great Britain can accept this option much less readily. A company from one of these countries that decides to remain a fully domestic operation is unlikely to achieve the production capacity and overall profits of their U.S. or Japanese equivalent simply because their market size is so much smaller. A corporation usually must rest on a more substantial foundation than a small to mid-sized domestic population can support, to create the funds required for large-scale or capital-intensive activities.

Competition can harm even those multinational corporations committed to selling their products globally if they are based in a nation with a relatively small population. Where a U.S. or Japanese multinational corporation might think of testing a product domestically before expanding on a global scale, the relative smallness of the domestic market in a country like the Netherlands makes such efforts less effective or less profitable. As a result, companies in small countries are likely to move at the earliest stages of production into the international arena. Such ventures, in turn, reinforce a tendency toward greater cross-cultural awareness.

In recent years, the issue of comparatively small domestic markets has given rise, in part, to such supranational organizations as the European Economic Community, or Common Market. Carlo De Benedetti, chairman of Italy's Olivetti Corporation, significantly observed that "companies [in Europe] have realized that a unified Europe is no longer an option. . . . Without at least a Continental dimension—in terms of market shares, production and commercial structures, access to the financial markets, and so on—it is impossible to cope with the dual competitive pressures from the U.S. and Japan" (1988).

The willingness to subordinate nationalist goals to form supranationalist unions predates the Common Market. The desire to join with others may even represent a business characteristic of cultures with small to mid-sized populations that is essentially foreign to larger nations.

Indeed, so many companies based in countries with small to mid-sized populations have merged across national boundaries that it is worthwhile to cite a few examples. Most notable among these transnational mergers, representing the height of cross-cultural awareness and leadership is Unilever, the world's largest consumer products company. Unilever came into being long before the Common Market. It resulted from the merger in 1930 of the Netherlands' Margarine Union and Britain's Lever Brothers. It has operated successfully for decades, with twin headquarters in London and Rotterdam, and has grown primarily by merging with (or actually taking over) other companies all around the world, including Harriet Hubbard (France), McNiven (Australia), National Starch and Chemical (United States), Gessy (Brazil), Batchelors (Great Britain), Vita (the Netherlands), Pepsodent (United States), Rondi (South Africa), Brooke Bond (Great Britain), and Perlina (Peru).

Likewise, the world's largest manufacturing company (when ranked by assets) and largest oil company (when ranked by reserves) is another Anglo-Dutch concern: the Royal Dutch/Shell Group. Like Unilever, Shell, which was formed in 1907, long predated any thought of the European Economic Community. Significantly, the Royal Dutch Petroleum Company and the Shell Transport and Trading Company entered into a joint venture, at least in part, specifically to battle the largest oil company in the United States, John D. Rockefeller's Standard Oil Trust (now Exxon). Here was a contest between firms in nations of great and of relatively small population size. Standard Oil's large domestic population (and significant domestic oil deposits) provided a base for expansion and entry into world markets. It is notable that Rockefeller solidified his position in the U.S. market before expanding internationally. By contrast, Royal Dutch/Shell, a company whose individually small home markets (and limited domestic natural resources) led to a transnational effort, focused from the very outset on international markets and sources of oil.

Companies in other countries with small to mid-sized populations have also created concerns operated jointly from more than one national base. Agfa-Gevaert, founded on a model like Unilever's, has two jointly owned operating subsidiaries. Agfa-Gevaert's parent companies in Germany and Belgium are divided 50–50 and act as holding companies. Similarly, though not a full merger, the joint management arrangement (or *Zentral Gesellschaft*) of VFW-Fokker has control divided between three Dutch and three German managers, although the company remains headquartered solely in Germany.

Not all cross-national cooperative efforts to increase domestic market size succeed. Dunlop-Pirelli, for instance, is a good example of a cross-national venture in which cultures did not mix well. The corporate marriage joined Great Britain's Dunlop with Pirelli, already a transnationally based operation divided between Pirelli SpA of Italy and the Société Internationale Pirelli of Switzerland. The cultures (both national and corporate) did not easily meld and contributed to the eventual demise of Dunlop-Pirelli.

Success or failure, however, is not the main issue here. Rather, the key point is that such efforts are relatively common in smaller nations, whereas corporate executives in more populous nations are less likely to establish transnational leadership with multiple headquarters of equipollent strength. Significantly, few major U.S. or Japanese corporations, no matter how global their sales or numerous their foreign subsidiaries, follow the binational patterns of Unilever, Royal-Dutch Shell or Agfa-Gevaert.

The large domestic markets of these nations and the resulting freedom to adopt ethnocentric principles to their overall strategy make truly international leadership culturally foreign. No necessity exists to force supranational cooperation, and thus nationalist tendencies become the norm even among the most multinational of Japanese or U.S. enterprises. The one notable exception is in the oil industry; such companies as ARAMCO and Shell/Esso in Europe and Caltex in the Pacific and Africa represent binational efforts. In that industry, though, the resource limitations of petroleum itself necessitate supranational cooperation.

The oil industry is, indeed, clearly an exception borne of an extraordinary situation. Such supranational coordinated endeavors are almost wholly absent among U.S. financial institutions, automobile manufacturers, pharmaceutical concerns, and computer firms, even though the companies in these services and industries themselves have a global presence. For example, IBM is among the most successful multinational corporations in the United States. It has subsidiaries throughout the world and is almost universally admired in terms of both sales and management in the many nations in which it has a presence. Because IBM allows scientists and computer experts to contribute to its laboratories and to the corporation itself wherever the labs are located, scientists can take part in computer research in such relatively small nations as Sweden and Austria, where otherwise no indigenous research operation would exist. Moreover, IBM's presence helps nations such as France, the Netherlands, Great Britain, and Germany—which already have or are working to develop computer companies—to advance their computer knowledge and promote greater opportunities for their computer experts.

Nevertheless, as Christopher Tugendhat has remarked, "the only completely self-sufficient, or potentially self-sufficient, country in the IBM network is the U.S." (1971, p. 155). Tugendhat goes on to explain that the reason for this rests in large measure on the population size of the

United States as IBM's home base. "Besides being its home country," he writes,

> the U.S. accounts for over three-quarters of the company's gross income. Because the market is so large IBM can product all the components needed for a computer. Elsewhere this would be unprofitable as the individual markets are too small to support a full operation while enabling the company to achieve the long production runs necessary for maximum profitability. (p. 156)

The point here is that countries with large populations can think on a global scale. IBM has one of the greatest international presences of any corporation. Indeed, a majority of the world's multinational corporations are based in the United States and Japan, not in those nations with smaller populations. Still, managers of companies in large countries may perceive themselves as having the choice to remain within their domestic market or at least to view their home market, as IBM does, as the most important one. In countries with smaller populations, such assumptions are either highly limiting or wholly impossible. Virtually no industrial leader in a country with a small population can think of its domestic market as its most important base and compete in a free market economy. If it did, it would find itself limited by the number of people to whom it could sell. More important, unless it was protected from external competition, it would be unable to compete against foreign companies that had either a large domestic base or that *did* think globally.

Ironically, companies based in less populous countries may find that the disadvantage of a small market forces them into an advantageous position in global competition. The traditional waterfall approach, practiced by multinational corporations based in countries with large domestic markets, may be obsolete. The waterfall model (see Figure 3.4), which has

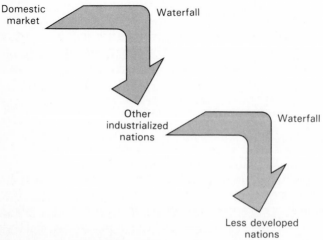

Figure 3.4 The waterfall model.

been used by the majority of U.S. corporations as well as by many firms in Japan and the larger European nations (France, Germany, Great Britain), is based on the practice of securing one's home market, then moving one's product to other industrialized nations and, finally, to the less-developed nations. Kenichi Ohmae, among others, warns that "the waterfall model . . . which has been used implicitly by many traditional multinational corporations (MNCs), has become obsolete. The assumption that the home country's strengths and success can be transferred to other [developed] nations, and to less-developed countries (LDCs) can betray a company, particularly in fast-moving high-technology industries" (1985, p. 21). In this respect, the global vision of the company based in a nation with an inherently inadequate domestic market may provide the alliances and global strategy necessary to penetrate foreign markets and compete effectively on a worldwide scale.

Population Density and Space Usage

Population density strongly influences underlying assumptions about how people use their environment. Such assumptions, in turn, directly affect business behavior and communication. Table 3.1, which lists the population density of selected nations, indicates the wide range of densities around the world.

Population distribution, as a subset of population density, also plays a role in the way people conduct business. A good example is Canada, which, as we have discussed, is a relatively sparsely populated nation. Nonetheless, in such urban centers as Toronto and Montréal, Canada may face some of the same problems as more densely populated nations. Still, the attitude toward the use of space even in these cities is more likely to be expansive than in a nation such as South Korea, which has over one and a half times the population of Canada, densely packed into an area of roughly one one-hundredth the size.

Population density and distribution have a significant impact on a wide range of activities. For example, in more crowded cities, transportation may be less efficient, and massive traffic jams make it harder for people to arrive at appointments on time. In densely populated Hong Kong, businesspeople have come to be more flexible about punctuality than either Britain or China, its two major cultural influences.

Shopping habits are also determined, to some extent, by population density and distribution. The H. J. Heinz Company lost an estimated $8–10 million investment in an effort to sell Frutsi (a popular Latin American processed orange juice) in Brazil at least in part because it misread the Brazilians' shopping patterns. Heinz, which sells Frutsi successfully in Mexico, did not adjust to culturally determined differences in distribution needs from one nation to another. "In Mexico," as at least one analyst indicated, "Frutsi sells well in neighborhood shops, where much of the shopping is done. So Heinz concentrated on neighborhood shops in São Paulo. But 75% of the grocery shopping in that city is done in

Table 3.1   POPULATION DENSITY OF SELECTED NATIONS

Density per square mile	Nation
11,325.0	Singapore
2,032.5	Bangladesh
1,454.7	Taiwan
1,116.8	South Korea
924.0	The Netherlands
846.8	Japan
845.1	Belgium
698.0	India
608.8	United Kingdom
583.8	Israel
519.7	Vietnam
494.4	Italy
423.8	Switzerland
335.9	Nigeria
317.2	Czechoslovakia
308.9	Denmark
306.7	People's Republic of China
283.8	Thailand
269.7	France
240.2	Indonesia
199.9	Spain
197.0	Greece
129.3	Ireland
110.6	Kenya
68.3	United States
49.1	Sweden
45.8	Brazil
41.8	Mexico
33.5	Soviet Union
32.8	New Zealand
16.3	Saudi Arabia
6.9	Canada
6.2	Libya
5.8	Australia
5.0	Mauritania
0.1	Greenland

Source: World Data Annual, Chicago: Encyclopaedia Britannica, 1991.

supermarkets, not the smaller shops" (Michaels, 1988, p. 61). Apparently assuming that all Latin American nations were fairly much alike, Heinz was not sensitive to the differences between village populations in Mexico and urban centers in Brazil.

Perhaps more than any other factor, land use is affected by population density. In densely populated cultures, land is at a premium. Avoidance of wasted space becomes of tantamount importance. Conversely, in sparsely populated nations, space is at considerably less a premium.

Businesspeople in densely populated regions are likely to be more aware of the efficient (or inefficient) allocation of space than those in sparsely populated areas. This tends to hold true even in sparsely populated regions of densely populated nations, because the attitude toward land use infuses the culture. This is why the use of space has so strong an impact on business communication.

The point may be best illustrated by a comparison between the United States (a relatively sparsely populated nation) and Japan (a very densely populated nation). It is important to note that the populations of Japan and the United States are not evenly distributed, as is the case in most nations. Thus the megalopolis stretching from Boston to Washington, D.C. along the U.S. Eastern seaboard is very densely populated, while areas in the northern Midwest and Southwest have vast stretches of sparsely settled land. Likewise, with the exception of the area surrounding Sapporo, the Japanese island of Hokkaido is relatively sparsely populated. Still, Japan averaged (in 1991) just under 847 people per square mile, while the United States averaged just over 68 people per square mile.

The scarcity of space in Japan as a whole affects the perceptions the Japanese hold, even in sparsely populated areas. Conversely, the relative abundance of land in the United States colors perceptions in crowded New York City as much as in the open spaces of Wyoming. Thus the U.S. penchant for big items — roomy cars, large living quarters — may derive at least in part from the fairly widespread availability of space. U.S. history has been dominated by the notion of westward expansion into what was seen as undeveloped or essentially empty land. Japanese history, long centered on the village, arguably had the seeds of large-scale urbanization well before its industrialization in the late nineteenth and early twentieth century. The difference between Japan and the United States in the perception of space usage can be readily seen in the way people park, set up their homes, and arrange their working quarters.

To use parking as just one example: in Japan, parking on the street is almost impossible and often illegal. Yet with limited space, the two-car garage, so common in the United States, is an extravagant use of land. One increasingly common solution among those Japanese with two cars is a double-decker home garage, in which the second car is raised on a mechanical lift directly above the first car. Similarly, while parking structures have been built in most U.S. urban centers, the amount of space required for a U.S.-style parking structure is increasingly untenable in Japanese cities. Increasingly narrow and difficult sites are being turned into parking towers, which have a computer-controlled conveyor and storage system much like a Ferris wheel.

Similarly, the way in which people use products is based directly on their perception of space. U.S. refrigerators, when introduced in Japan, proved to be a dismal failure. The reason had little to with Japanese protectionism or even competition. As we noted earlier, the refrigerators exported to Japan from the United States simply did not fit into the Japanese kitchens, which were so tiny by North American standards as to be inconceivable to U.S. manufacturers. In a related issue, the Japanese, having less refrigerator space, shop more often for perishable or frozen goods, a factor that differentiates the way in which these goods would be marketed in the United States and Japan. Similarly, the need for storage has made such products as Tupperware a great success in Japan, not for the preservative quality touted in the United States but because Tupperware containers stack neatly and so conserve space.

In a densely populated society, even a product like baby powder can represent a challenge to marketing departments. Because the Japanese place a strong cultural value on cleanliness, they change their babies' diapers frequently. They seemed, as a result, to U.S. baby powder companies to be an ideal market for baby powder. In test trials, Japanese consumers indicated that they would like to powder their infants, but sales were dismal when the U.S. companies actually introduced the product to the Japanese market. Again, the reason did not rest in overt Japanese trade barriers or competition. Instead, it was discovered that the cloud of powder associated with the standard U.S. sprinkle-on can was incompatible with the small Japanese living quarters. One shake would cover nearly a whole living room, kitchen, or dining room (the usual Japanese places for this procedure) with powder (Fields, 1983).

Perhaps most significant for the business communicator is the difference in the way U.S. and Japanese offices are arranged. The majority of Japanese companies employ the open-space format in their offices. Here people of all ranks work in large rooms without intervening walls to separate their desks. Each person has his or her assigned work space, usually arranged by work group and rank, but in such a situation, virtually everything that takes place in one section of the room is possible to hear in another part. Privacy and secrecy have no role in such an environment, and teamwork is reinforced by the physical layout. By contrast, the majority of U.S. offices provide individual rooms or cubicles, each set off from the others by walls and usually doors. Such an arrangement—by its physical layout—encourages privacy and secrecy as well as independent thought and work. Moreover, one is often able to determine rank by the physical trappings of the room, including its size. Such useful cues in the United States, however, have no meaning in the open-space Japanese system.

Other features of contemporary society besides land use result from population density differences in the two countries. Billboards are popular in both the United States and Japan in heavily populated areas. However, since they can count on heavy pedestrian traffic as well as traffic jams, the Japanese employ, at least in Tokyo, Mobotrons—giant, wheeled VCRs that move like trucks throughout the city. While the expense would be questionable in all but the most crowded U.S. cities, these mobile video billboards are cost-effective in Tokyo. Similarly, on Japanese public transportation — which advertisers can almost always expect to be heavily used — Japanese businesses buy time on recorded tapes reminding passengers that this or that stop is near their store or service center.

While dozens of other examples exist, ranging from obstruction of sunlight to noise reduction, the key issue is that businesspeople are unlikely to consider space (crowded versus roomy conditions) in planning products linked to life style precisely because it seems so universal. As a result, businesspeople may misread subtle messages conveyed in a cross-cultural setting.

For example, the misguided U.S. visitor to a typical Japanese office might well misinterpret the message conveyed by the large undivided space to mean that the Japanese do not place much value on status or rank. The Japanese are very much concerned with rank and status differences. What the U.S. visitor would have to recognize is that the Japanese communicate these concerns in ways other than through office size and decoration.

Still, the use of work and living space does reflect cultural values. As suggested earlier, the use of space and population density may reinforce or even shape attitudes toward privacy. For example, Germans have been noted to place greater stress than Americans on such environmental features as soundproofing, double doors, and heavy curtains, as well as shrubs or other barriers to shield yards from neighbors. It has been asserted that such preferences result from, or at least reinforce, a social distance that is greater than that in the United States (Condon and Yousef, 1985; Hall, 1966).

The Relative Availability of Natural Resources

The relative abundance of natural resources and the existing ecological factors or interrelationship of people to their environment remain an influence on any country's historical development and subsequently on its culture in general, and on business communication in particular.

On the most elementary level, the relative availability of one item over another affects the tastes in food and other everyday items. Cultural preferences for certain foods, for instance, in part originally result from their availability. Local tastes in food then create an environment where consumers expect those foods to be *made* readily available. One can attribute much of the success abroad of the McDonald's restaurant chain to adjustments it has made to suit culturally based preferences. Without changing its basic concept of the U.S.-style burger, fries, and shakes, McDonald's has modified its products slightly as local palates have dictated. The company sells vintage wines along with its soft drinks in France and local beers in Germany. Acknowledging the Japanese fondness for sweet foods, McDonald's added more pickles to its hamburgers and more sugar to its buns. In Malaysia, customers can select not only chocolate and vanilla shakes but *durian*-flavored shakes, as an accommodation to that nation's taste for the popular Southeast Asian fruit.

A more important issue, however, is the relative accessibility of sources of energy, water, and other basics. For example, a nation poor in resources is more likely to stress conservation than one with superfluous resources. Again, we can examine culturally imbued differences in attitude in the United States and Japan. Akio Morita, chief executive officer of the Japanese electronics giant Sony has observed that

> the attitude in America is much more easygoing as far as raw materials are concerned than in Japan. America has so much of everything—oil, coal, copper, gold, uranium, timber—that even today Americans do not seem to take conservation seriously. I am reminded of the American expression, "There's plenty more where that came from" We have no such expression. (Morita, 1986, p. 259)

It is significant that Morita illustrated his observation by pointing to the fact that Japanese has no counterpart to the U.S. figure of speech he quotes. The way in which we view the world directly affects the way in which we communicate in business.

A culture rich in one resource but poor in another will, if it has run the survival course of history, adapt itself to those conditions. As several experts (Leach, 1965; Kaplan and Manners, 1972; Prosser, 1985) have observed, culture is the primary means through which people adapt to and control their environment.

Such relative richness has enormous effects on business behavior in particular. Indeed, the discovery of vital natural resources early in a nation's industrial development may shape its whole business culture. U.S. business behavior is often characterized by lack of concern for conservation and by expansiveness (as Morita's observation indicates). Such attitudes may reflect the wealth of natural resources mined and harvested, and rapid Western expansion, during the first 150 years of U.S. history.

The link between early discovery of resources and national development, however, is nowhere clearer than in the relationship between Australia and the natural resources giant Broken Hill Proprietary, Ltd. When Australia's rich mineral deposits at Broken Hill were discovered in 1883, Australia was just emerging as a nation (it received independence only in 1901). The founding of Broken Hill Proprietary—the largest company in Australia, accounting for 10 percent of the value of all shares listed on the country's stock exchanges—dramatically shaped not only the way in which Australians conduct business but the nature of Australian culture. According to George Blainey,

> it is unlikely that any significant mining field of the future will exert as much influence as did Broken Hill on Australian life. This can be said with some confidence, less because the finding of another Broken Hill is so improbable than because of the fact that a major mineral discovery is more

influential when it is made early in the life of a nation. As a nation becomes more populous and its institutions and economic life become more settled, it is less malleable to great mineral discoveries and similar events. (1982, cited in Moskowitz, 1987, p. 111)

Indeed, when Saudi Arabia, the Persian Gulf states, and Iran discovered the potential of their great oil deposits, their cultures were less able than that of Australia to adapt to the impact of such enormous wealth. Their difficulty in adapting was — as Blainey's comment would seem to indicate — precisely because the Arab and Iranian societies had a long and rich tradition. Unlike the fledgling Australian nation, which could grow socially as well as economically with its newfound natural wealth, the Saudis, the peoples of the Gulf states, and the Iranians had to accommodate their traditional life style, including the way in which they conducted business, to the Western structures necessary to produce the oil and sell it in the global marketplace. "Tradition and progress," as one expert on Saudi Arabia has commented, "were engaged in a titanic struggle to maintain an impossible equilibrium. Western advisors designed mechanisms that would allow Saudi Arabia to function the way the Saudis believed they wanted it to function, and the culture, dominated by Islam, rose up to do battle against the kingdom's quantum leap into the future" (Mackey, 1987, p. 178).

Cultural attitudes toward natural resources may also affect the way in which businesses use those resources. The belief among many Plains Indian tribes in the sacredness of their land, for example, kept them from developing their resources or from compromising with white settlers over land allocation. The subsequent destruction of these cultures by combined U.S. government and business interests was a drastic response to conflicting views of the environment; one would hope that such brutality will never be repeated.

Still, cultural differences in attitudes toward the environment still come strongly to play. Less industrialized nations may consider resources to be their primary means of entry into financing industrialization — as a kind of national treasure. This view has dominated, for instance, at Petroleos Mexicanos (Pemex), the world's fifth largest oil producer and the largest company in Latin America. Pemex's representatives have consistently resisted foreign interference even while allowing foreign investment. Mexico received independence around the time that oil became important to the industrial world. As one of the earliest major oil producers, Mexico has long associated its oil with the welfare of the nation itself. As a result, Mexicans are more likely to look askance at foreign interest in its oil. This attitude was recently demonstrated to U.S. bankers who suggested that Mexico could reduce its foreign debt by selling its oil reserves. As one spokesperson for Pemex observed: "Oil is as sacred as the Virgin of Guadaloupe for many Mexicans" (Moskowitz, 1987, p. 457).

Nations rich in resources, however, may not necessarily be rich economically. Conversely, because cultures adapt to the physical environment around them, nations that are poor in resources may develop their human resources to overcome the environmental handicaps they face. Indeed, Kenichi Ohmae, managing director of the Tokyo office of McKinsey & Company, has gone so far as to suggest that wealth in natural resources may be a greater hindrance than benefit. He points to the way such resourceless nations as Japan, Singapore, South Korea, and Taiwan economically surpass such resource-rich neighbors as Indonesia and Australia. "Today, the basis of the world's wealth," Ohmae asserts, "is shifting from natural resources to advanced technology. The natural resource superpowers are watching the relative worth of their assets dwindle while nations with intelligent human resources are expanding their trade and accumulating surpluses" (1987, p. 4).

Ohmae in particular cites Switzerland as the model of the resourceless nation achieving economic success through education and training. A further cultural adaptation the Swiss have added, in contrast to the Japanese, is a quiet growth in foreign markets to keep potential antagonisms in check among those nations with whom they must maintain a trade surplus to prosper.

PERCEPTIONS OF TECHNOLOGY, CULTURE, AND PHYSICAL ENVIRONMENT

How people view technology, or the way in which they manipulate their environment, significantly affects the way they view the world. Thus, in countries like the United States, Japan, Canada, Australia, and the nations of Western Europe, people customarily assume that others have at least a basic communication technology. Yet such assumptions often result in business communication breakdowns. The telephone, for example, has an international range of per capita distribution spanning from 89 telephones for every 100 people in Sweden to 0.4 in Indonesia and under 0.3 in Ethiopia. To illustrate how such disparity can affect international business communication, we can cite how differences in telephone distribution between the United States (77 telephones per 100 people) and Poland (10 telephones per 100 people) undermined at least one business negotiation. The incident was related by cross-cultural consultant Marija Dixon:

> Dixon tells the story of an American who went to Poland on business. An important meeting needed to be scheduled but the American wasn't sure about timing, so he asked the Poles to call him in the morning to set a time. They never called, the meeting didn't happen. "It was a big deal for him, he was very disappointed. He assumed the Poles weren't interested. The Poles, on the other hand, assumed everyone knew the phones in Poland are not always reliable — on a bad day, it can take two hours to get a call put through, if you can get a working line" (Decker, 1990, p. 23).

Perhaps more important, culturally influenced beliefs regarding the relationship of people to their environment can vary substantially. The way in which people view this relationship seriously affects both how they use technology to solve work problems and how they communicate about the role they believe technology should play in the workplace. As one expert has observed, "neither the environment nor culture is a 'given' but . . . each is defined in terms of the other, and . . . environment plays an active, not just a limiting or selective, role in human affairs" (Hardesty, 1987, p. 270). In other words, the use of technology both influences and is influenced by the host culture. Culture and the environment are thus in a "dialectical interplay" (Kaplan and Manners, 1972, p. 79), and technology is the prime manipulator of the environment. In short, cultural differences regarding the relationship of people to the technology they use to interact with their environment needs to be considered in intercultural business communication situations.

"Technology and the way it is used," Herbert Schiller has written,

> affects the basic infrastructure of social communication. Thus the acceptance of a "developmentalist strategy" in a nation introduces more than industrial techniques and equipment. The way human beings are related to each other in work and in their community and family life is largely, if not overwhelmingly, determined by the nature of the technology employed, how it is employed, and the social relations that govern its use. (1976, p. 48)

The way in which people use the resources available to them—that is, their level of technology—often shifts notably from culture to culture. As some have observed: "Culturally-engrained biases regarding the natural and technological environment can create communication barriers" (Borisoff and Victor, 1989, p. 131). Businesspeople accustomed to the application of technology particular to their culture should anticipate differences in other cultures' technological development and adjust their communication strategy accordingly.

Such technology-related differences manifest themselves in a wide range of business subjects. Many of the differences are relatively easy to overcome as sources of misunderstanding, especially if they are based, at least in part, on lack of *knowledge* rather than on intrinsic values. As several authors have observed (Seelye, 1984; Borisoff and Victor, 1989), communicators can eliminate or reduce sources of nonproductive conflict by examining variations among cultures in those environmental areas (discussed above) that technology is most likely to affect.

Understanding a culture's *attitudes* toward technology differs from understanding how a society's technology affects the behavior of its members. This distinction is important because technology and culture act on each other, as mentioned above, in a relationship of reciprocal causality. As Mesthene observes, "Technology can lead to value change either by: (1) bringing some previously unattainable goal within the realm of choice or (2) making some values easier to implement than heretofore, that is, by changing the costs associated with realizing them" (Mesthene, 1969, p. 500). "Technology," Terpstra and David note, "affects values because a

society's technology sets limits on the range of social goals that are feasi-
ble" (1985, p. 152).

These larger issues of culture-technology reciprocity play a significant
role in any long-term interaction between cultures and thus merit the
attention of researchers. The immediate concerns of day-to-day cross-cultural business communication, however, rest more on the *attitudes* a
culture's members hold regarding technology than on the dialectal interplay of a given culture and its available technology. In understanding a
culture's attitudes toward technology, it is possible to select the most
appropriate means to communicate about the use of technology when
interacting with businesspeople from that culture.

Attitudes toward the use of technology in resolving problems in the
work environment can be divided into three major categories:

1. control,
2. subjugation, and
3. harmonization.

Table 3.2 is a partial list of cultures representative of these three
catagories.

Control

Those who hold control attitudes toward technology see technology as a
positive good. Members of societies with a control attitude believe that
their environment is meant to be mastered and that technology is the tool
by which they can master it. Relatively few cultures fall into the control
category. However, the impact of this bias toward technology is far-
reaching, as this is the view primarily held in such major industrialized
nations as the United States, Canada, Australia, Great Britain, Germany,
Israel, the Netherlands, Luxembourg, and the Scandinavian countries.

Control cultures generally emphasize the concept of self-determination: will-power and drive enable one to achieve a desired goal. As Copeland and Griggs point out (regarding North Americans, though the point is
applicable to those with shared views): "Underlying much of American
enterprise is the conviction that individuals and organizations can substantially influence the future, that we are masters of our destiny, that we
can make things better" (1985, p. 12). Technology is the means to attain
those goals.

The technology of control cultures derives in large part from a belief
in the rational, scientific approach to reality. The structure of nature is
seen as mechanistic and directly tied to the cause and effect reasoning
in which technological innovation — or at least experimentation —
flourishes. By emphasizing analytic-deductive reasoning, control cultures
have, as Johnson observes, "tended to define spiritual and 'immaterial'
phenomena as potentially superstitious and dangerous." The debunking
of spiritual or nonanalytical explanations of reality, in turn, has "yielded

Table 3.2   WORK ENVIRONMENT PERCEPTIONS

Control cultures	Subjugation cultures	Harmonization cultures
Australia	Algeria	China
Canada	Bolivia	India
Denmark	Burma (Myanmar)	Japan
Finland	Burundi	Singapore
Germany	Chad	Sri Lanka
Great Britain	Colombia	Taiwan
Iceland	Ecuador	
Israel	Guatemala	
Luxembourg	Hondurus	
The Netherlands	Iran	
Norway	Jordan	
Sweden	Libya	
United States	Malawi	
	Malaysia	
	Mali	
	Mauritania	
	Oman	
	Peru	
	Qatar	
	Rwanda	
	Saudi Arabia	
	Sudan	
	Tanzania	
	Turkey	
	United Arab Emirates	
	Yemen	
	Zaire	

to a progressive demystifying of the physical environment, through the outstanding accomplishments of research and technological development" (1985, p. 124).

Technology for control cultures has, at least to some extent, taken the place of the spiritual or religious. If a problem occurs in a control culture and the members of that culture wish to correct it, they turn to scientific research and technological innovation. For example, if a major river begins to flood regularly and cause serious damage, technicians design a dam to control the river. Society does not accept the flooding as inevitable and people simply adapt their life styles to the new set of circumstances. That is, farmers do not change the crops they grow — say, by switching from wheat to rice, which requires flooding. Similarly, the culture tends not to turn to spiritual sources, such as prayer, to stop the flooding.

In control cultures, a tendency exists to judge those with a view toward technology that varies from their own as operating on a lower level, not just of technology but of civilization as a whole. Technology, as the means of controlling the environment, is also the means of interpreting the quality of life. From the perspective of the control culture, the more one is able to control one's environment, the higher the quality of life.

This perception affects the way in which business executives communicate about the use of technology. Control culture members speak of themselves as the "developed nations" and the rest of the world as "developing" or "underdeveloped." Even astute and otherwise sensitive international business observers from control cultures characterize their country's level of industrialization as the seemingly obvious highest stage. They generally assume, moreover, that other cultures wish to attain a similar stage (for example, Ohmae, 1985; Terpstra and David, 1985; Garland and Farmer, 1986). Such assumptions are not wholly valid, as we will explore in the next section.

Subjugation

Subjugation cultures perceive technology as at best neutral and often as something negative. Members of cultures with a subjugation attitude are likely to believe that they are subject to their environment. In direct contrast to control cultures, subjugation cultures see their environment not as something to harness but rather as something that utterly masters them. Such cultures may interpret their environment in two ways: (1) impossible to control or (2) undesirable to control.

Subjugation cultures in the first group view natural forces as too overwhelming to control. Placing little emphasis on the scientific and analytical bias that is the philosophical foundation of control cultures, subjugation societies tend to consider technological innovations as doomed from the outset. Technology is perceived not so much as negative but as simply a waste of effort.

Because many subjugation cultures are in less industrialized regions of the third world, control cultures, as noted above, may consider subjugation views as backward or even foolish. Such an ethnocentric bias, however, is often unreasonable. When control cultures attempt to manipulate subjugation environments, they may find that massive technological efforts are needed to accomplish even the most minor of adaptations, a fact which increases their condemnation of the subjugation culture. As with any ethnocentric attitudes, such biases are likely to lead to conflict between subjugation and control culture members.

When subjugation cultures attempt to introduce levels of technology comparable to that in the control cultures, they may face great obstacles. It is how people use technology and not merely the technology itself that creates the so-called technology gap between these cultures. To implement technology in a subjugation culture, one must first change its members' views toward their environment. The culture's values as well as its level of analytical knowledge must be altered. In such cases, as Rybczynski notes, "There is a desire for the fruits of modernization, but only a partial grasp of the changes that are required to achieve them" (1983, p. 28).

The question then arises whether the introduction of the foreign technology into the culture is not a form of technological imperialism. To adapt to the technology, the subjugation culture must cease being the society it had been. The two may not be able to coexist.

A host of experts on technology transfer and culture clash have been concerned with this issue. Ellul (1964) has suggested that technology transfer does not parallel the pouring of new wine (the technology) into old bottles (the receiving cultures) but the breaking of the bottles in the process of pouring so that the wine no longer has a container to hold it. Similarly, Drucker (1970), Illich (1977), and Rybczynski (1983) have all suggested that the non-Western cultures — at least the subjugation cultures — are disappearing under the flood of Western, or control culture, technology. The tendency of technology to destroy certain cultures that attempt to adopt it is likely to increase resentment on the part of the culture being destroyed. Such hostility would cast a pall over any communication about technology directed toward members of a subjugation culture. Consequently, both the giver and the receiver of the technology should be aware of this possible source of resentment.

While the first type of subjugation culture considers the environment as not amenable to alteration, the second type views technology as a negative force. To members of such subjugation cultures, many aspects of their environment are not so much unchangeable as *undesirable to change*.

A culture may view the world as having been created the way God intended it to be. To use technological innovations to change the existing order could be interpreted as akin to sacrilege. "Self-determination is a concept almost outside the comprehension of many peoples," Copeland and Griggs have written. "In Moslem countries from Libya and Turkey to Indonesia, the will of Allah influences every detail of life and many feel it is irreligious to plan for the future. Although many Moslem executives do think in terms of strategy and plans, even they will regard their efforts in the context of what God wills" (1985, p. 13).

Similarly, superstitions — arguably a form of religion — need also to be considered: "Making light of superstitions when doing business with other cultures may prove to be an expensive mistake. In parts of Asia, for example, ghosts, fortune telling, palmistry and soothsayers are all integral parts of culture and must be understood as influential in peoples' lives and in business dealings as well" (Phatak, 1989, p. 36).

Whether based on religion or superstition, the resistance to tampering with the natural order may be deeply rooted in the culture. The attitude on the part of control cultures that the beliefs of such subjugation cultures somehow make them undeveloped or even backward is strongly ethnocentric. People behave within their own societies in ways that are logical within their own cultural parameters. They act as they do, in short, because it makes good cultural sense to do so.

As this concept is likely to meet resistance among control culture members and as this discussion is directed in large part either to members of control cultures or those who have adopted such values, a further point of illustration may be appropriate here. Members of control cultures tend to judge their success on their material well-being, precisely because their technology allows them to manipulate their environment in a manner enabling them to achieve great material success.

Such behavior, however, was not always the case in most control cultures. In pre-Renaissance Europe, for example, before the advent of technological innovations on a massive scale, Christians — who comprised the majority of the population — held a subjugation attitude toward technology. Pre-Renaissance Europeans were cautious about disrupting the natural order. Technology was seen as interfering with God's design of the world. As Condon and Yousef have observed, "testing and questioning is considered destructive or blasphemous. Much of Christian thought before the Renaissance reflected this orientation, as all works of man were to glorify God and not to examine his works" (1985, p. 108). What is important to remember is that cultures may succeed in ways other than the economic or material markers used to measure success in control cultures.

Harmonization

The final category of cultural approaches toward technology is that of harmonization. In harmonization cultures, people are seen as neither mastering nor being subject to their environment. Instead, members of such cultures view themselves as part of their environment.

Even in such a culture as Japan, whose technological level is as sophisticated as that of Europe and North America, substantial differences exist in the role technology is seen to play in the culture. Technology, to summarize in very general terms, has (at least traditionally) been seen as a means to maintain the balance in nature, or *wa*, that people disrupt by their actions (DeMente, 1981). The use of technology for its own sake must be measured against its place in the natural order. More important, the application of technology is measured against its effect on the social whole of interpersonal relationships of the group.

In Hindu culture, the material world affected by technology influences only the physical sphere of being, the basest level of existence. Many Indians draw a distinction in daily life between the secular (into which realm the use of technological innovations falls) and the spiritual. As Bharati observes, "it is the secular teacher who has to teach people important skills, and it is the holy man whose sole duty is to show the way to unification with the higher self. Social work or medical services are all right in their own domain, but they must not intrude into the circle of total purity" (1985, p. 217). Indeed, as another study has noted, "The self as the basis of important human achievements, such as scholarship, artistry, or *technological invention,* is totally ignored in Indian philosophical texts" (DeVos, Marsella, and Hsu, 1985, p. 3, *emphasis added*).

Similarly, Chinese thought generally emphasizes reasoning from a whole rather than the analytical deduction characteristic of control societies. Gregory-Smith, in contrasting Western and Chinese approaches to science, has observed that

> Western modes of cognition are deductive and analytic, emphasizing causal relationships and the perception of substrata. Chinese epistemology, its logical complement, is inductive and synthetic, emphasizing temporally defined dynamic relations and the systematic perception of functions. (1979, p. 228)

The Chinese stress on functions, or the way things work within the whole, rather than on causal relationships has a profoundly different effect (from that of control cultures) on the perceived role of technology.

The examples of Japan, India, and China reflect the harmonization culture's understanding of technology's role in the environment. Technology is neither — as in most control cultures — necessarily a positive good in its own right nor — as in subjugation cultures — a futile, negative, or unspiritual force. It is a subset of a larger system of thought that builds on existing aspects of the culture.

CULTURE, BUSINESS COMMUNICATION, AND THE THREE APPROACHES TO TECHNOLOGY

Since it is relatively easy to slip into a judgmental ethnocentrism regarding the use of technology, it is important to stress that all three approaches work well within the cultures in which they are employed. No one approach is right or wrong. All three approaches to technology have pros and cons. Whether we view these traits as advantages or difficulties is itself culturally linked. What is important is that no approach is superior or inferior to the other. Each view of technology works within its own society to achieve ends that are considered valuable for that culture's overall goals. The effective business communicator ought not to pass judgment on any one approach toward technology described here. Again, people behave as they do in a culture because within the parameters of their own culture it makes good sense to act in that way.

The control culture approach has arguably made the use of technology among its most definitive traits. For its members, technological innovation does not threaten the native culture; it *is* the culture.

However, as Frank Johnson has observed: "The overall effect may be to produce a way of thinking that concentrates attention onto material objects and applies rationalistic models of explanation to immaterial 'things.' The preference for such explanations may contribute to a loss of the sense of the mystical, and a tendency to consider pathological that which is not 'rational' or 'logical'" (1985, pp. 126–27). Moreover, as technology becomes increasingly sophisticated, overall comprehension may be severely diminished. While technology is honored, actual knowledge of the various spheres in which the technology acts is absent. As Johnson writes: "the acceptance of the mechanical and logical characteristics of a world of objects also constitutes a 'belief system.' The *psychological* experience of this 'belief' in science, in complicated technology and materialism may not be so different to [sic] 'superstitious' interpretations of reality" (pp. 124–25).

This attitude is potentially dangerous, particularly in control cultures that are democracies. As Rybczynski notes:

> Increasingly one must be an expert to understand even a single aspect of the technological environment, and few experts can master more than a small part of the whole. Yet in a democracy people are compelled to form opinions and to make decisions about technology that are far outside their intellectual and emotional acquaintance. . . . the only way to form opinions on most subjects is on the basis of secondhand experience. (1983, p. 26)

The control culture's deference to science is thus not much different in some respects from the subjugation culture's approach to religion. However, the resistance to change of the subjugation culture makes its members resist the introduction of technology. While reluctance to accept technology enables subjugation cultures to preserve their way of life, economic or material advancement may well be threatened in a global economy characterized by increasingly sophisticated technological advances.

The harmonization culture blends the preservation of tradition of the subjugation culture with the acceptance of technological development of the control cultures. This stance would seem an ideal compromise of the two positions. However, the ideal and the reality of harmonization may not be particularly in line with each other. For example, the pollution rampant in Japan might suggest that the Japanese have lost some of the cultural ideal of harmony with nature. Similarly, the antitechnology attacks of the Cultural Revolution in the People's Republic of China may be interpreted as at least a temporary rejection of the harmonization approach in favor of subjugation.

What is essential, however, is not to pigeonhole cultures conveniently into one of the three classifications we have discussed. Instead, the business communicator should be aware that attitudes toward technology are deeply rooted in a society's overall culture. As these views affect the way in which members of the culture communicate about technology, business executives should assess and take into account the views toward technology in both their own culture and the culture with which they communicate.

ACCOMMODATING DIFFERENCES IN THE PERCEPTIONS OF ENVIRONMENT AND TECHNOLOGY

Unlike many of the issues raised in this book, accommodating cultural differences in perception of environment and technology is relatively straightforward. Differences in such areas as authority conception, contexting, and social organization are likely to become tinged with an ethical bias toward right and wrong as determined by the businessperson's home culture. By contrast, variations from culture to culture in the perception of environment and technology are more likely to appear as different rather than acceptable or unacceptable.

The most important exception to this precept comes in the contrast between control cultures and cultures in which religion or superstition serves as a barrier to technological change. Here ethnocentric biases favoring or condemning efforts to alter the environment are often emotionally charged. Accommodating such differences demands great flexibility. Most conflicts that arise from cross-cultural differences in the perception of environment and technology, however, are more likely to occur from ignorance of these differences than from an ethnocentric bias. Consequently, business communicators have less to overcome in this respect than in other, more emotionally entrenched issues raised elsewhere in this book. In most cases, we need merely to recognize the variations to accommodate them.

This is easier to suggest than to put into practice. Therefore, the following recommendations for discerning cultural differences in attitudes toward the environment and technology may prove useful.

Assess the possible impact of environmental factors likely to affect work behavior. Determine in what ways a culture differs from your own regarding climate, topography, population size, population density, and the relative availability of natural resources. Consider to what extent these differences might affect business behavior. Whenever possible, view photographs or films of workplace and living quarters of cultures with which you have no firsthand experience.

Compare the target culture's view of technology with your own. Ask yourself how, if at all, the target culture differs in the way its members regard technology. Determine to what extent the culture in question falls into a control, subjugation, or harmonization category. Be aware that most cultures are likely to share attributes of more than one category.

Interview those who are familiar with the target culture. Talk with those from your own culture who have recently returned from the target culture as well as with those from the target culture itself. Experts at universities, national trade associations, and the commerce divisions of your country's embassy in the target culture are also good sources of information. Ask in particular about the work and living conditions and the level of technology available. Formulate your queries to elicit specific responses to the concerns raised in this chapter; most people will not have thought of these issues in the abstract terms of environment or technology.

Read. In no other area raised in this book is information as useful as in examining environmental and technological differences. Since most difficulties arising from these differences stem from ignorance rather than from more deeply rooted cultural biases, the more information you can gather, the less likely environment and technology will hinder the communication process. Read about the target culture not only to assess workplace and living environments but to determine geography and demographics. Since lack of information is probably the most likely source of difficulty, reading is arguably more useful on these issues than in any other variable affecting international business communication.

SUMMARY

Culture shapes our attitudes toward the environment and technology. Such attitudes, in turn, affect our underlying perception of the world, including the way in which we communicate in business.

Our view of the environment is determined by many factors, but five physical elements are most likely to influence directly our business behavior: climate, topography, population size, population density, and the relative availability of natural resources.

In dealing with its environment, each culture employs technology somewhat differently. These differences in the use of technology may be divided into three broad approaches toward the environment: control, subjugation, and harmonization. The sophistication level of a country's technology is increasingly central to how it conducts business, and so these three views of technology are likewise increasingly important. The three approaches are particularly significant to cross-cultural business communication because the way in which a culture views technology profoundly affects how its members will use and communicate about technology. The international businessperson should be aware of all three approaches in formulating a communication strategy.

As lack of knowledge is the primary source of difficulties created by environmental and technological considerations in international business communication, gathering information on the target culture is the primary means for accommodating cultural differences. To the extent that perceptions go beyond mere levels of awareness, the need for cultural sensitivity, here as in all the variables discussed in this book, comes into play.

Chapter
4

Issues of Social Organization in International Business Communication

*S*ocial organization may be defined broadly as the common institutions and collective activities shared by members of a culture. The influence of these institutions and collective activities shapes the behavior of people in all aspects of life, including business. Unlike the other variables discussed in this book, social organization can be seen as an overt, external influence on individuals.

Most of the variables we have examined may seem so natural that individuals may be unaware that the particular formulation of that variable is not universal. The exact opposite is true for social organization. Individuals almost always understand the artificiality of social organization. Even so, people may be critical of deviations from their system of social organization. While people often do not recognize the influence of internal factors—for instance, the way their language limits or extends their ability to express themselves—they are likely to be aware of the way social institutions (an external influence) restrain or extend the limits of acceptable behavior. To this extent, Sigmund Freud's notion of the individual's superego may be seen as the counterpart to social organization for a culture.

Social organization manifests itself in each culture's enduring structures and institutions. Collectively these institutions form the underlying social values of the culture to which they belong. Alfred Radcliffe-Brown defines social values as follows:

> When two or more persons have a *common interest* in an object, that object can be said to have a *social value* for the persons thus associated. If, then,

practically all the members of a society have an interest in the observance of the laws, we can say that the law has a social value. (1987, p. 131)

Although the values that collectively make up social organization are numerous, these values tend to be reinforced by specific social structures. Those social structures that most interest the businessperson (because of their influence on the workplace) include the following ten areas:

1. kinship and family structure
2. educational systems and ties
3. class systems and economic stratification
4. gender roles
5. individualism and collectivism
6. religion
7. occupational institutions
8. political and judicial system
9. mobility and geographic attachment
10. recreational institutions

Each of these ten categories is complex enough to have provided material for entire books. Still, it is important for the international communicator at least to be aware of how these factors shape business behavior from culture to culture. Only then can he or she adjust strategies accordingly. We will examine each element and, at the chapter's close, suggest steps for anticipating and accommodating the role each culture's social organization plays in business communication.

KINSHIP AND FAMILY STRUCTURE

In several economically powerful cultures—notably, the United States and the nations of northern Europe—business concerns and family ties are kept fairly separate, but the majority of the world's cultures place considerably more stress on kinship. Throughout virtually all of North Africa and the Middle East, most of Latin America, much of Asia, and portions of southern Europe, family ties are of central importance to most aspects of life, including business dealings. For example, Margaret Nydell, in discussing Arab society, has observed that "family loyalty and obligations take precedence over loyalty to friends or the demands of the job" (1987, p. 75). According to Boye DeMente, an expert on Asian business practices, "Family background . . . plays a vital role in both business and society in Korea today" (1988, p. 29). Moreover, in many cultures (particularly in Africa and Asia), the principal wage earner has an obligation to support the extended family. Table 4.1 lists relative strengths of kinship ties by cultures.

The degree of indifference to family ties and the separation of family and business matters in North America and northern Europe often surprises those from other cultures. A visitor from Indonesia to the United States contrasted these two countries by noting that "in America, people

Table 4.1 KINSHIP TIES IN SELECTED CULTURES

Kinship and Business Ties Relatively Weak	Kinship and Business Ties Relatively Strong
Australian	African*
British	Arabic*
Canadian	Chinese
Danish	Greek
Dutch	Indian
German	Indonesian
Icelandic	Iranian
Norwegian	Italian
Swedish	Korean
U.S.	Latin American*
	Portuguese
	Spanish
	Turkish

*Category includes many nations sharing a common liguistic or geographic unit.

show hospitality to strangers, but do not care for family members" (Kohls, 1981, p. 9). John Condon, in his discussion of the contrasts between Mexican and U.S. loyalty to family, perhaps best describes the difference between cultures with relatively strong and relatively weak familial ties:

> The family forms a much less important part of an individual's frame of reference in the U.S. than is usually the case in Mexico. Neighbors, friends or associates, even some abstract "average American," may be the basis for the comparison needed in evaluating oneself or others. "Keeping up with the Joneses" may be important in New York or Chicago, but keeping up with one's brother-in-law is more important in Mexico City. In the same way, the Mexican depends upon relatives or close friends to help "arrange things" if there is a problem or to provide a loan. While this is by no means rare in the United States, the dominant values of the culture favor an institutional response, which is seen as both efficient and fair. . . . In Mexico one is more likely to hear of a person's "connections" or "influence," which is frequently through the family system. (1985, pp. 24–25)

Not only are kinship ties more important in most cultures than in the United States, Canada, and northern Europe, but the concept of family is much broader. In the United States and Canada (and to a lesser extent in northern Europe) the concept of family is essentially limited to the nuclear family. "When [North] Americans use the term 'family,'" Gary Althen has observed,

> they are usually referring to a father, a mother, and their children. This is the so-called "nuclear family." Grandparents, aunts, uncles, cousins, and others

who might be labeled "family" in many other countries are "relatives" in American terminology. These usages reflect the fact that, for most Americans, the family is a small group of people, not an extended network. (1988, p. 48)

For most other societies, family and kinship have a much wider meaning. In Arab society, "The degree to which all blood relationships are encompassed by a family varies among families, but most Arabs have over a hundred 'fairly close' relatives" (Nydell, 1987, p. 75). The notion of family can extend even beyond blood relationships. "Families," Condon says in regard to Mexico, "are extended beyond blood-lines through the institution of compadrazco, godfather relationships. To be a godparent is often much more than an honor; it is a means through which advice or loans or favors may be sought and granted" (1985, p. 25).

The cultural difference in the way people view family and kinship has major implications for international business communication. For example, in most major U.S. corporations, the customary first step in obtaining a job is a résumé sent to the company's personnel department in response to an advertisement or job posting. The applicant and the personnel manager are not likely to be acquainted. Even if the two do know each other, the applicant probably would not stress this fact in either the résumé or the cover letter. In fact, the closer the relationship between the hiring manager and the applicant, the more likely others in the corporation will be suspicious of the applicant's résumé. Because the charge of nepotism (hiring one's relatives) is a serious accusation that calls into question the potential employee's abilities, in most large firms personnel managers would prefer to hire a stranger based on the qualifications laid out in a résumé and confirmed in an interview or trial employment period.

In many other cultures the U.S. practice seems at best odd and in many people's eyes preposterous. Nepotism and favoritism (discussed in the sections on educational ties and class systems) are seen in the United States as potentially leading to corporate corruption, whereas much of the world views nepotism as a positive good. The logic in such cases asserts that it is impossible to trust a stranger. A stranger has no innate reason to be loyal to the hiring manager and therefore no reason to be loyal to the corporation. It would be better to hire a relative whose blood ties to the employer ensure loyalty than to hire a stranger, even if the stranger has somewhat greater qualifications. Indeed, to hire an outsider of truly superior talents could destroy an organization. To see the logic in this view, think of the multitude of U.S. computer and high technology companies founded by less than loyal employees of corporations who could not hold on to them.

Family and kinship ties are not limited to hiring. The role of the family is central to a wide range of business situations, ranging from establishing an environment of respect and trust in negotiations to securing a loan from a bank. Even marketing is affected, as consumers may buy products only from those in the family or those with ties to relatives. Similarly, key management strategies can be affected by kinship issues. Terpstra and David cite an example of differences between India and the United States regarding the role of family ties:

> Recently, an American businessman suggested to his Indian joint venture partner that the latter use a standard market-portfolio model (à la Boston Consulting Group) to plan his business expansion. His partner refused to invest unequally in the five existing businesses because each was managed by a son. Unequal investment would cause family discord. (1985, p. 187)

To the extent that kinship ties influence each culture's business practices, international executives must adjust their business communication to accommodate differences in the role family plays from culture to culture.

EDUCATIONAL SYSTEMS AND TIES

On the surface, education may seem to affect business communication only to the extent that it contributes to the level of literacy and familiarity with basic areas of learning (mathematics, science, religion, foreign languages). While we should not diminish the importance of this aspect of education, perhaps a more significant (because less readily identifiable) role of education involves the network of ties linked to educational institutions. Both the nature and distribution of education and the networking associated with educational institutions merit our attention here. These variables differ markedly between nations that have little or no educational infrastructure and nations that have such an infrastructure.

Weak or Absent Educational Infrastructure

The nature and distribution of education varies from nation to nation. The clearest difference occurs between those nations that have a system of widespread education and those countries whose people receive little or no formal training.

In nations that do not provide widespread educational opportunities to their populations, people tend to fall into two categories: the uneducated masses and the educated elite. Most business communication — aside from marketing — is conducted with the elites. The elites are themselves often educated in the schools and universities of Western Europe, the United States, or the Soviet Union. In such cases, they may conduct their business communication much like the people in the country in which they were educated. Thus they may behave less like a person of their own culture than they do a British, French, Dutch, German, U.S., Soviet or other foreign businessperson. The degree to which foreign-educated elites hold allegiance to the culture in which they received their education varies.

To adopt an appropriate communication strategy, the international executive should assess the amount of foreign influence both for elites educated abroad and the fewer number educated in their home culture. Because of a number of factors, ranging from borrowed technology to former colonial associations, even those schools and universities based in the home culture may reflect marked foreign influence. Members of the educated elite in such cultures may feel slighted if they are treated little differently from other members of their society. Indeed, such people may be quick to acknowledge openly the European, U.S., or Soviet influence on their behavior. An elite trained in England may, for example, feel the need to be treated *more* like a Briton than an actual Briton would.

Business communicators, however, cannot automatically assume a foreign influence simply because a person belongs to the educated elite or has received a foreign education. Foreign training and influence do not necessarily indicate the wholesale adoption of a foreign culture. Religion, nationalist feelings, familial ties, and other factors are equally strong in shaping cultural outlooks. People from certain cultures are therefore more likely to be affected by foreign influence than others, and some cultures are more susceptible to cultural domination by particular foreign nations than others. Thus people from some former French colonies might accept French cultural values if educated in Paris; they would not be likely to adopt German cultural values if educated in Berlin.

While most business communication conducted in countries without universal schooling takes place with the educated few, it is not always the case. Moreover, the degree of training needed to be considered a part of the educated elite may be considerably lower than in societies in which education is widespread. Such a disparity can create deep-seated cultural conflicts. This is well illustrated in the oil boom of the 1970s in Saudi Arabia.

> The glorious oil boom was in reality immensely threatening to the Saudis. With inadequate education and skills, a tiny elite was called on in 1973 to manage the largest infusion of wealth and the most rapid change thrust on any country in modern history. Within a few years, this core of managers was supplemented by a new foreign-educated middle class that entered business or fleshed out the bureaucracy. With few exceptions, those who came home to assume high-level jobs still lacked the experience or sophistication to function efficiently in a world dominated by Western-style institutions and mechanisms. They had no choice but to recognize their inadequacies publicly and hire the expertise Saudi Arabia needed. A Saudi possessing any education rapidly moved from being solely a member of family and tribe, proud in his sense of who and what he was, to being a cog in a new economic system dependent on foreigners. In the Saudi psyche, the Westerner rose up as a person whose superior technological skills threatened to shame him. (Mackey, 1987, p. 121)

Sometimes the international businessperson must interact with the general population—for instance, to manage the workforce of a factory, train service people, or market the company's goods or services to the general public. When businesspeople are given such assignments, they must assess the degree to which the people with whom they deal lack the skills the communicators themselves may take for granted.

Literacy, knowledge of basic mathematics, and familiarity with technical terminology may not be widespread. A Western European multinational corporation faced a serious problem when trying to sell its baby formula to the largely illiterate nations of sub-Saharan Africa. The company provided directions indicating that the formula had to be mixed with boiled water; however, most people could not read the directions. The difficulty was compounded by a lack of fuel for boiling water. That boiling water kills bacteria may have seemed to be basic knowledge to most Westerners but was largely unknown to (or at least not taken as seriously by) the generally uneducated sub-Saharan cultures. The company was therefore selling what essentially amounted to suspension vehicles for disease.

A similar debacle, again involving the sale of baby food, also took place in Africa. Attempting to accommodate the region's large-scale illiteracy, the baby food company followed a business communication practice common in such countries: it placed a picture of its product on the package label. The illustration led to serious misunderstandings, however, as one observer has explained:

> This very logical practice proved to be quite perplexing to one big company. It tried to sell baby food to an African nation by using its regular label showing a baby and stating the type of baby food on the jar. Unfortunately, the local population took one look at the labels and interpreted them to mean the jars contained ground-up babies! Sales, of course, were terrible. (Ricks, 1983, p. 31)

Perhaps the most important consequence of global differences in educational opportunity is that those nations whose populations receive little or no formal training are increasingly less able to compete economically with nations that provide widespread education. Indeed, training *creates* the economic advances of the so-called developed countries. As Peter Drucker observes:

> In the developed countries now about half of all young people undergo formal schooling beyond secondary school, developing the human resources needed to make the new technology operational, productive, and beneficial. In turn the new technology creates the employment opportunities for the new work force of the developed countries. (1986, p. 325)

This creates a self-perpetuating source of tension, dividing the world into developed and lesser developed nations. Kenichi Ohmae takes this a step further in asserting that the educational system in the developed countries, in teaching people to use similar technologies, increasingly eliminates cultural differences:

> As educational systems enable more people to use technology, they tend to become more similar to each other. It follows, therefore, that education

leading to higher technological achievement also tends to eradicate differ-ences in life-styles. (1985, p. 23)

By contrast, those who live in the less developed nations are becoming increasingly alienated precisely because they have no way to use the new technology and thus little means of communication with the rest of the world. Such differentiation and isolation make these countries even less accessible and thus perpetuate the dilemma. To the extent that these people represent wasted human potential, the issue merits the serious attention of the business world.

Established Educational Infrastructure

Among nations with established educational infrastructures, three factors that are of concern to the international business communicator come into play: (1) the relative accessibility of the infrastructure, (2) the importance of educational ties and the network of personal connections linked to educational institutions, and (3) the nature and emphasis of the schooling provided.

Accessibility   In most nations with a well-established educational infra-structure, holding a university degree is important to professional ad-vancement. Still, the comparative accessibility of higher education to the average person differs from one country to the other, affecting the society as a whole and particularly its ruling elite, including the upper-level managerial and business class. Basically, four major access systems exist: the two-track, the U.S., the Japanese, and the Soviet.

In some nations — mostly in Western Europe — access to higher edu-cation is limited to a relatively small portion of the population. The structure takes the form (with minor variations from country to country) of a two-track educational system. In most West European countries, children at about the age of 11 or 12 are separated into two tracks, or groups: a vocational or technical track and a university-bound track. As might be expected, such division helps create an elitist group based on education.

The elitism in the two-track system is arguably less dramatic than that of the foreign-educated elite in countries with a weak or absent educa-tional infrastructure. Nevertheless, students placed in the advanced track have access to the key business (as well as political and social) positions in the culture, whereas vocational-track students usually do not. Generally, the students placed in the advanced track are the children of the current ruling elite. "The tradition of separating academic education of the social elite and the vocational education of the working class," one observer has written, "is still alive and pervasive" (Haitani, 1986, p. 75). In short, the two-track educational system perpetuates a class system based on access to education.

In several other countries with established educational hierarchies, by contrast, education serves less as a means to maintain the privilege of an entrenched elite than as a means to undercut social differences. Most notable among these are the United States, Japan, and the Soviet Union. All allow relatively open access to their educational systems by placing primary emphasis on screening examinations and ability of the student when he or she is ready to enter the university rather than on family connections or ability of the student as a child.

Even though other considerations exist that influence business position and relative status in the United States, Japan, and the Soviet Union, the opportunity-equalizing effects of education are pervasive. Moreover, in all three nations, higher education is widespread. Yet these countries differ in the nature of the access to the educational infrastructure.

In the United States, universities are relatively open to any student who can meet the school's entrance requirements (which vary from institution to institution, even when state-run) and can afford to pay the tuition and other expenses. This last factor is perhaps most significant, since in the United States, wealth remains the most important determinant of social status. Still, most higher education is affordable not only to the rich but to the upper middle class. Because the rich and the upper middle class can pay for university training—a main source of economic advancement—they are able to perpetuate themselves. Also, since it is possible to enter the upper middle class without a university education, many successful people who do not have a college degree are still able to send their children to college. Moreover, most universities and the federal and state governments attempt to counteract the role wealth plays by offering government-sponsored student loans and scholarships. Also, many students from lower-income families work to put themselves through school. In short, higher education in the United States remains relatively open to the majority.

In Japan, access to higher education is about as widespread as in the United States. As in the United States, entrance to Japanese universities is based on examinations, although the Japanese exams tend to be more stringent and more standardized than their U.S. counterparts. Since the national universities are much less expensive than in the United States, wealth plays much less of a role in Japan and, in fact, access to higher education can be seen as based wholly on ability. As Kanji Haitani has observed, "The relatively low cost of attending national universities and the fact that entrance is based strictly on merit combine to make these [Japanese] institutions effective conduits of upward social mobility of gifted children of low-income families" (1986, p. 67).

In the Soviet Union, education holds a somewhat schizophrenic position. The educational system is advanced and well-established. Official Soviet doctrine—while currently undergoing change—at least traditionally does not recognize an educated elite but attaches white-collar workers to either the working class (industrial proletariat) or peasantry (agricultural workers). Although political power rather than wealth or education remains the engine driving advancement in Soviet society, white-collar workers, political leaders, and technical and scientific experts who graduate from the universities dominate the power elite. Moreover, as several observers (Smith, 1976; Willis, 1985) have noted, through preexamination tutoring and their network of political influence, the power elite customarily has unofficial access to specific schools. Still, most experts (Park, 1969; Willis, 1985; Haitani, 1986) agree that the educational system works in such a way as to allow access to higher levels of power among the lower classes while perpetuating the status of those already in the power elite.

Other nations with established educational infrastructures exist outside Western Europe, the United States, Japan, and the Soviet Union. These nations generally follow one of the access systems practiced in these countries and so do not need special discussion here.

Importance of Educational Ties and Networks The emphasis placed on the institution from which a businessperson has received a degree is not universal. In some cultures, such as the United States, while place of schooling remains important, educational ties remain comparatively weak. Factors such as job performance and identified potential may move graduates who hold appropriate degrees from less prestigious schools up the corporate ladder. In other countries, notably Japan and France, few factors are more important than the university from which the degree was awarded; moreover, the businessperson's educational ties remain crucial throughout his or her career.

All nations with established educational infrastructures rank universities based on various factors, ranging from accreditation by independent bodies to the quality of faculty. Each culture recognizes its elite schools. In the United States, which in business puts less emphasis on the university from which a degree is received than many other industrialized countries, graduation from elite schools (such as the Ivy League, Michigan, or Stanford) plays a role in initial hiring and in the rise to prominent positions. On the whole, however, alumni networks and university ties are secondary to individual accomplishments and job experience.

By contrast, three major industrial nations—Japan, France, and, to a lesser extent, Britain—place considerably more weight on educational background. Few factors in Japan and France are more critical to advancement in the business world than the school group to which one belongs. As one analyst has written: "In Japan, to a much greater extent than in the U.S., your university is your destiny" (Wysocki, 1988, p. 1).

Japan. In Japan, almost all key business posts are reserved for the graduates of a handful of universities, led by Tokyo Daigaku (Tokyo University or *Todai,* as it is known in common parlance). As Boye DeMente has noted:

Japan's young know only too well that if they do not get into Todai they are probably forever barred from several top-ranking companies and ministries because these institutions hire mostly Todai graduates. By the same token, those who succeed in getting into Tokyo University know they have it made for rest of their lives. (1981, p. 34)

While Tokyo University leads Japan in its position as number one and therefore in the patronage it receives from businesses, a parallel arrangement exists with each successive rank of university and company. Thus the largest companies take their leadership from *Todai*, while the second largest companies call their executives from those universities ranked immediately below *Todai*, and so on.

The new hires from these graduating classes form a sort of school clique, which the Japanese refer to as *gakubatsu*. A strong bond is formed within these cliques among employees who maintain allegiance not only to the school alumni but to those in the same year of graduation. The *gakubatsu* system thus encourages group loyalty and a web of obligation based on favors traded, both important features of Japanese organizational behavior. Throughout an employee's career, alma mater and year of graduation remain important points of identification. Many non-Japanese, unaware of this attachment, may feel surprised at the degree of interest the Japanese show even to foreigners regarding where and when they graduated from their university. International businesspeople should recognize that Japanese inquiries into their education would not fall into the category of small talk but represent an important part of the Japanese businessperson's overall assessment of their counterparts.

France. Like the Japanese, French businesspeople place great emphasis on the university from which one graduates. Elitism is cultivated in France through a handful of select institutions collectively called the *grandes écoles*. Unlike Tokyo University, which is the undisputed leader among universities, the French have several influential *grandes écoles*, each with a distinct emphasis and philosophy and—through a powerful network of alumni in leading positions—backers who prefer to recruit among their graduates. For example, among the leading *grandes écoles* (although this is not a complete list) are the Ecole Polytechnique and the Ecole Centrale, which emphasize production management and engineering, the Ecole Nationale d'Administration, or ENA, with its stress on government service and diplomacy; the Ecole Normale Supérieure, which concentrates on education and the teaching profession; and the Ecole des Hautes Etudes Commerciales (HEC), which focuses on business administration.

Entrance to the top positions in business and government is not completely limited to graduates of the *grandes écoles*, but alumni of these institutions looking for high-level positions are treated favorably. As Kanji Haitani has written, "The access to the top French bureaucratic order in both government and business is through grandes écoles" (1986, p. 76).

Many *grandes écoles* alumni (particularly those from the two leading schools, the Ecole Polytechnique and the ENA) move into careers in the so-called *grands corps*, the upper stratum of the French civil service. The *grands corps* carry enormous prestige, power, and influence in both government and business. Moreover, many members of the *grands corps* leave their ministries to take over key executive positions in the private sector.

The education offered in the *grandes écoles*—though relatively narrow and specialized—is of the highest quality. It is not, however, the excellence of training that gives these schools and the *grands corps* associated with them so much influence in the business world. Instead, it is the web of networking among alumni that creates a sort of club of carefully scrutinized and limited membership among the ruling business and government elite. "Each school and corps has its active old-boy loyalties," according to a British observer, John Ardagh:

> All this may bear some relation to the days when the British Cabinet and Whitehall were dominated by Etonians, Wykehamists and Balliol men; but whereas in Britain these old-school-tie networks are today weakening and becoming largely social, in France they have become stronger since the war and more specifically professional. Moreover, the prestige of the great Écoles and the grander Corps, and the golden careers they offer, may explain why so much of France's young talent is tempted to join them. (Ardagh, 1987, p. 90)

As one graduate of ENA said, "This school makes you ambitious: you realize power is held by only a very few people, and so you feel obliged to try to get the highest rank, in order to get power, difficult though you know it may be to enter the 'charmed circle' that controls it" (Zeldin, 1984, p. 161).

The implications of the *grande école* educational network for international business communicators are twofold. First, while the talent or level of education of a French businessperson educated in any major university may be as high as or higher than that of a graduate of the *grandes écoles,* the graduate of the *grande école* will be viewed differently by most French businesspeople. For example, the Institut Européen d'Administration des Affaires (INSEAD) at Fountainebleau, a leader in management studies, is a relative newcomer to the field (founded only in 1959); its deservedly strong international reputation probably is greater in European countries outside of France than in France itself. Second, because business connections in the upper levels of French society are generally tied to the *grandes écoles* alumni cliques, foreign businesspeople (if not themselves *grandes écoles* graduates) are likely to remain outside the network of key decision makers, even if they have graduated from such comparable institutions as Tokyo University, Harvard, Oxford, or Cambridge. It is, therefore, important in facilitating business dealings for the business communicator in France to network through associates who are alumni of the *grandes écoles.*

Britain. Interestingly, John Ardagh's comment on the *grandes écoles* quoted earlier underplays the strong networks of the exclusive English public schools and of the "Oxbridge" alumni, graduates of Oxford or Cambridge universities. These ties remain strong in modern Britain, even if, as Ardagh noted, they have weakened considerably since World War II.

While public school backgrounds and Oxbridge ties are less influential than the French *grandes écoles,* such connections are far from negligible. As late as the 1980s, 57 percent of the leading U.K. managers had public school backgrounds (Fidler, 1981, pp. 84–85). Similarly, a public school and/or Oxbridge education was shared by 8 of the 12 chairmen of Britain's major life insurance companies, 14 of the 17 chairmen of its leading accepting houses, 5 of the 6 chairmen of its clearing banks, and all 18 governors of the Bank of England (Sampson, 1982, p. 274).

Significantly, public school and Oxbridge influence is most dominant in the nonindustrial sphere of banking, financial institutions, and insurance companies. By contrast, leaders of only 10 of the top 30 British industrial companies held similar educational backgrounds. While this figure remains important, it is markedly lower than in nonindustrial business positions. The disparity results from the fact that, in Britain, elite education typically is a function of class. The British sociologist Martin Joseph has observed that, "while it may be possible to quote examples of the sons and daughters of dustmen having attended a prestigious school, or Oxford or Cambridge universities, it will normally be the children of higher-status parents who attend these elite institutions" (1989, p. 42). The upper class connection to the elite educational institutions, in turn, reinforces the traditional disinclination of the British upper classes toward industrial positions (discussed later in this chapter).

The British upper-class connection to the elite educational institutions is significant in business communication. The unspoken network of the public school and Oxbridge training represents both a class affiliation and generally a nonindustrial (and arguably even an antibusiness) bias. In this respect, the British public school and Oxbridge educational background is quite different from the *grandes écoles* of France. In Britain, class determines education; in France, education determines class. In Britain, an elite education has engrained within it the nonindustrial bias of its aristocracy. In France, by contrast, the *grandes écoles* specifically train their students to become France's business and industrial leaders. Thus it is primarily in the strong network and influence of their alumni that the British and French elite schools demonstrate close similarity.

Nature and Emphasis of Education   The sort of education students receive varies among nations with well-established educational infrastructures. As a result, graduates of the universities in different countries vary in their strengths and weaknesses and philosophies in approaching business.

While a cross-cultural comparison of the nature and emphasis of education is beyond the scope of this text, for the purposes of this discussion we can point to three broad categories of educational training as it relates to business: humanistic education, technical training, and apprenticeship.

Humanistic education. Most nations in Western Europe that follow the two-track system also follow the humanistic education approach. This approach provides a broad-based, generalist background emphasizing the humanities and learning for its own sake. For these cultures, "Education is not regarded as primarily a means of facilitating economic development of the country or improving social mobility of individuals" (Haitani, 1986, p. 75). While it promotes an intellectual love of knowledge that is useful in encouraging leadership, interpersonal skills, innovativeness, and creativity, such a system represents distinct drawbacks for business. The difficulties may be most evident in the United Kingdom: "In Britain, many undergraduates taking arts subjects realise only at the last moment they are likely to go to industry. Like reluctant maidens, they go to a shotgun wedding putting aside their tender thoughts of the Foreign Service, the *Guardian* and the BBC" (Ivens, 1965, pp. 21–22). And one French business expert, writing about the British emphasis on learning for learning's sake rather than for any industrial application, has observed:

> This may account in large part for the reluctance of top managers to deal with technical matters and their greater ability to comprehend financial and marketing matters, production being more technology-loaded than finance and marketing. In turn marketing and to a lesser degree finance is more 'arts-like.' (Horovitz, 1980, p. 150)

Technical training. At the other extreme are cultures that emphasize a technical approach designed to provide students with specific skills and applied learning. Because most U.S. business schools, French *grandes écoles,* and Soviet universities follow this pattern, their graduates tend to possess expertise in narrow fields. The U.S., French, and Soviet business worlds are filled with experts who can accommodate the increasingly technical organization of the workplace. "The educational backgrounds of managers in France clearly show the predominance of technical training," Jacques Henri Horovitz has observed. "Over two thirds of top managers come from engineering whereas it is less than one third in Great Britain" (1980, p. 156).

Yet the emphasis on the technical, while helpful in dealing with specific, complex technical issues, may create problems of its own. Managers who are the product of such specialized training may not be able to see what in the United States is called "the big picture" — that is, they are often limited to their own areas of expertise. This results in a sort of cookie-cutter approach to business strategy and problem solving. In France in particular, as Horovitz has indicated, the networking of the *grandes écoles* may actually exacerbate the problem:

> This high representation of engineers coming mostly from the *grandes écoles* is certainly causal to the emphasis on production control. However, one may

argue that this has been given too much emphasis. Chief executives who come from *Polytechnique* will trust anybody else coming from *Polytechnique*. As a result, because they come from the same prestigious backgrounds, production managers are the ones who obtain so much autonomy . . . that the grasp of control is loosened in that area. (1980, p. 156)

In the United States, the predominance of technical expertise in business training contributes to an overlooking of the nontechnical sides of business. Especially the late 1970s and the 1980s, it surfaced in the form of a series of business scandals and a growing concern among business leaders and educators alike with the lack of ethics and corporate responsibility in the U.S. business world. Steven Muller, president of Johns Hopkins University, in addressing the issue of a technical emphasis in higher education, indicated that the university system is producing "potentially highly skilled barbarians: people who are very expert in the laboratory or at the computer or in surgery or in the law courts but who have no real understanding of their own society" (1980, pp. 30–31).

Apprenticeships. The last broad category of emphasis in business education is that of the apprenticeship system. Apprenticeship, or learning on-the-job skills through practical experience, takes two forms, which are perhaps best illustrated by the German and the Japanese training approaches, both with roots that reach well into the last century.

In Germany, those not earmarked for college through the *Gymnasium* (college preparatory schools) enter the labor force through an apprenticeship system. These apprentices, who made up roughly 6 percent of the preunification German work force, divide their time between work and schooling in an academic setting. In an article on apprenticeships, *Fortune* magazine noted that German companies are strong advocates of the program, saying that such training offers the following advantages:

> Students learn good work habits on up-to-date equipment at a young age; employers train workers for future openings; and companies and students have three years to decide if the match is a good one. ("West Germany's Competitive Advantage," 1989, p. 136)

In learning a skill or a subject, apprentices receive both applied practice in the workplace and theoretical instruction in the classroom. These young worker-students thus have the opportunity to apply in the workplace what they have just learned in the classroom and, conversely, to practice in the workplace what they will discuss in the abstract at school. "They thus," as Peter Drucker notes, "simultaneously receive both practical experience and theoretical learning, becoming at the same time skilled workers and trained technicians." Indeed, Drucker goes so far as to claim that the German form of apprenticeship education is the key to Germany's long-term economic success:

> This is in large measure the explanation for Germany's success in raising productivity steadily: it creates not only the right attitude but also the theoretical foundation. It also creates receptivity to change. (1986, p. 84)

The Japanese model of apprenticeship differs notably from the German practice. Japanese apprenticeship takes the form of on-the-job training and occurs only after the student has graduated. Thus, unlike its German counterpart, it takes place wholly outside the classroom. The actual university education in Japan is not particularly focused, following a generalist's model. Once a major Japanese company hires its graduates, however, it trains them (or at least those earmarked for administrative functions) in a wide variety of specific job areas:

> There are institutes and academies of a universally applicable art of management, but within the firm the emphasis is on thoroughly learning a business. Future administrators, most of whom have general degrees in law, commerce and economics, go through a short induction course and then begin work on the shop floor. Thereafter they spend some time in different parts of the firm before joining the department to which they are assigned. Trainees thereby gain an understanding of how the firm works and what the business involves. (Clark, 1979, p. 57)

The Japanese apprentice system produces two results that differ from that found in most U.S., Canadian, and West European companies. First, the average employee in an entry-level position of importance will be significantly older because of the additional years such training takes after the initial hiring. The *wunderkind* (bright and promising young employee) who is relatively familiar in the West, particularly in the United States, is entirely absent in the traditional Japanese corporate setting. Second, the Japanese apprenticeship system reinforces job stability because so much of the training is specifically tied to the individual company. "At the end of such training," Clark notes,

> their views of industry and company are likely to be rather different from those of Western marketing men or accountants, who think of their skills as serviceable in many industries, and of firms merely as particular contexts in which their skills may be used. (1979, p. 57)

The educational systems just described affect the training and general business philosophy of those who have passed through them. The international business communicator should therefore understand the sort of business outlook the graduates of these systems are likely to have and adjust his or her strategy accordingly.

CLASS SYSTEMS AND ECONOMIC STRATIFICATION

Inequalities of relative power, wealth, and privilege exist to some extent in all countries. For some societies, particularly those with aristocracies, such differences can be formalized and inheritable. In nations without aristocracies, the social stratification tends to be more informal, with varying degrees of social mobility.

Differences between countries that have and do not have marked class stratification can create an ideological stumbling block in cross-cultural business communication. A 1988 Gallup poll, for example, surveyed how U.S. opinion leaders compared the United States and West Europe. When asked to respond to the question of whether the society "places a great importance on a person's family social position,"only 13 percent agreed for the United States, versus 70 percent for West Europe. The difference proved to be even more dramatic in response to the statement "gives everyone an equal opportunity to succeed"; 81 percent agreed with this statement in reference to the United States while a mere 4 percent agreed for West Europe ("American Attitudes Toward Europe: A New Gallup Poll," 1988, p. 24). The rift in opinion can be significant in U.S.–West European relations when one takes into account the importance U.S. society as a whole places on equal opportunity.

Class differences, regardless of cross-cultural distinctions between societies, may also have an impact on the people with whom one works within a society. For example, the British upper classes tend to have a predilection for government and nonindustrial service rather than business, which traditionally has been deemed below their station. In the words of one British historian, writing on the decline of the U.K. economy, "The aristocratic scale of values . . . was indeed dominant. Being 'in trade' was indeed an awful stigma" (Hobsbawm, 1968, p. 154). More recently, the British sociologist Martin Joseph reasserted the antitrade bias of the British upper classes:

> An aversion to things industrial lies deep in British thinking, and needs to be understood. Indeed, it seems that the country is best at pre-industrial activities; farming, banking and finance, insurance and merchanting. Industry does not seem to have status and therefore does not attract high-status people. (1989, p. 24).

As discussed earlier, such class-linked biases are reinforced by upper-class influences on the elite British educational institutions.

At the same time, Bass and Burger's international assessment of managers notes that "strong social class conditions and entrance into management as a result of social class . . . was still commonplace" (1979, p. 177). Thus British employers still tend to favor those members of the upper class who seek industrial positions (despite the strong class bias against such occupations). In the 1980s, the chief executives of 14 of the 30 largest British industrial companies (including 6 of the United Kingdom's 12 largest) included members of the upper class. These business leaders comprised one earl, three lords, and nine men who had been knighted (Sampson, 1982, pp. 343–344).

In the United Kingdom and other nations with similar class systems, employers are often faced with a very limited pool of highly qualified potential employees, and those that are available may be viewed by others as social climbers. Moreover, when (as in the United Kingdom) the upper classes usually disdain business as beneath them, the entire culture is likely to reflect a less favorable attitude toward business. The comments of Lucian Camp, creative director of Valin Pollen Public Relations in London, epitomize this phenomenon when he compares the approach to marketing in the United States and the United Kingdom:

> In advertising it's very different. The best US advertising is PROUD to be selling you something. In the UK we are slightly embarrassed to be selling you something. 'We are sorry to be a nuisance, and we hope you think well of us, but we do have this nice product to sell you.' In the US, it's 'Wow, do we have a fantastic product for you—it's the greatest, we're the greatest.' (Gordon and McGoon, 1986, p. 26)

While the influence of formal aristocracies is most influential in nations with strong and active monarchies such as the United Kingdom, Thailand, or many of the Middle Eastern states, formal titles may still remain a force in countries with weak or even overthrown monarchies. Theodore Zeldin has observed that vestiges of the French aristocracy retain some influence 200 years after its overthrow. While he admits that a title of French nobility carries weight mostly for others with titles, such rank nonetheless remains "more than the mark of membership of a genealogical society, for the nobles have the largest family network in the country, having devoted endless attention to advantageous marriages. So they have still more than their fair share of top jobs in industry" (1984, p. 187).

Similarly, John Ardagh observes of the role of the aristocracy in a republican Germany: "It is thus significant, if at first sight paradoxical, that in this new semi-classless society the one class that does survive most distinctively is the old aristocracy. Today it holds no formal status; but it still uses its titles, and it is quite widely respected and not solely out of snobbery. . . . Today they tend to behave discreetly, even usefully, and are seen as a link with tradition. The aristocracy no longer exerts power as a class: but many individuals are in positions of public influence." (1987, p. 150)

In countries with strong egalitarian traditions, whether they are republics, like the United States, or monarchies, such as in Scandinavia, class differences may be downplayed. Indeed, organizations and their leaders may consciously attempt to communicate egalitarianism. Rolf Sklar, founder and, until recently, chief executive officer of Norway's giant minicomputer producer Norsk Data, explained the practice:

> We go to extremes to avoid class differences. Take a look at my office. It's not that I am thrilled to have a small office. Maybe it would be more comfortable to have a bigger one. I know, however, that I am setting standards. Therefore, the size of my office is irrelevant. Nor will I fly first class when none of the other employees do. . . . Some of these rules may sound funny to an outsider, but in reality it is the small details that matter. These details ultimately amount to a spirit, a tone, a philosophy of relationship between people of equal worth. (Moskowitz, 1987, p. 442)

It is significant that Sklar selected such details as office size and first class flights to emphasize egalitarianism. Such distinctions may be generally too subtle to recognize to the person from a culture with more pronounced class differences.

Indeed, in egalitarian cultures, status is more likely to be attached to achievement. By contrast, in cultures with formal, inherited class ties, achievers who attempt to break out of their social class may be considered tainted and be looked down upon as bounders, both by the class they attempt to enter and the one they attempt to leave.

Relative wealth also creates class differences. Money in particular helps determine one's relative worth — and therefore one's social class — in several otherwise egalitarian cultures. This is especially true in the United States. Robert Settle and Pamela Alreck, both marketing strategists specializing in U.S. consumer behavior, have observed that "status symbols such as automobiles are commonly promoted as indicating the owner's worth. For instance, GM used magazine ads for the Pontiac Grand Am showing the car on a dock by an impressive power boat. The headline: "'So no one has to ask you how you're doing'" (1986, p. 226). Still, these differences may have less effect in the workplace than in nonwork settings. Moreover, in many cultures emphasizing egalitarianism, wealth is not as fully admired as achievement. In the United States, for instance, the self-made millionaire is the most admired; those who have inherited their money — even though it may exceed that of people who make their own fortunes — are usually less admired, because of U.S. cultural ties to egalitarianism. As one observer, explaining the U.S. business culture for Mexican managers, has indicated:

> Status in U.S. society is based mainly on achievement and, to some degree, its concomitant wealth. In their work, U.S. executives seek opportunities for achievement because they know this will bring recognition and wealth. Wealth and the possession of material goods have become identified with status. But the "idle rich" do not generally have status; the respectable wealthy are admired because of their achievements, not just their wealth. (Kras, 1988, p. 41)

Nevertheless, unofficial aristocracies often exist in egalitarian societies. Thus the Boston Brahmins or Black Aristocracy of New Orleans provide members with a network of connections nearly as exclusive and influential as a formal aristocracy.

Cultures with the most overt class distinctions often use their religious or legal systems to enforce these differences. Even among foreigners, the rigidity of the class structure directly affects business communication practices. The system of apartheid in South Africa legally places blacks and other nonwhites in a lower station than whites, and the social condemnation of attempts to change the order is unmistakable. George Morris, formerly vice president of labor relations worldwide for General Motors, related to the author how GM's efforts to integrate even the cafeteria of its South African operations ended in failure. Black and white employees shared — as ordered — the same room but both voluntarily sat at opposite ends of the room, self-segregating themselves into two groups. Similar efforts, including a plan to construct integrated neighborhoods, also failed.

In India, the socioreligious ideology of the caste system represented an impregnable establishment of inherited classes. Following the efforts of Mahatma Gandhi to make the caste system illegal, much of the influence of the caste system waned. Still the traditional caste roles have by no means been eradicated in India.

Foreigners with egalitarian value systems may find it hard to adjust to such social stratification. Visitors in South Africa who treat blacks as equal to whites or do not recognize the remaining effects of the caste system in India will face difficulties. They may hold onto their ethical or cultural values but will not be appreciated by those in power in the host countries. Thus U.S. executives who choose to promote a black South African to an executive position may — regardless of the ethical issues involved — find that they have cut off their own chances of success. Unless one decides not to conduct business in countries with offensive cultural values, it may be necessary to conform to the prevailing class distinctions to maintain useful communication. James Livingstone addressed this problem well when he wrote: "A society preventing upward movement may in time come apart at the seams, but in day to day terms it can make difficulties for the enterprise in limiting its choice of executives to those which will be acceptable in the role to the rest of the community" (1975, p. 199).

GENDER ROLES

In almost every culture one is expected to communicate in a certain manner depending on whether one is dealing with a member of the opposite or of the same sex. In virtually every culture, men and women are brought up according to different standards. In particular, they are taught to communicate in different ways, using distinct types of phrasing and language. Indeed, in many languages the very form of the words men use differs from that used by women. Moreover, the majority of the world's languages reinforce sexual distinctions through gender-linked differences in word construction. For example, even English — which is relatively genderless compared to many other languages — distinguishes between male and female in the third person singular (i.e., *he* and *she*).

The psychologist Lillian Breslow Rubin asserts that because of gender-related differences in language, men and women are raised in such a way that they develop different aspects of their personality: "They are products of a process that trains them to relate to only one side of themselves — she, to the passive, tender, intuitive, verbal, emotional side; he, to the active, tough, logical, nonverbal, unemotional one" (1976, p.

116). While Rubin's statement may exaggerate the degree to which this difference in upbringing affects the individual's personality, her point still holds: men and women in every society learn to communicate differently. Since the nature of this difference grows out of the culture in which the individual is brought up, the impact of gender-based communication style varies from culture to culture.

The comparatively recent entry of women into the work force in Europe, India, East Asia, and the Americas has made gender differences in communication of interest to businesspeople. And to the extent that Rubin's statement holds true, the two sexes represent distinct cultural approaches to the work environment.

Significantly for international business communication, much sex-trait stereotyping is universal. Williams and Best (1982) studied characteristics assigned to men or to women on the basis of gender in 29 countries and found that people in each country attached the same traits to the same gender. Regardless of cultural differences, Williams and Best found, the respondents associated men with such attributes as "adventurous," "dominant," "forceful," "independent," and "strong-willed," while they associated women with such qualities as "emotional," "sentimental," "submissive," and "superstitious" (p. 16).

Yet despite the widespread similarities of sex-trait stereotyping across cultures, how strongly members of a particular culture allow these differences to affect behavior and communication in the workplace varies. Although it is impossible to categorize whole cultures according to women's and men's roles, it is possible to characterize the way in which cultures manifest sex-trait stereotyping in the workplace. These differences fall roughly into three basic configurations we might coin here as

1. collegial interaction attempting to ignore gender stereotypes
2. collegial interaction attempting to cultivate gender stereotypes
3. noncollegial or absent interaction

In many nations, as women enter the upper levels of the workforce in increasing numbers, both sexes have attempted to redefine their relationships by ignoring the sex-trait stereotyping they have learned through their culture. For example, it is a societal ideal in the United States to deemphasize gender differences in the workplace and, as necessitated by legal requirements, to treat men and women in as similar a manner as possible. Admittedly, in the United States such efforts have eliminated differences neither in pay for equivalent jobs nor proportionate distribution of key corporate positions between the sexes. Still, gender equality remains, generally, a legal and corporate ideal of expected behavior.

Facing the increased demand for collegial interaction in the workplace, many other nations have sought to emphasize sex-trait stereotypes as a way to bring distinct human strengths and qualities to the fore. Thus more women than men may be called on to use interpersonal skills they are perceived through culturally learned sex-stereotyping to have in greater abundance than men. Conversely, more men than women may be assigned tasks involving analytical skills that they are perceived to have in greater abundance. This position is clearly illustrated in a statement, made by Mariko Sugahara Bando, regarding the increasing opportunities for women in Japan's still highly sex-segregated workforce. Bando, a counselor at the prime minister's office and author of books on women and the elderly, indicated that the increased presence of women in upper-level positions will help dissipate the image of Japanese workers as "economic animals": "Japanese businessmen are faces without names. They're organization men. Women tend to be more human. And more of them working can create a new image for Japan" (Solo, 1989, p. 158).

In some cultures, no interaction occurs in the workplace between men and women. Saudi Arabia, Libya, Qatar, and many other Islamic countries enforce a strict segregation of the sexes and hold to the Islamic belief in the subordination of women. In other societies, women are accepted into the workplace but have very limited opportunities; they are held in dead-end jobs. While this is still true of virtually all countries, the degree of unequal division of labor varies. Among the most highly industrialized nations, for example, considerably more opportunity exists for women to advance to positions of relative influence than in less developed nations.

The one major exception to this is Japan. Thus, Kazuyoshi Kamioka, president of Hakuoh University, while discussing the advances of women in the workplace, can still bluntly state that, "As Japanese society is still male-oriented, the demand for women in business remains low" (1988, pp. 173–74). Indeed, an article in the *Wall Street Journal* recorded that "over half of all Japanese companies offer no opportunities for women's advancement" (1988, p. 17). Signs of change are, however, apparent. While it remains minuscule by U.S. and European standards, the number of women in Japan "with managerial titles increased 50% between 1982 and 1987," as one observer has noted. "Now for the first time large numbers of college-educated women are being set on the management track" (Solo, 1989, p. 153). Still, the opportunity for women to advance has not gained widespread acceptance. Perhaps nowhere were these mixed reactions more apparent than in the July 1989 vote for the upper house of Japan's Parliament. In the most serious setback in Japanese history for the unbroken rule of the Liberal Democratic Party, the Japan Socialist Party won 46 of 126 seats in the upper house, 10 seats more than the Liberal Democrats won. The significance of this accomplishment goes beyond politics and into the realm of gender relations, since the Socialist Party was led by a woman, Takako Doi. Yet as a sign of the ambivalent feelings toward her gender, then Agriculture Minister Hisao Horinouchi could publicly attack Doi for being a woman, saying, "It is wrong for women to come to enter the forefront of politics" (Smolowe, 1989, p. 24).

The relatively high level of inequality between the sexes in the workplace in many Third World nations can be explained only partly as stemming from cultural roots. The changing gender roles in the workplace of Europe and North America, for example, have occurred despite similarly deep-rooted cultural biases. The strength of the continued inequality of Third World women in the workplace may be reinforced or even promoted by the developed nations themselves. Several experts (Boserup, 1970; Blaxall and Reagan, 1976; Lim, 1983) have suggested that multinational manufacturers set up labor-intensive operations in nations with low wages to reduce costs. The manufacturers are particularly attracted by the lower wages paid to women based on a discriminatory division of labor. It seems likely that, because employers can offer jobs with no opportunity for advancement at lower pay to women, multinational corporations with home bases in developed countries hire significantly more women than men in their Third World operations.

While in virtually every culture people hold to sex-based stereotypes, it is difficult to determine the validity of these beliefs. Cultures such as the United States that attempt to ignore the stereotypes may assert that perceived differences are based on prejudice rather than on any innate evidence. Conversely, cultures that emphasize sex-based traits either by capitalizing on them in the workplace or by discouraging collegial interaction are likely to believe in their inherent validity. Whether innate differences based on gender actually exist is therefore subject to debate from culture to culture. Traits considered masculine or feminine, however, do occur in human behavior.

The Dutch management researcher Geert Hofstede conducted a highly important study on cultural differences in the perception of gender-linked traits in the workplace (1984). He did not assign the traits to either gender but merely studied their frequency in what he termed a masculinity–femininity index. He surveyed workers in 40 countries on their views toward various societal norms that could be considered *masculine* in outlook versus *feminine* in outlook.

Hofstede tallied as *feminine* those responses that indicated people orientation, interdependence, fluid views of sex roles, leveling (rather than excelling), quality of life, sympathy for the unfortunate, intuition, emphasis on service (rather than achievement), a "work to live" philosophy, and a belief that differences in sex roles should not mean differences in power. He tallied as *masculine* those responses that indicated a materialistic orientation, emphasis on performance and growth (over quality of life), clearly differentiated sex roles, excelling (rather than leveling), decisiveness, sympathy for the achiever, a "live to work" philosophy, and a belief that men should dominate in all settings (p. 205). From these, Hofstede found dozens of work-related correlations, ranging from the manager's role to stress levels in the workplace.

Hofstede ranked the countries surveyed according to the numerical ratings of their responses:

> The list of countries in order of Masculinity Index shows Japan at the top. German-speaking countries (Austria, Switzerland, and Germany) tend to score high; so do the Caribbean Latin American countries Venezuela, Mexico, and Colombia, and Italy. The Anglo-American countries (Ireland, Great Brit-

ain, South Africa, the United States, Australia, New Zealand, and Canada) all score about average. On the lower side we find other Latin countries (France, Spain, Peru, Portugal, and Chile) and Yugoslavia; at the lowest end are the four Nordic countries (Finland, Denmark, Norway, and Sweden) and the Netherlands. (1984, p. 191)

As we indicated, Hofstede did not link to either gender the categories of masculine or feminine behavior. Still, he determined specific correlations between the degree of masculinity or feminity and the actual differentiation between men and women in certain areas. The findings directly affect the strategy business communicators should take in the surveyed countries. Hofstede observed that "in more feminine countries more working women are in the more qualified jobs, and in higher education the *same* courses tend to be taken by women and men" (pp. 203–204). Moreover, Hofstede concluded—citing as additional evidence the study conducted by Bartova (1976) as well as his own findings—that "there is also some evidence that in more masculine countries fewer men are positive toward the idea of seeing women in leading positions" (p. 204).

While the role of women and what is perceived to be their proper behavior at work vary, this does not necessarily mean that women must conform to the attitudes of the foreign culture in which they conduct business. Frequently members of one culture find the behavior of foreign businesswomen acceptable even when that behavior would be wholly unacceptable on the part of a woman who *is* a member of the culture. For example, according to the female vice president of Bank of America's Asia Division, "Being a foreigner is so weird to the Japanese, that the marginal impact of being a woman is nothing." Marlene Rossman has observed of her experience as a U.S. business consultant abroad:

> As a businesswoman you are seen much more as a "foreign executive" who happens to be a woman than as a "woman" who has a more traditional role in the local society. Especially in developing countries, the fact that you *look* different from the locals helps your clients to see you as "executive," not as "woman." (1986, p. 93)

The degree of acceptance of women should influence the communication strategy of the female business executive. It is not mandatory for executives from, say, Europe and North America to avoid sending women to countries in which women have a subservient role or even to countries where women are almost wholly absent from the workplace.

Barbara Stewart, a U.S. investment manager, talked about her successful business negotiations in such countries traditionally unaccepting of women as Saudi Arabia, Tunisia, Jordan, and Iraq: "If they want your product and you are a professional they will accept you anywhere" (Rossman, 1986, p. 75). Still, the insensitivity to cultural differences suggested by Stewart's observations borders on arrogance, based as it is on power (wanting the product badly enough) rather than on understanding (recognizing cultural differences in the perceived role of women). Moreover, blind insistence on the superiority of one's own system (whether the belief in the innate equality *or* inequality of the sexes) is unlikely to lead to effective cross-cultural business communication. Sondra Snowden, an expert in international protocol, recorded the sort of difficulty that can occur:

> I learned a lesson in protocol while running the international protocol services for a major banking concern. I was given the responsibility to meet a plane on which a very important sheik, a client of the bank, was arriving. I was to greet him officially. We at the bank were unaware that by sending a woman to the airport, we were, in keeping with his custom, offering the company of the woman to him during his stay. We had a very unhappy customer to contend with when he learned this was not the case. (1986, p. 25)

The point here is that international businesspeople of either gender should adjust for, though not in every case necessarily accommodate, differences in the perception of the role of women in the workplace.

Finally, businesspeople, regardless of sex, should remain cognizant of cultural differences in the attitude of women. Such awareness should help them be flexible to gender-linked communication differences that may be wholly unacceptable in their own country but are proper in the foreign culture in which they are working. It will also be useful in other ways for developing an informed communication strategy — for example, in determining the degree of resistance (compared to the home culture) a businesswoman who has risen to a position of importance can expect to face in a foreign culture.

INDIVIDUALISM AND COLLECTIVISM

A set of 12 statues representing national virtues rings the main theater of the U. S. pavilion of the World Showcase at Disney World's Epcot Center in Orlando, Florida. The statues are supposed to embody "the Spirits of America," those traits held most dear by Americans. Among the symbols of the U.S. spirit are four statues representing "Individualism," "Self-reliance," "Independence," and "Freedom." To most U.S. visitors, these four traits seem fitting and little different from "Compassion" or "Knowledge" or any of the remaining virtues the other statues symbolize. The very selection of these virtues at Disney World's patriotic showcase is a telling example of how different cultures view the relative merits of individualism.

Few visitors from other countries would be likely to consider "Individualism" and the three kindred traits represented by the U.S. pavilion statues to symbolize what they believe are their own national virtues. It is, indeed, a unique feature of the United States to value individualism and such other related qualities as virtues. In a majority of cultures, individualism is considered a counterproductive force, equated with selfishness, unpatriotic feelings, or disruptive behavior that undermines harmony within the community.

This difference in viewpoint can be illustrated by two expressions. In the United States, one common sentiment bandied about the workplace is the paraphrase of the English writer John Heywood's "Every man for himself" (with the ending "and God for us all" usually forgotten or dropped). By contrast to this rally to individualism and self-reliance, the Japanese often cite a wholly different proverb: "The nail that stands up will be hammered down."

In short, cultures can be assigned some point on a continuum that stretches from high value placed on the individual (and little concern with group identification) to low value placed on the individual (and great concern with group identification). In the first type of culture, people see themselves primarily as individuals and stress such traits as self-freedom and self-reliance. In individualist cultures, people usually identify themselves only weakly with the groups to which they belong. Their strongest loyalties are to themselves (and perhaps to their immediate family). In collectivistic cultures, people generally view themselves more as group members than as individuals. They derive their identity in large part from the groups to which they belong and consequently hold a great deal of loyalty to those groups.

In individualist countries, employees are likely to see themselves as free agents relying on their own skills as they jump from one organization to the next.

The degree of individualism in a culture may even affect the attractiveness (or lack of it) of larger corporations. Thus, as the need for *larger* financial backing and productive capacity grew in the face of the increased demands of global competition in the late twentieth century, small business and entrepreneurism reached a nearly unprecedented resurgence in the United States, Canada, Australia, and New Zealand and other countries with cultures that emphasize individualism. For instance, Michael Bliss, among the most thorough observers of Canadian business, attributed the enormous increase in entrepreneurialism in Canada in the 1980s to a Canadian cultural emphasis on individualism so deeply embedded that it

> appeared to have both spiritual and structural roots. Big corporations could make executives rich, and sometimes even famous. But generations of high-achieving entrepreneurs had testified to more important satisfactions of business life relating to the joys of ownership—the sense of having created an ongoing organization, of having built something useful, of having been one's own boss, subservient to no man. As large organizations struggled to accommodate and nurture the entrepreneurs in their midst . . . the haunting possibility was that no amount of stock options or profit-sharing could substitute for real ownership, no amount of freedom within a tolerant, caring organization could truly accommodate a thorough-going individualist or self-starter. By definition the individual was not an organization man, or woman. (1987, p. 569)

Nor are such effects of individualism limited to Canada. Similar views are as deeply engrained in other individualist cultures, including Australia, New Zealand, and the United States.

In collectivist cultures, conversely, individuals are unlikely to change groups, seeing their skills as secondary to their role within the group. Indeed, people in collectivist cultures are much more likely to distinguish between in-groups and out-groups. Because group relationships in such cultures are usually nurtured over long periods, the outsider has not experienced (and may not be able to receive access to) the web of interrelationships among the group members.

It is important to note that no culture is wholly individualist or wholly collectivist. Aspects of both occur in any society. Nonetheless, the degree to which the two elements are emphasized from culture to culture varies greatly. The value attached to achieving individual or group goals is of particular importance to business communication, since virtually all business communication must take place in an organizational or group setting. As Hofstede has put it, "The level of individualism/collectivism in a society will affect the organization's members' reasons for complying with organizational requirements" (1984, p. 153). If the work-related value of self-gain and individual achievement is most important in a culture, business communicators would do well to stress the needs of the individual. Conversely, if group harmony and collective success is most significant, then the business communicator should focus on the needs of the group rather than of its individual members.

As part of the study referred to in the discussion of gender, Hofstede surveyed people in 40 countries to assess the relative effect of culture in determining individualism or collectivism in the workplace. Basing his survey on 14 questions regarding work goals, he ranked the 40 nations according to the survey respondents' views of six main goals most closely tied to individualism: personal time, freedom, challenge, use of skills, physical conditions, and training.

Not surprisingly, Hofstede found the highest individualism in the United States. Significantly, five of the six nations defining the top of the individualism scale were English-speaking — Australia ranked second, Britain third, Canada fourth, and New Zealand sixth. Only the Netherlands ranked fifth, was not a part of this English-speaking culture cluster of Britain and her former colonies. The upper portion of the scale below this extreme consisted of (in descending order) Italy, Belgium, Denmark, Sweden, France, Ireland, Norway, Switzerland, West Germany, South Africa, and Finland. At the middle of Hofstede's index were Austria, Israel, and Spain. Those just below the midrange were India, Japan, Argentina, Iran, Brazil, Turkey, Greece, and the Philippines. Those nations with a low individualism rank consisted of Mexico, Portugal, Yugoslavia, Hong Kong, Chile, Singapore, and Thailand. The five lowest-ranked nations were Taiwan, Peru, Pakistan, Colombia, and Venezuela (p. 158).

Hofstede's rankings provide the global-minded businessperson with a means to predict the importance of the six features measured. While care must be taken not to stereotype people based on this information, Hofstede's findings give the business communicator a way to determine the likely organizational norms prevalent in various cultures. As he notes: "More collectivist societies call for greater emotional dependence of members on their organizations; in a society in equilibrium, the organizations should in return assume a broad responsibility for their members." He also observes, borrowing the terms "moral" (working with the group by doing what is right) and "calculative" (working with the group for self-interest) used by Etzioni (1975), that "We can assume more "moral" involvement with the organization where collectivist values prevail, and more "calculative" involvement where individualist values prevail" (p. 153).

Individualist cultures place greater emphasis than collectivist cultures on internal controls (such as self-assessment) and, arguably, on democratic principles in which each individual has a vote. By contrast, as the Hong Kong-based research team of Michael Bond, Kwok Leung, and Kwok Choi Wan have observed, "collectivism entails the need to preserve group harmony and will consequently result in a more egalitarian assignment of rewards and punishments for a given task input to a group product" (1982, p. 187). Collectivist cultures, in other words, are likely to stress the maintenance of surface harmony, censure by the group, and face-saving (which we will discuss in more detail in Chapter 5).

A culture's relative individualism or collectivism determines in large part whether communication is likely to be dyadic, or one-on-one (the preferred mode in the United States, for example) or intergroup (as is strongly emphasized, for instance, in Japan). This choice, in turn, affects the degree to which group formation, solidarity, and consensus-building are deemed more important than direct confrontation and individual action. Moreover, the relative value placed on individualism or collectivism is not easily recognized by members of any given society. These values are learned so early in life and are so deeply ingrained that, to members of a culture, they appear to be universal. To stress group behavior in an individualist society or individualism in a collectivist society would seem at best *very* foreign and at worst wrong or even immoral.

Because Hofstede was interested primarily in other factors besides business communication concerns, not all countries on his index reflect a precise parallel to cultural preference on group versus individual communication preferences. For instance, a stress on loyalty or working conditions may not indicate a nation's cultural emphasis on the particular issue of individual or group communication. Hofstede's survey, therefore, should function only as an initial predictor that the international business communicator can use as a starting point but should not consider absolute.

For example, the Japanese place a great deal of emphasis on consensus management, including the use of group communication. Perhaps more than any culture Hofstede surveyed, the Japanese prefer to avoid dyadic communication. Virtually all business meetings among the Japanese are conducted between teams. Moreover, individuals within the teams are unlikely to respond without the tacit approval of other team members. It is common in Japan for negotiation team members to refer questions to other team members with more expertise, even when questions are directed specifically at a different individual. Finally, as a culture, the Japanese are adverse to personal self-disclosure because it highlights individualism. As Dean Barnlund concluded from his studies of U.S. and Japanese communicative behavior:

> the Japanese communicate significantly less of their inner feelings and thoughts even with their most intimate acquaintances. Americans, in contrast, appear to express themselves across a wider variety of topics at a significantly deeper and more personal level. (1975, p. 144)

Yet because of other variables less related to communication style measured in Hofstede's individualism index, the Japanese do not (as such behavior would indicate) define the bottom end of the scale (as the United States does the top end).

A similar situation, though for different reasons, is that of Israel. Two organizational values, with wholly different emphases on individualism and collectivism, play a part in Israeli business. The standard Israeli business community is one of relatively strong individualism. By contrast, the collective *kibbutz* system, which dominates agriculture and remains influential in certain industries (including high-tech areas), is the most purely collectivist managerial system of any culture. The collectivist principle of the *kibbutz* is described by Brian Dicks:

> In its strictest form the *kibbutz* (derived from the Hebrew word meaning "group") is a communal and collective village governed by the general assembly of all its members. Its structure is based on equality in everything: work, housing, food, clothing, and the raising of children. The basic principle is that every member gives to the community to the best of his abilities and in return receives from it his needs. (1977, p. 41)

While the *kibbutz* members represent only a fraction of the Israeli population, their relative importance lies not only in their productive contribution to the economy but in their role as the pioneer leaders and state founders (they have at times represented up to seven times their number in the Knesset, the Israeli Parliament). As a result, the *kibbutz*, with its emphasis on collective behavior and paternalistic oversight of common group behavior, is symbolically important to non-*kibbutz* members, forming what the Israeli journalist Amos Elon called a "value elite" (1972, p. 325) in which "the ideal of *kibbutz* life was often worshipped, at least verbally, by those personally unprepared to live by it" (1972, pp. 324–325). As a result of the attempt to assimilate these two different value systems, many Israelis may prefer business communication styles favored by individualist countries while being influenced by the group ideals and pressures of the collectivist cultures. Thus Israel's ranking at the middle of Hofstede's individualism index may prove to be deceptive.

In any case, the international business executive should assess the role individualism or collectivism plays in any given culture. It is important not to pass judgment based on one's own standard. Thus a U.S. executive meeting with a Japanese company team might communicate hidden messages by passing culturally biased judgments. To the Japanese executives, the U.S. representative's insistence on one-on-one communication might seem arrogant. Indeed, the use of a lone U.S. company representative might even convey to the Japanese that the U.S. company found them too unimportant to send a full team. Conversely, the U.S. executive might determine that the Japanese emphasis on the group represented a lack of preparedness or even of expertise, since the group members would customarily pass off questions to one another or confer among themselves. At the least, both sides, by not accounting for the cultural preferences, would find their counterpart's communication approach offsetting and confusing.

RELIGION

The role of religion in business has long been discussed. Max Weber, in his now classic philosophical treatise *Die protestantische Ethik und der Geist des Kapitalismus (The Protestant Ethic and the Spirit of Capitalism*, 1904–1905), asserted that countries in which the majority of the population adhered to religions that place strong emphasis on the world to come are less successful in business than countries in which most people belonged to religions that stress the here and now, or this world. Weber's main contention dealt with his turn-of-the-century observation of "the fact that business leaders and owners of capital, as well as the higher grades of skilled labour, and even more the higher technically and commercially trained personnel of modern enterprises, are overwhelmingly Protestant" (1958, p. 35). According to Weber, the this-worldly focus of Protestantism creates the business edge; it resulted, he said, from what he saw as the Protestant work ethic, a sort of live-to-work philosophy.

Weber's assertions, while once highly popular, must be viewed with great caution. While religion is an important aspect of culture, it is not (as we have seen throughout this book) the *only* factor.

Moreover, a religion's relative importance among its adherents varies greatly from culture to culture and from religion to religion. Weber's view of the world can also be seen as somewhat myopic. As a European, he was primarily concerned, in his cross-cultural study, with the dominant European religion—Christianity. As a result, he took no account of Confucianism, which arguably places greater emphasis on work than Protestantism. In grossly simplified terms, Christianity asserts that a person works as penance for the fall from grace; it is thus possible even in Protestant

Christianity to overwork—that is, pay too much penance. In Confucianism, again in greatly simplified terms, one lives on in the memory of one's ancestors; therefore, greater productivity only provides more good works by which to be remembered, and, as a result, one cannot overwork.

Nevertheless, in one major respect, Weber was correct: religion does play an important role in determining the priorities and goals of the people who adhere to it. Figure 4.1 is a map showing the distribution of the world's major religions.

Three aspects of religion merit our attention here: the theological values of the religion and their influence on business behavior; the details of the religion and their effects on day-to-day interactions; and the degree to which adherents accept, tolerate, or refuse to deal with nonadherents. These three factors play a role in interreligious (as is often the case with international) business interactions.

Theological Values

The influence of theological values on behavior represents the thesis of Weber's treatise. To some extent, though religion never acts in isolation and is subject to a myriad of other factors, it does shape its adherents' value system. Religion *does*, therefore, affect the way people behave in the workplace and the way they conduct business communication.

A comparative discussion of religions is beyond the scope of this book. What is important is that certain religions tend to emphasize particular approaches to problem solving, conflict management, long-term planning, and other business functions. For example, a difference exists between one's life style and one's religion for most North and South Americans, Australians, and Europeans (mostly Christians and Jews). By contrast, most followers of Islam and Hinduism in much of northern Africa and southern Asia make no distinction between religion and life style; in these faiths, religion *is* a life style. Spiritual beliefs, therefore, will more strongly influence decision making in predominantly Hindu or Muslim nations than in Europe, Australia, and North and South America. It is not unheard of, for example, for a Muslim businessman to confer with a religious leader for advice on a commercial transaction; such a practice is uncommon among executives from Europe, Australia, or the Americas.

Views of the future are also affected by religion. Adherents to Islam believe that one should submit to God's will and that the future is in God's hands. Similarly, many animist religions believe that careful planning for the future may anger the governing spirits; such *hubris*, they believe (as did the ancient Greeks), may cause the spirits to turn on the individual who is too self-confident.

Such religious beliefs can have specific impact on business communication. For instance, an animist may see a Christian's desire to buy an insurance policy on a project as placing the project in jeopardy; such a policy would almost certainly enrage the spirits, who would then attack

RELIGIONS

The majority of the inhabitants in each of the areas colored on the map share the religious tradition indicated. Symbols show religious traditions shared by at least 25 percent of the inhabitants within area units no smaller than one thousand square miles. Therefore minority religions of city dwellers generally have not been represented.

Roman Catholicism

Protestantism

Eastern Orthodox (including Greek and Russian Orthodox)

Independent churches of Eastern Christianity (including Armenian, Coptic, Ethiopian, East and West Syrian)

Christianity undifferentiated by branch (chiefly mingled Protestantism and Roman Catholicism, neither predominant)

Islām, predominantly Sunnī

Islām, predominantly Shī'ah

Buddhism

Hinduism

Chinese and Korean religions*

Japanese religions**

Traditional, tribal, and animist religions

Uninhabited

☆ Judaism   † Undifferentiated Christian populations

Equator

*Chinese and Koreans frequently hold plural religious beliefs, with strong influences deriving from Confucianism, Buddhism, and Taoism.

**Most Japanese have plural religious affiliations. The major Japanese religious influences include Shintoism, Confucianism, and Mahayana Buddhism.

Figure 4.1 Distribution of the world's major religions.

the project to teach the arrogant policy buyers a lesson. Citibank faced such a situation when it entered several Muslim countries, as Terpstra and David have described:

> Inshallah, "God willing," is an expression of submission to the will of Allah. As a corollary for some Muslims, insurance policies are an attempt to defy the working of Allah's will. As a result, Citibank finds itself financing the uninsured inventories of Muslim merchants. The prohibition against charging interest is circumvented by charging a "commission" instead. However, if the bank must go to a court to collect, the Muslim court will award only the principal. (1985, p. 101)

To the extent that God's will determines the individual's success in life, religion can also be seen as influencing its members' attitudes toward work. This is the basis of Weber's theory of the Protestant work ethic. Again, it is important to note that such an attitude is neither exclusive to Protestants (similar nonfatalistic philosophies are notable among Confucianists, Jews, and others) nor an indicator of the work ethic of all adherents to more fatalistic and hereafter-oriented faiths. Even though Weber's conception of a religious-based work ethic is far from the absolute work-behavior determinant he conceived his theory to be, the international business observer should not reject Weber's notions out of hand. His ideas are still relevant regarding attitudes about the need for work to achieve goals.

For example, the view common in the United States that material possessions are earned through effort rather than awarded by fate influences U.S. attitudes toward labor-saving devices and respect for hard work. Settle and Alreck observe that in the United States, people "are a little skeptical about goods that promise effortless results or that eliminate the need for hard work." They go on to note that labor-saving devices are best introduced in cultures like the United States, using a business communication strategy justifying the devices' practicality in increasing the user's work output. Simply advising that effort can be saved is inadequate without a rationale informing users that "the device will let them devote their time and effort to some other activity" (1986, p. 225). They cite as an example how the U.S. food processing giant

> Beatrice uses magazine ads to promote the "Soup Starter" line of "Homemade Soup Mix" with the headline, "Soup from a can is okay for lunch . . . but dinner calls for something more." They note that "you add your own fresh beef or chicken." The appeal is based on the homemaker's distrust of things that are too easy. With this product, they save time but still contribute some effort. (1986, p. 226)

Moreover, what may be thought of in one culture as not being in the realm of religion may be taken very seriously in another society. Superstitions, for example, are often treated casually and frivolously in North America and in Europe. Few Western businesspeople consult fortune tellers or astrologers for business advice. In many other cultures, however, spiritualists and seers are highly respected and their advice taken very seriously. "Making light of superstitions when doing business with other cultures," Arvind Phatak writes, "may prove to be an expensive mistake. In parts of Asia, for example, ghosts, fortune telling, palmistry and soothsayers are all integral parts of culture and must be understood as influential in peoples' lives and in business dealings as well" (1989, p. 36). Indeed, so many Japanese turn to fortune tellers for advice on matters ranging from finance to naming children that a whole industry has been built on their services. Leonard Koren describes a supermarket for one-stop fortune-telling shopping in one of Japan's priciest areas:

> In Tokyo's trendy Harajuku section, a building where thirteen fortune tellers are on call at one time, each in his or her own parlor, is open from 11 A.M. to 8 P.M. every day of the week. . . . The smorgasbord of prophecies includes Chinese systems like the I-Ching and other systems from around the world like Tarot, astrology, geomancy, and palmistry. There are two hundred in all. (1988, p. 100)

Religion and Day-to-Day Behavior

Religious precepts affect the day-to-day nature of behavior. If a religion is dominant enough within a culture, it may influence the daily patterns of business.

For instance, in many Christian countries, shops and businesses in general close on Sundays in recognition of the Christian Sabbath. Even in nations with no state religion, such as the United States, Christianity's dominance is evident in the work patterns of the whole culture (the stores are closed on Sundays to non-Christians as well). In Israel, a predominately Jewish state, most shops and businesses close on Friday nights and Saturdays, the Jewish Sabbath. In most north African and Asian nations where Islam is the majority religion, businesses close on Thursday afternoon and Fridays (the Muslim day of rest); in many countries (Saudi Arabia, for example) government offices close all of Thursday as well as Friday. Countries with no religious preference for a day of rest may find nothing wrong with keeping businesses open every day of the week, although the tendency in some nations (Korea, Japan, the Soviet Union) is to follow the pattern of the economically powerful Christian countries, with Sundays off.

Holy days or holy seasons may also become a feature of the business calendar. The end of December is traditionally a very poor time to conduct business in Christian countries because of the celebration of Christmas. Similarly, the observance of daylight fasting and abstinence during the month-long holy season of Ramadan in Muslim countries frequently creates substantial drops in productivity and delays. However, both the Christmas and Ramadan seasons increase consumer spending and national levels of consumption.

Prohibitions of certain products may also be problematic in intercultural relations. For example, the Islamic ban on alcoholic beverages makes the hiring of employees from many Western nations difficult. "The ban on beer," in Saudi Arabia, according to one observer, "severely hindered the recruiting efforts of German companies and threatened to hobble some of the Saudis' favorite construction companies" (Mackey, 1987, p. 86). To many Germans, accustomed by their culture to drinking beer liberally (Germany is consistently among the top two nations in per capita beer consumption), placement in a desert climate without their national drink was unthinkable. A compromise was reached for a while, when the Schlitz breweries invented near beer to solve this particular dilemma. Incidentally, this beverage was later outlawed, along with fruit juice in foil-wrapped bottles and carbonated grape juice, as being too reminiscent of beer, wine, and champagne, respectively; fundamentalist Islamic leaders feared that consumers might imagine intoxication because the packaging and taste mimicked that of alcoholic beverages.

Religion and Group Membership

As with any cultural trait, religion helps its adherents define their sense of community. For followers of any religion, the world can be divided into believers and nonbelievers.

Some religions — the Protestant sect of Unitarianism, for example — promote toleration of other faiths. On the whole, however, most religions assert their own infallibility as the true way and, as a corollary, the waywardness of other faiths. The degree of intolerance can affect business communication to the extent that adherents of one religion do not trust or tolerate those of other faiths.

Islam, as it is practiced in many nations, is especially intolerant of nonbelievers. Sandra Mackey, speaking only of Saudi Islamic Wahhabism, has suggested that

> their particular hostility to other religious groups seems to express a great fear that somehow the beliefs and legalisms of Wahhabism will not stand up to examination by or exposure to other ideas. In reality, religious intolerance is another form of the Saudis' all-consuming need to preserve their honor and their traditions. (1987, p. 84)

The anthropologist Claude Lévi-Strauss has gone so far as to assert that the gulf between adherents and nonadherents of Islam was impassable. Islam is based, in Lévi-Strauss's analysis,

> not so much on revealed truth as on an inability to establish links with the outside world. . . . [Moslems are] incapable of tolerating the existence of others as others. The only means they have of protecting themselves against doubt and humiliation is the "negativization" of others, considered as witnesses to a different faith and a different way of life. . . . The truth is that contact with non-Moslems disturbs Moslems. (Ajami, 1981, p. 16)

The intolerance of other faiths and the numerous prohibitions on non-

Muslims creates unique problems in conducting business in many Islamic cultures. Mackey notes the difficulties Bell Canada faced in Saudi Arabia:

> Bell Canada, responsible for the kingdom's telephone system, maintains offices in both holy cities of Mecca and Medina. Since the cities are barred to Christians and other non-Moslems, the company is plagued with the problem of trying to match an employee's skills with his religion to keep the in-town offices functioning. Since it is seldom able to keep them fully staffed with Moslems, auxiliary offices and housing compounds for non-Moslem employees are maintained on the outskirts of the cities. These people live in a type of exile, for they cannot enter either city. To shop for food, the women living near Mecca take a bus to Jeddah, an hour away, several times a week. For the employees in Medina, more than 300 miles from the nearest accessible large town, the company maintains a general store and operates a grueling once-a-week shopping excursion to Jeddah. (1987, p. 86)

Actually, the preceding discussion may be somewhat misleading. It is important to keep in mind that the Koran recognizes other "people of the book" (Christians and Jews) and that the teachings of Islam are viewed as a fulfillment and completion of the Jewish and Christian revelations. In this respect, Islam holds Judaism and Christianity in much the same relationship that New Testament Christianity holds Old Testament Judaism. Common theological sources, however, do not necessarily breed tolerance or acceptance.

Still, as Margaret Nydell writes, "Arabs place great value on piety and respect anyone who sincerely practices his religion, no matter what religion it is." The greatest intolerance in Islam is not for the non-Muslim but for the atheist. As Nydell warns:

> Religious affiliation is essential for every person in Arab society—there is no place for an atheist or an agnostic. If you have no religious affiliation or are an atheist, it is best to keep it to yourself. Shock and amazement would be the reaction of most Arabs, along with a loss of respect for you. (1987, p. 87)

The international businessperson should be aware that fundamentalist groups exist in many of the world's major religions and, whatever their ethical strengths, their influence should not be underestimated in promoting intolerance for nonbelievers.

Religions are rarely monolithic. Sects and divisions separate coreligionists often more markedly than differences between religions. Christianity is divided into Roman Catholic, Orthodox, and Protestant faiths, among others. Islam is divided along Shia and Sunni lines. Buddhism has its divisions of Theravada and Mahayana, among others. Often these sects create pronounced tensions within the religion, forming distinct groups among their adherents. This is notably the case in rifts between Catholics and Protestants in Northern Ireland and between Shi'ites and Sunnis in many Muslim countries.

Religion and group membership does not always reflect the role of a culture's dominant faith. Often, religious minorities wield economic and cultural influence in their societies far disproportionate to their numbers. Nowhere is this more evident than in the case of India's Zoroastrian Parsees: "Although they represent only .02 percent of the population, the Parsees have left their mark in India. Well educated, sophisticated, and open to Western ideas, they were doers—but not mindlessly so. In India they became successful merchants, traders, and industrialists, with many of them building into their businesses a strong ethical component" (Moskowitz, 1987, p. 575). India's largest private enterprise, the Tata Group, was founded by and is still largely represented by Zoroastrians. "The Tatas," Milton Moskowitz notes, "are emblematic of India's small but influential Parsee community" (1987, p. 575).

Similar disproportionate economic and business power is held by religious minorities in various nations. As minorities, often prejudiced against and always theologically different from adherents of the majority religion, these coreligionists may develop strong group feelings. Sharing a minority religion, in short, may reduce distrust and promote better relations; this creates a sort of in-group and out-group mentality. Thus, the international businessperson should be aware of the relative importance of minority religious groups.

Religion, whether as a majority or minority within the culture, merits the international business communicator's attention. Still, one should keep religion's role in culture in perspective; it is but one of many factors. Terpstra and David offer sound counsel for assessing the role of religion in the business environment. They suggest three pieces of advice:

> First, [international managers] should learn to avoid quick stereotypes about the impact of religion on economic development. Second, they should consider the degree of religious heterogeneity in a nation and the impact of religious figures and institutions in mobilizing support for social and political movements. . . . Third, they must become informed on details of religious beliefs that, just as in their home country, specifically affect operations. (1985, p. 106)

OCCUPATIONAL INSTITUTIONS

The way in which people view their workplace, occupational institutions, and business in general varies greatly from culture to culture, largely because each society seeks to mold the attitudes toward work and business its members hold.

Culture teaches people to view in a particular way their roles, or function, within their work organization. This perception creates a culturally constructed organizational reality. Vijay Sathe, an expert on corporate culture, has written:

> Organizational reality is socially constructed. What an individual sees is conditioned by what others sharing the same experience say they are seeing. Shared beliefs and values influence this process by providing members of the organization with shared interpretations of their experience. (1985, p. 30)

While this passage deals with internal corporate culture, Sathe's observations are useful in understanding the influence of national culture on the way the occupational institution is viewed. The occupational institution, because of its organizational setting, places the individual in constant contact with others. To the extent that other workers have the same national-cultural referents, their "shared beliefs and values" will reinforce national-cultural values.

The international business communicator should ask two questions regarding the way in which people view occupational institutions: First, how do the leaders of occupational institutions (i.e., corporations, companies, government agencies) view the role of the corporation in society? Second, how do the employees of occupational institutions view their workplace? We will examine each issue in detail.

The Role of the Occupational Institution

Sathe suggests that "Culture . . . helps people in an organization make sense of their actions by providing justifications for it" (1985, p. 30). It follows that, to the extent that different cultures hold to different values, their members will justify their actions differently.

The role the occupational institution is supposed to play in society is far from universal. Views range widely within a national culture and even within the same industries in a country. Still, national cultures tend to emphasize specific functions for their occupational institution; views of what constitute corporate responsibility vary.

One philosophy is that the occupational institution exists to benefit society at large. Arguably, although such a view may be considered an ideal in most societies, it is closer to reality in certain cultures than in others.

Konosuke Matsushita founded Matsushita Electric Company, the Japanese electronics giant better known in the English-speaking world by its brand names Panasonic, Quasar, National, and Technics. Matsushita, though himself somewhat of a nonconformist by Japanese standards, expressed what may be the quintessentially Japanese philosophy of the role the occupational institution should play in society:

> A business should quickly stand on its own, based on the service it provides society. Profits should not be a reflection of corporate greed but a vote of confidence from society that what is offered by the firm is valued. When a business fails to make profits it should die — it is a waste of resources to society. (Pascale and Athos, 1981, p. 72)

Matsushita's philosophy, to use the words of Kazuyoghi Kamioka, is one of "national service through industry — not solely to gain wealth or to display industrial strength, but to contribute to the progress and welfare of the community and the nation" (1988, p. 70). It is, as Richard Pascale and Anthony Athos note, "a management philosophy tying business profitability to the social good in a kind of Darwinian paradigm" (p. 72). The emphasis on the corporation's tie to the "social good" is embedded in Buddhist and Confucian ethical precepts and is thus firmly anchored in the Japanese cultural view of business in society. It is also rooted in the Japanese conception of face, which we will discuss in Chapter 5 at greater length.

Such a philosophy is by no means limited to Matsushita Electric. It is espoused by a remarkable number of the founders of Japan's major corporations. Virtually the same viewpoint, for instance, is held at Nippon Gakki (Yamaha), the world's largest producer of musical instruments, fiberglass boats, and snowmobiles and the second largest maker of motorcycles. Nippon Gakki's president, Hiroshi Kawakami, has summarized the corporate philosophy of his grandfather, Torakusu Yamaha, the company's founder: "My grandfather propounded three major principles: think creatively, ruffle no one's feathers, and make a contribution to society" (Moskowitz, 1987, p. 655). Similarly, in a 1985 address to the quadrennial International Industrial Conference in San Francisco, the chairman of NEC (the world's biggest producer of semiconductors and Japan's fourth largest electronics company), Koji Kobayashi, warned that in automating factories, corporations should not "forget their responsibilities as members of society" (Moskowitz, 1987, p. 383).

The Japanese cultural stress on the occupational institution and society has far-reaching implications. Because profits are downplayed relative to societal contribution and the public status of the corporation, the Japanese and societies like them emphasize long-term results, in direct contrast to the short-term approach, focuses on quarterly or yearly profits, favored in such cultures as the United States and Canada. The successful Japanese company must gain public confidence and devotes great energies to do so. The most visible sign of public confidence, in turn, is market share. The company with the largest market share must, according to this logic, be the one producing the goods or services that most meet the needs of society. As Peter Trasker observes:

> Japanese companies are so obsessed by their position in the market that they often seem unconcerned whether they are making any money at all. As a result conventional [North American] performance measures, such as sales margin and return on capital, are miserable for even the best-quality Japanese firms. However, market dominance eventually brings its rewards in terms of customer acceptance, economies of scale and the gradual inexorable squeezing of competitors. (1987, p. 46)

In addition to market share, Japanese companies can measure their success in terms of pure production. Moreover, the Japanese generally believe that the larger a producer is, the more it benefits society; in short, size in itself brings status. Rodney Clark explains that

> the aims of the Japanese company can usually be expressed in terms other than financial, in units of production; and production is something everyone can agree to increase without reservation. But production need not be an end in itself. The more a company makes of a thing, the bigger the company

becomes, and the bigger it becomes the better respected not only the company but also its employees will be. (1979, p. 96)

Although the cultural emphasis on the social responsibility of the corporation finds its apex in Japan, it is not confined to the Japanese. The massive influx of foreign capital into the Persian Gulf states of Qatar, the United Arab Emirates, Kuwait, and Saudi Arabia has instilled a belief that all citizens of their countries should benefit from the infusion of wealth. Still, such companies as Kuwait Petroleum, Qatar's Mannai, and Saudi Arabia's Aramco may show social concern for different reasons other than the more purely long-range concern for social responsibility prevalent in Japan. Instead, they may demonstrate social concern because of their close ties to the state governments and because of the massive surplus of foreign capital they receive for the oil they sell. Unlike the economy of Japan, powered by the manufacturing of goods and services, the Gulf states' production of natural resources does not lend itself to the same concerns for market share. Nevertheless, the value Arab executives place on status and prestige (since they have little short-term cause for concern regarding profits) produces a similar public-spirited attention to social responsibility; status and prestige may be seen as resulting from public benevolence.

Perhaps a national pattern more closely aligned to the Japanese philosophy is found in India. In a 1962 interview, J. R. D. Tata, head of India's largest private sector conglomerate, set forth the company philosophy:

> Every man has an innate desire to be useful to others, and in India the cause of lifting our people is such a crying one that service is easier than in a completely industrialized country. We here at Tata are so obsessed with our people's poverty that we don't deserve special credit for having public service on our minds. (Moskowitz, 1987, p. 579)

To some extent, Tata's own analysis is correct in differentiating the company's philosophy from that found in more industrialized nations such as Japan. Still, it is a philosophy, like that of Japan and the Gulf states, that is essentially foreign to many Western nations.

Business philosophy in the United States represents the opposite extreme of that in Japan, the Gulf states, and India. The U.S. view of the philosophical foundation of the corporation generally emphasizes self-preservation through quick private gain and short-term profitability. Few U.S. business leaders would agree with the stated philosophy of Shibusawa Eiichi, the founder of Japan's Dai-Ichi Kangyo Bank, among the world's three largest financial institutions. Eiichi included among his frequently quoted sayings that "to become rich without moral principle is not to succeed, even though it is to become rich" (Moskowitz, 1987, p. 169). Indeed, the majority of U.S. business leaders would probably assert that the exact opposite is nearer the truth.

U.S. executives tend to see themselves as accountable not to society but to their stockholders or (especially in the case of privately held companies) to themselves. This attitude has been summarized by one analyst of U.S. business philosophy: "For the most part, America's business leaders think first in terms of their own personal economic and financial well-being. Next, they think of the profitability of their company; and third—finally—they think about those who consume their products or services. Generally speaking, any benefit to the United States is incidental" (DeMente, 1987, p. 123).

In response to this philosophy, most U.S. consumers look suspiciously on big business. In Japan the public believes that the larger a company is, the greater the probability that it is working for the public good and the greater its sense of social responsibility. By contrast, in the United States, the larger the company, the more likely that the public will suspect that the company is taking advantage of them.

To some degree the situation has been changing in the United States since the mid-1960s—not, however, as the result of a culturally imbued role of the corporation. The philosophy of Barnumism ("There's a sucker born every minute") is still culturally expected; if a business can get away with something, the national mentality promotes the belief that it will. Instead, what caused this shift is the success of a different aspect of U.S. culture: individualism and the spirit of protest. U.S. consumers followed the lead of a lone protester who, unattached to university, the government, or any other formal organization, symbolized the quintessential ideal of individualism and reform: Ralph Nader.

In 1966 Nader single-handedly took on the largest U.S. corporation —General Motors—and won. Yet when Nader attacked General Motors for producing unsafe cars, U.S. corporations had little concern for Japanese-style social responsibility. Their main concern was for short-term profits and the enrichment of their executives and shareholders. In direct counterpoint to Japanese business, U.S. business had in David Halberstam's words, come to represent "bigness and power without apparent accountability" (1986, p. 490).

The United States, if extreme, is not alone in the role its culture assigns the occupational institution. Most European countries hold similar views. For instance, Helmut Maucher, the German-born president of the Swiss multinational Nestlé, in a 1985 speech at the University of Guadalajara (Mexico), felt that high ideals make bad business. "We need leaders and managers more than ideologists," he claimed, asserting that "in my opinion one of our present world problems comes from too many idealistic people with too much power" (Moskowitz, 1987, p. 404).

Ivar Kreuger, founder of Swedish Match—until its recent takeover, the world's largest match manufacturers and second largest producer of flooring—was equal to any U.S. monopolist of the nineteenth century. Kreuger epitomized the self-benefit aspect of business, once noting:

> Today the world demands balance sheets, profit-and-loss statements once a year. But if you're really working on great ideas, you can't supply those on

schedule and expose yourself to view. Yet you've got to tell the public something, and so long as it's satisfied and continues to have faith in you, it's really not important what you confess. (Moskowitz, 1987, p. 571)

While Kreuger's philosophy should not be considered typical of current Swedish business practice, his statement shows that such views are not exclusive to the United States.

Most national cultures are characterized by views of the role of occupational institutions that fall somewhere between the two extremes we've described. Some cultures — most notably the Soviet Union and those following the Soviet model — emphasize full employment. Most of these countries guarantee employment in their constitutions.

Other societies may feel that it is business's place to further national culture. For example, Franco Bollati, chairman of Bonifica (a division of Italy's largest company, IRI), explained its reasons for selecting in 1985 a depressed area in the United States to build an industrial park: "For us, it's a matter of pride. We come to the South Bronx to introduce ourselves to the United States and show off the fruits of our experience" (Moskowitz, 1987, p. 305). Moreover, in Italy itself, IRI is often a major backer of losing enterprises that provide large-scale employment. As a result, despite highly profitable divisions, when IRI broke even in 1986, it was for the first time since 1973.

Similarly, Unilever, the British-Dutch consortium, though significantly more profitable than IRI, was once called by London's *Financial Times* "the nearest thing British commerce has to civil service" (Moskowitz, 1987, p. 625). In the case of the Société Générale de Belgique, Belgium's huge holding company, the distinction between civil service and private enterprise is even more blurred. The main mission of the Société Générale is to promote trade and industry in Belgium; it is still largely considered to be the private business venture of Belgium's king.

Another view of the role of the occupational institution is that of the bearer of national aesthetics. For some cultures, including the United States (though this is changing), such ideals seem irrelevant or relatively unimportant niceties with little intrinsic value. Still in some cultures aesthetics — the role of art and design — is often a major concern. Camillo Olivetti, founder of Italy's office equipment giant, once said, "A typewriter is not a gadget or a toy. Aesthetics must be considered" (Moskowitz, 1987, p. 186). In fact, Olivetti typewriter designs have found their way into collections of modern art.

Similar philosophies dominate in nations with major artisan industries, such as Ireland (Waterford crystal), Italy (the Murano glass works) and others. Discussion of aesthetic issues in certain cultures may vary substantially from considerations of the topic in other societies. Where the U.S executive may become impatient if aesthetic issues are raised as a primary concern, an Italian executive might grow irritated if such concerns are cast aside as of secondary importance.

Finally, aesthetic issues may surface in more subtle ways, ranging from emphasis on personal appearance and document design (discussed more fully in Chapter 7) to the expressiveness and rhetoric used in speech (discussed more fully in Chapter 5).

The Employee Perception of the Occupational Institution

Employees perceive the part they play in the occupational institution differently from culture to culture. Views range from the employee's self-perception as a cog in a huge and impersonal machine to that of an integral and valued member of a team.

Within any society, a spectrum of views are likely to coexist from employer to employer. Thus employees at Company A may see themselves as nameless entities who can easily be replaced and who feel little loyalty to the company, whereas employees performing the same tasks at Company B, in the same country, may view themselves as valued team members. Much of the difference rests less on national culture than on the corporate culture, which in turn, results from the particular management styles of the occupational institution's leaders.

To the extent that occupational institutions in a society reinforce one style of leadership and management over another, we can say that the national culture encourages a specific type of perception. Although it may not be universal within the culture, that view nevertheless predominates among that nation's occupational institutions.

In Chapter 6, we will discuss cultural influences on authority conception and motivation. What concerns us here is the view of the employee toward the workplace itself. While the topic is too complex for more than a cursory discussion here, we can briefly demonstrate the cultural origins of varying employee conceptions of the workplace. To illustrate these differences, we will look at two cultural approaches that reinforce different employee attitudes toward occupational institutions: the *mechanistic* (as in the United States and the Soviet Union) and the *humanistic* (as in Saudi Arabia and Japan).

The Mechanistic Attitude   The United States exemplifies the contractual, mechanistic approach to the employee–employer relationship. Under this arrangement, employees work for the employer in exchange for wage and benefits under a contract. The situation is generally understood to exist even when no formal, written contract is signed. Individuals agree to work for the employer as free agents; if they can receive better wages and benefits elsewhere, they are free to leave. In turn, if the employer feels the employee is not holding to his or her part of the contract—in other words, is not performing the expected work—the employee can be dismissed.

The contractual approach leads to a mechanistic view of the occupational institution. The employee offers the employer his or her labor, which is viewed by the employer as a commodity. The human element in this exchange becomes relatively unimportant. What *is* important is the amount and quality of the labor (what the employee can do) and the amount and quality of the recompense (what the employer pays). Such an attitude inhibits the degree of loyalty and sense of belonging that characterizes other systems.

In the Soviet Union, no such contractual arrangement exists, although an equally mechanistic approach prevails. Under this system, which is *involuntary*, the employee is generally assigned to a job and has little control over what or where the work is. Employees cannot choose to leave the job (although they may be permitted in certain cases to do so); in fact, they are required by law to work at the assigned job. Failure to work is a criminal act. As in the United States, the relationship between the employer and the employee is mechanistic—it is based on the exchange of labor for wages and benefits. To this extent, the employer and employee enter into an informal societal contract. However, because employees are not free agents, as most U.S. workers are, dissatisfied Soviet employees have no formal options open to them. Passive aggression and even sabotage against the employer are the only outlets available. Since the employee cannot quit, they may, for example, work slowly on purpose as a means of harming the employer.

The Humanistic Attitude   In the humanistic approach to the employee-employer relationship, employees are encouraged to think of themselves as part of a group with close personal ties. Employees are less likely to see themselves as selling the commodity of their labor than as gaining membership into a sort of family. Work output is only one goal of such an organization; a sense of belonging and the growth of interpersonal relationships is equally important.

In certain societies (as we discussed earlier in this chapter), kinship relationships predominate in the workplace. If most employees are family members, their work relationships extend beyond that of the free agent. For example, many Saudi Arabian occupational institutions are run by families; their employees are related to the owners by various kinship ties. Such workers are much less apt than their U.S. counterparts to think of themselves as free agents. A worker who decided to leave the organization would be letting down family members. Moreover, the organization leadership infrequently allows a mechanistic view to predominate. The human element matters because the employer will have to deal with the employee as a relative both on *and* off the job.

In other societies, humanistic approaches occur even though the workplace does not practice nepotism or necessarily have kinship bonds. Most major Japanese companies, for example, offer a form of lifetime employment to workers as a way to promote long-term loyalty and dedication. This practice reinforces the Japanese cultural view that it is the employees themselves the corporation seeks, not the commodity (their labor) they offer. One of the creators of lifetime employment in modern Japan was Sazo Idemitsu, founder of Japan's third largest oil company, Idemitsu Oil. Idemitsu taught (as paraphrased by Boye DeMente) that "a salary should not be the price of a person's labor, but a guarantee of the employee's livelihood" (1987, p. 101).

Idemitsu was far from alone in emphasizing the human side of the employment relationship. An extreme symbol of corporate bonds to the individual employee is the Kyoto-based ceremics giant Kyocera, a leader in denture technology, artificial gemstones, and the world's largest maker of semiconductor packaging. Kyocera built a company tomb to hold the remains of its employees. As Kyocera's founder, Kazuo Inamori, explained, "We are all members of one family, so it is natural to stay together after we die" (Moskowitz, 1987, p. 337). The philosophy appears to be successful: "Kyocera is now the fastest developing company in Japan, with 8,000 local employees. With its overseas subsidiaries, the company employs a total of 20,000 workers. Inamori feels that it is his responsibility to 'feed those 20,000'" (Kamioka, 1988, p. 139). On the negative side, as Joel Kotkin and Yoriko Kishimoto (1986) have noted, a concern for self-identity beyond the boundaries of the corporation affect the Japanese psyche in the workplace. Without practical alternatives, most Japanese employees—whether at the executive level or lower— feel driven to see the corporation as both the means to maintain their expected lifestyles as well as the final arbiter of their self-worth.

The Japanese have also carried this philosophy outside Japan. For example, when Toyota Motor Corporation began hiring for its automobile assembly plant in Georgetown, Kentucky, it tested all potential employees, even for entry-level shop-floor jobs, for a minimum of 14 hours. The *Wall Street Journal* reported how several U.S. personnel consultants criticized Toyota for this practice. One human resource consultant called it "overkill," while another questioned "how so much testing could be relevant to a job" ("Labor Letter," 1987, p. 1). What these U.S. personnel experts did not understand (and what the article never explained) was that Toyota was not hiring people to perform a job; the company was hiring them to have loyalty to the organization, and the testing was little different from the screening performed before granting admission to a club. In the United States, screening for low-level positions rarely extends beyond an hour, and even those seeking high-level positions generally receive significantly less preemployment testing than Toyota gave its line workers in Georgetown. The contrast reflects a cultural difference in the feelings about the workplace. Toyota viewed the hiring decision as humanistic; most U.S. employers would view the same decisions as a mechanistic commodity exchange. The U.S. company usually seeks the necessary skills; the Japanese company generally looks for proper attitude and loyalty.

POLITICAL AND JUDICIAL SYSTEM

A nation's political and judicial system affects business more powerfully than any other factor in social organization. A country's administrative and legal systems help shape culture itself, since they determine how people are allowed to behave on a day-to-day basis. To the degree that the political and judicial system has an impact on the workplace, it is relevant to the international business communicator.

The subject of comparative political and judicial systems as a whole goes far beyond the limitations of this book. It is, therefore, highly recommended that international communicators familiarize themselves with the political and judicial climates of the countries in which they conduct business by consulting the appropriate trade embassies and exploring the vast literature available on virtually every country.

Because even a cursory discussion of comparative political and judicial systems exceeds the scope of this text, we will focus on just two examples to illustrate their impact on the atmosphere in which international business negotiations takes place. We will look briefly at the Soviet Union to show how the political system in that country influences cultural attitudes toward business. We will then turn to Japan to examine how attitudes toward the judicial system are intertwined with Japanese culture as a whole.

Soviet Political System

The atmosphere in which business communication takes place in the Soviet Union differs to a large extent from that in Western nations. First, most business communication is conducted through government ministers who oversee the individual state-run enterprises as part of the management of the national economy. Second, the fact that the political system guarantees employment and that all business enterprises are state-owned affects overall attitudes toward motivation and work behavior.

As a centrally planned economy, Soviet business is run largely from the *Gosplan* and related ministries in Moscow rather than at the actual production sites. The international business communicator would most likely deal almost exclusively with central planners rather than with the stewards (managers) of the individual enterprises. Thus, most business communication would probably be handled through one or more intermediaries — government planners, ministers, and officials who explain the needs of the enterprises to the foreign businessperson and the needs of the foreign businessperson to the state-run enterprise. Even if the businessperson tried to deal with the stewards, not much could be accomplished because they have little authority themselves. The factory, or any other productive enterprise, is an operational unit of the Soviet government (which owns all property, land, equipment, and assets) and is therefore run by the appropriate government ministries. While the Soviet system as it affects business is of course much more complex than this description indicates, it can be seen that the political system creates an intermediary rather than direct system of communication.

A second point regarding work motivation and business communication is the matter of full employment and state control of much managerial decision making. In the Soviet Union, all citizens able to work have a constitutional right and obligation to do so. The benefit of such a guarantee is the reality of full employment. Only students and mothers of small children are unemployed, and their time is, by Soviet cultural standards, acceptably accounted for. Indeed, full employment is considered a point of national pride. The system's major drawback is that, for political reasons, "the Soviet leaders have a vested interest in maintaining a high rate of employment however it is achieved. There is thus a strong bias against dismissing workers even if they are redundant or incompetent. This implicit policy results in the absence of fear, on the part of workers, of unemployment and consequently in lax labor discipline" (Haitani, 1986, p. 123).

In direct contrast, the Soviet manager is in a position of great instability. Usually acting on directives from a central planning committee, managers have very little control over what they must do; they are more or less outside the decision-making mechanism. Moreover, because managers must encourage a labor force to work productively with little incentive, they are in an untenable situation. Managers who fail in a task face severe punishment—not only dismissal from the job and transfer to another area, but actual prosecution. Since the government owns the means of production, managerial failure can be viewed as a crime against the state. Robert Campbell has observed that Soviet managers

> are held to a very strict accountability for their actions and are often judged arbitrarily. Failure to achieve fulfillment of the planned targets may bring an accusation of criminal negligence or of economic crimes against the state and the responsible persons could be imprisoned or shot. At the same time, a manager's best efforts to meet the plan targets may lead him afoul of the multitudinous legal prohibitions that circumscribe his freedom of action. For instance, the materials supply system works ineffectively and he may have to resort to illegal means of procuring materials in order to fulfill the plan. Many of these legal restraints are not rigorously enforced but enterprise officials always place themselves in a potentially dangerous position by violating them. (1966, p. 70)

It is important to note that much has changed in the Soviet Union since Campbell's observations were made in the mid-1960s. Much of the terror of negative sanctions has been mitigated to promote greater motivation. Even as Campbell was writing, the system had grown less harsh than it had been at the time of Stalin, leading Campbell to conclude that "negative sanctions work best if they lurk more or less in the background" (p. 70).

Still, the underlying principles of the Soviet system remain unchanged. Reform in the administration of punishment in the workplace has primarily broadened the number of offenders subject to punishment. This is particularly true of the quality control reforms instituted in the late 1980s under Mikhail Gorbachev. As Marshall Goldman has written: "Under the new incentive policy, if factory output is rejected because of its poor quality, the entire workforce will find its salary and bonuses reduced accordingly" (1987, p. 78). Thus the worker and the manager share in the negative sanctions that would result.

The system itself, under Gorbachev's *perestroika* (or restructuring) efforts, may be in the process of limited change. As part of *perestroika*, the Soviet Union is attempting to redistribute authority between the central departments and the enterprises. Gorbachev himself has said that "the broadening of the rights and economic autonomy of enterprises, the changing functions of central economic and sectoral departments and the transition from predominately administrative methods to mainly economic methods of management call for radical changes in the managerial structure" (1987, p. 91).

Even with the changes Gorbachev has proposed, the Soviet political system has an enormous influence over the workplace. As a result, the communicator doing business in the Soviet Union can primarily expect to interact not with the people who run the factory or other business enterprise but with the government officials who do the planning. The business communicator may never get close enough to the factory or enterprise to know what is happening; negotiations with the people who do the actual work is almost always conducted through an intermediary. Demands by a businessperson from abroad for, say, higher quality products may initiate a string of counterproductive measures down the Soviet hierarchy. Therefore, even seemingly simple requests must be considered for their far-reaching ramifications.

Japanese Legal System

To illustrate the effect of the legal system on international business communication, we might look at Japan. The discussion is not meant to represent even a brief outline of how the judicial system in Japan operates, but rather to focus on the Japanese view of the law. Indeed, the Japanese legal system itself is not unique, since, following the post–World War II U.S. military occupation of Japan, much of its judicial apparatus was based on U.S. and European legal institutions. Instead, our concern is the manner in which the Japanese use (or refuse to use) their legal system. The Japanese are among the least litigious of cultures. In Japan, a nation with roughly half the population of the United States, there are under 15,000 lawyers, less than in the state of Illinois alone. In the United States, there are over 650,000 attorneys; at one point (during its divestiture) a single U.S. company, AT&T, maintained an in-house legal department of over 1,000 lawyers. Such a practice is incomprehensible in Japan.

One may argue that since Japan imported its legal system (and even then did so under duress), the Japanese are less accustomed to using the law to resolve conflicts than those nations in which the law grew out of a long, evolutionary development. Still, the Japanese have had some form of legal code since as early as the seventh century.

Rather, the lack of litigation seems to be culturally grounded. Culturally, the Japanese dislike using the courts or turning to lawyers to mediate disputes; the law is the system of absolute last resort. The Japanese culturally shun win–lose situations—loss of face and the public airing of grievances by both winner and loser creates a situation that makes both winner and loser seem at fault. The Japanese as a culture believe that almost all matters can be resolved without filing a formal lawsuit, through traditional emphases on *wakai* (compromise) or *chotai* (conciliation). If a suit is filed, this means that both parties, regardless of who wins the suit, are at fault, because neither party tried hard enough to reach a *wakai* or *chotai*. To file a lawsuit is to defy this cultural mind-set, creating a disruption in the surface harmony from which, in the Japanese view of the world, no good can come. This Japanese attitude is well explained by Paul Lansing and Marlene Wechselblatt:

> If there is a tendency not to use the court system nor seek the counsel of a lawyer in settling a dispute, how then do the Japanese resolve conflicts? As we have seen, the Japanese long-standing dislike of litigation remains; only when persons have stepped outside of the community of thought can disputes arise. In such a case, all parties are, to some extent, culpable, and harmony is to be restored only by reconciling the parties, not by determining which party was right and which party was wrong. (1983, p. 653)

In most Western cultures, and most notably in the United States, with its puritanical origins, the desire to attribute blame is one of the strongest motivations for using the legal system. Culturally, the United States and many other Western nations are inclined to find blame in business before resolving a matter. This is simply not the case in Japan.

On the other hand, Japanese companies often avoid litigation because of the willingness of corporate leaders (including company CEOs) to take responsibility for incidents for which an employee was responsible. For example, in 1982, a Japan Air Lines plane crashed as a result of pilot error. The pilot was in fact a schizophrenic whose mental illness had gone undetected. Many passengers were killed and many more injured. Evidence surfaced that the company had had some hints before the crash that the pilot was mentally unstable. Yet only one passenger sued the airline —not because the passengers would lose such a case under the Japanese system but, rather, because the president of JAL apologized in person to every family with a relative killed or injured in the crash. The company also paid a monetary sum to show its sincerity. Such behavior on the part of the president of a major company is virtually unheard of in the United States, Canada, or most European countries, as unlikely as having only one lawsuit filed after a major airplane wreck for which the company was responsible. What JAL paid in accepting responsibility and seeking *chotai*, or conciliation, however, was significantly less than one might expect in a similar situation in a Western country.

The reaction of the president of Japan Air Lines is the rule, not the exception. Enormous social pressure exists for the highest officials to take responsibility in such cases. George Fields, in his description of a major Japanese hotel fire that had a number of fatalities, tells what happens when the highest officials do not take responsibility:

> The president in this case refused to acknowledge liability and a number of lawsuits resulted. He has, as a result, been totally ostracized and the mass media has had a field day dragging before the country every aspect of his past, present, and private life with what seems to be little regard for any verification of truth or falsity. It's as if the media found it necessary to explain why anybody would behave in such a socially unacceptable manner. As he is beyond the pale of society, he was considered un-Japanese and is currently everybody's favorite villain. (1983, p. 192)

Lawsuits are possible in Japan, but they occur primarily when someone has stepped beyond the boundaries of acceptable behavior. The law is used as a vehicle to shame the litigants. "The Japanese aversion to law," Kim and Lawson write, "is really an aversion to the use of law in the legal process, to the shame of the courtroom, to the judgment that blames" (1979, p. 505). Thus, when the hotel chain president, by refusing to take responsibility, went "beyond the pale of society," lawsuits followed; but more important, he was also villified in the public eye.

To the international businessperson, the Japanese attitude toward the law presents a double problem. First, he or she is by definition non-Japanese and therefore much more likely to act in a manner "beyond the pale of society" (however, the Japanese as a culture tend to overlook much behavior by foreigners that would be unacceptable by native Japanese). The second problem is more serious. The attachment to the law — particularly among North American and northern European cultures — finds no parallel in Japan. Boye DeMente explains why:

> American companies habitually use attorneys to negotiate for them or bring in attorneys as members of their negotiating team. . . . The attorney mentality is anathema to the Japanese. . . . Their way of doing business is diametrically opposed to the detailed, legalistic approach practiced by attorneys. They do not deal in absolutes; they do not deal within hard, unchanging narrowly defined rules. They demand flexibility, room for changing with circumstances. (1987, p. 129)

Thus the U.S. executive would expect, as part of routine communication, to rely on lawyers in nearly every step of interaction, particularly in the field of international business, in which so many factors are not clearly delineated. The Japanese executive, as we have discussed, would be unlikely to rely on attorneys in routine business communication and might even question the reasoning behind foreigners' insistence on using their attorneys. In turn, non-Japanese executives may view their Japanese counterparts' reluctance to use attorneys as evidence of lack of commitment or even as somewhat underhanded. This variance in approach does not reflect a difference in legal or judicial systems; rather, it illustrates the cultural factors behind the way a nation uses its legal and judicial systems.

MOBILITY AND GEOGRAPHIC ATTACHMENT

Nations vary in their views of distance and their attachment to where they live. While rapid improvements in the means of transportation make the *ability* to travel easier in most societies than ever before, in only a handful of cultures does the *desire* to travel parallel the increased means to do so.

Instead, a connection exists between the length of settlement of a nation and its mobility patterns. According to a study published in *The Wall Street Journal*, "People in relatively new 'frontier' countries move around more than the populations of older, settled European nations" ("Young People, Nations Have Higher Mobility," p. B-1). As a result, the percentage of people relocating annually varies from 6 percent in Ireland and under 10 percent in both France and Great Britain, to almost one-fifth of the population in New Zealand at 19 percent and nearly as high in Canada (18 percent), the United States (18 percent), and Australia (17 percent).

Cultures can be divided into three categories related to their views of mobility: high mobility, static mobility, and phasic mobility. Each category reflects an attitude toward travel and attachment to one's own region. Such attitudes reflect the willingness to travel for a number of reasons, ranging from brief business trips to permanent relocation (for example, to accept a promotion in a different city).

High Mobility

In cultures with a high-mobility orientation, people either do not mind moving or like moving from place to place. The classic example of a high-mobility culture is the United States. In general, people in the United States do not view geographic distance as a major barrier. Large numbers of U.S. businesspeople travel for a living, and relocation to a permanent residence away from one's place of birth for educational or business reasons is common. As Condon and Yousef have indicated, for the United States, "the norm appears to be constantly shifting in an effort to better oneself" (1985, p. 79). They cite as support such business expressions as "the man on the go" and "let's get moving" as reflections of this attitude. In the United States, they note, the term "exile" has limited meaning, since the concept is relatively foreign (1985, pp. 75–76).

Static Mobility

In static cultures, movement is limited and attachment to one's birthplace or geographic region is very strong. Such attitudes affect not only the willingness of employees to be relocated but also the economic well-being of whole national regions, as those in depressed areas are reluctant to seek work by moving to areas that are better off. A static-mobility mentality also may play a role in determining how readily foreigners are welcomed. In static cultures, it may be difficult to understand why a person would want to leave his or her home to live in the host region permanently. Thus, even after years of living in some communities, a relocated individual may still be perceived as a foreigner or newcomer.

Phasic Mobility

In phasic cultures, people are relatively willing to move to another location for a limited period or phase. The expectation is that they will return home after a certain period of time. They do not anticipate setting down roots in their new location. Phasic travelers may include executives abroad or migrant workers; both expect to return after they have accomplished a specific task or goal.

One subset of phasic workers merits particular attention—the *Gastarbeiters*, or guest workers (briefly discussed in Chapter 1). This group is important because in many developed countries, they constitute a major component of the work force and because the attitudes toward them varies markedly among the host countries.

In general, guest workers travel to a foreign country that has a higher standard of living than their native land. While they may reside for years in the foreign country, they usually make no attempt to become citizens. Often, they send their earnings back to their families, who remain in the home countries, contributing to the guest workers' rootlessness in the foreign culture. Generally they perform tasks that native workers (because of their high standard of living) consider menial; however, some guest workers compete with native workers for certain jobs (usually manual labor and repetitive factory jobs). Although the guest workers' living standards are often far below those of citizens of the foreign country, such standards may actually be as good as or even superior to that in their home countries. Also, they may be willing to work for less money than native workers to perform the same tasks—a fact often resented by members of the host nation. Finally, because guest workers tend to favor specific foreign countries over others (i.e., Turks in Germany, Algerians in France, Mexicans in the United States), national stereotypes often follow.

Since the international businessperson as negotiator, trainer, or manager will likely encounter guest workers, it is important to recognize attitudes of the host culture and the guest workers regarding each other. Basically three approaches exist for dealing with guest workers.

The first approach is the *nonaccommodation model*. This model, practiced widely in France, Switzerland, and Germany, treats the guest workers as foreigners, not fully covered by the laws and standards that protect nationals. The guest workers are kept at a lower standard of living than native workers. While the guest workers provided the labor such countries required during growth periods, problems arose when recessions in the early 1980s slowed the economic growth needed to support them. Since guest workers were not fully protected as citizens, their work permits were not renewed and many were deported. As unemployment rises in nonaccommodation cultures, guest workers may also be sought out as scapegoats, even though the jobs most hold are those that native workers refuse to accept.

As a consequence, unemployed native workers may refuse government efforts to help them if it involves cooperating with guest workers. For example, they may refuse to live in subsidized housing that is occupied by guest workers (as was the case when French workers were asked to share low-cost housing with Arabs in the late 1970s). Scapegoating may also take the form of legislation. In Switzerland, a national referendum to reduce "overforeignization" by slashing the number of aliens allowed in the country was only narrowly defeated. The rise of the extreme right-wing National Front Party, led by the openly racist Jean-Marie Le Pen, won 15 percent of the French vote in 1988 on a platform of tougher immigration laws and strong sentiment against guest workers in France, where 7 percent of the population consists of immigrants. In less overt political reactions, governments may try to encourage or even force guest workers to leave, in order to appease their unemployed citizens, even though they would be unlikely to take the jobs the deported guest workers vacated. In France and Germany, guest workers laid off from their jobs were given cash bonuses or repatriation assistance and asked to leave.

A second approach to guest workers is what we might term *accommodation*. This approach gives guest workers rights that are equal, or nearly so, to those accorded to workers who are citizens, and the culture takes great care to provide equivalent services to foreign and native workers to reduce the economic disparity between them. Accommodation is practiced, arguably, in its most extreme form by the Swedes. Sweden was the first country to give immigrant workers (of three years' residence) the right to vote and even to hold local office, despite the fact that they were not citizens. All of the roughly 1.1 million guest workers receive the same benefits as Swedes. As the result of the 1968 Commission on Immigration, Sweden adopted a statute regulating the equality of Swedish and foreign workers as well as the encouragement of a cultural choice for guest workers to be Swedish or remain nationals of their home countries. Another law, passed in 1973, requires employers to give their guest workers "240 hours of paid leave of absence to attend lessons in Swedish provided free of charge." At the same time, "a determined effort has been made to give immigrants and their children a knowledge of their ethnic background. State grants go to national immigration organizations — Finnish, Yugoslav, Greek, Italian, and others — which have 80,000 members" (Childs, 1980, p. 162). In Sweden, as a result, there are significantly less tensions between guest workers and citizens than in France, Switzerland, or Germany. Nevertheless, employers and taxpayers have had to bear the expense needed to create the cooperation among Swedish workers and guest workers.

The third approach to dealing with guest workers is the *minority native* model. This describes the role of the guest worker most notably in the Persian Gulf Arab states, where foreigners comprise the majority of the work force. Natives of the cultures in question are minorities in their own countries. For example, by the end of the 1970s, fully 75 percent of the workers in the United Arab Emirates were foreign; and approximately 80 percent of the workers were foreign in Qatar (Birks and Sinclair, 1980, p. 139). The approach toward guest workers in minority-native situations is often two-sided. With such drastic imbalances between native and foreign population, the natives (many of whom do not work at all) may become a privileged class, served by foreigners. On the other hand, the number of foreigners who, in the absence of qualified natives, hold key positions in these countries is substantial. The imbalance between foreigners and natives also poses serious questions regarding the autonomy of the host nations.

RECREATIONAL INSTITUTIONS

How people in a culture choose to relax and the emphasis they place on recreation, while not directly linked to business, nonetheless remains an influence on social organization in the workplace.

On the most elementary level, the terminology of recreation often finds its way into the workplace — particularly in the United States, where a tendency to favor colloquialisms encourages this practice. Thus businesspeople use such terms as those listed in Table 4.2 on a regular basis. Such terms, however, because they come from sports that may be unfamiliar to foreigners, can provide serious barriers to international communication. The effective businessperson from the United States should avoid using these and similar expressions while trying to learn some of the colorful recreational phrases used in other countries.

The influence of sports on the workplace, however, goes well beyond mere use of special terminology. As we have seen, attitudes toward work are culturally influenced, and so are attitudes toward recreation. What interests us here, however, is less the flip side of the live-to-work attitude we have discussed — although a work-to-live attitude is just as pertinent. Rather, we are interested in how people in a culture spend their free time and, in particular, what that culture's recreational institutions are.

Table 4.2 U.S. SPORTS TERMS COMMON IN BUSINESS COMMUNICATION

Phrase	Source	Meaning
"To touch base"	Baseball	To keep in contact, as a baserunner does after successfully reaching base
"To go the whole nine yards"	Football	To muster one's full efforts in a gamble for successful completion, as a football player does when attempting to cover the remaining 9 of 10 possible yards to obtain a first down to keep possession of the ball
"To slamdunk someone"	Basketball	To make a point forcefully or overrule an idea, as a basketball player does by jumping above the basket and shoving in the ball to prevent any defensive measure by the opposing team
"To be out in left field"	Baseball	To behave in a manner that suggests that one is not fully aware of what is taking place or to be ill-informed, as the left fielder is to some extent in baseball; left field is the position to which batters are least likely to hit the ball

The first factor to consider is a people's devotion to or involvement in athletics or other recreational activities. In some cultures sporting events are national pastimes, while in other cultures the populations are not such avid fans. And just as the passion aroused by a particular sport differs in intensity among some societies, so do the types of games or events favored. A sport or other recreation that is highly popular in one nation may be unknown everywhere else.

The amount of time people spend on recreational or leisure activities varies from country to country. For example, surveys indicated that the average Japanese spends just 5¾ hours per week on discretionary activity; in the United States the estimated figure is 23.6 hours; in the United Kingdom it is 40.8 hours (*Britannica World Data Annual*, 1991).

How people spend their leisure time varies from culture to culture as well. For example, Britons watch approximately 28 hours of television per week, while people in the United States spend approximately 9.6 hours per week in front of their sets. The Japanese, in turn, spend only 2 hours and 18 minutes a week watching television, listening to the radio, and reading magazines and newspapers combined (*Britannica World Data Annual*, 1991). Such demographic differences suggest that the business communicator may have to determine the best way, in a particular country, to reach people during their leisure time.

The most important difference across cultures regarding nonwork activities, however, is in the actual recreational institutions around which activities occur. For example, the degree of censorship or the type of TV programming in the United Kingdom, the United States, and Japan may have an even greater influence on behavior than the disparities in time spent watching the programs. The same point applies to all types of entertainment in the culture, including radio, theater, opera, popular magazines and papers.

Perhaps no institution has as powerful a role in solidifying a culture's values than its sports. Harry Edwards indicated the importance of athletics in symbolizing a culture's central values when he noted that

> sport . . . has primary functions in disseminating and reinforcing the values regulating behavior and goal attainment and determining acceptable solutions to problems in the secular sphere of life. . . . This channeling affects not only perspectives on sport, but . . . affects and aids in regulating perceptions of life in general. (1973, p. 90)

Leonard (1984) believes that the sports hero functions as a means to reinforce the social structure of a culture by acting out its values, norms, and expectations and, in doing so, creating social solidarity.

Several sociologists of sports have noted how a society's dominant sports change to reflect shifts in national attitude. According to Louis Zurcher and Arnold Meadow (1972), for instance, protests in Mexico against the violence and inhumane treatment of animals in the national sport — bullfighting — reflect a lessening of the importance ascribed to *machismo* and even of the importance assigned to authority in Mexican society as a whole. Similarly, Murray Ross (1977) has suggested that the shift of national sport in the United States from baseball to American football represents a move away from the pastoral ideal (baseball) to the glorification of heroism, combat, and use of technology (reflected in the armor used) of football.

For international business communicator, recreational institutions, like any other important aspect of a culture, provide clues to the dominant values of that culture as a whole.

ACCOMMODATING SOCIAL ORGANIZATION IN INTERNATIONAL BUSINESS COMMUNICATION

Social organization as a cultural factor affecting international business communication is relatively easy for foreigners to detect. Precisely because social organization tends to reflect external (that is, societal) influences on personal behavior, its manifestations are generally more uniform than many of the other variables we discuss in this book. Even those who consider themselves iconoclasts are likely to recognize and (to the degree that they rebel against accepted restraints) be influenced by the culture's ideals of social organization. This is largely because, within each culture, social organization follows a set of prescribed norms.

As is usually the case in international communication, business travelers and executives should continue to observe a culture's social organization while they conduct business in that country. Moreover, appropriate questions to staff members in the business section of one's embassy as well as to businesspeople living in or returned from the nation will provide useful information, particularly if the questions relate to the ten factors discussed in this chapter. Communicators do not, however, have to limit their preparation to interviews with those already in the country. In general, the principles of social organization are not learned passively or naturally by natives (as are, for example, language or views regarding the environment); rather, the ideals from which a culture's social organization is constructed are taught from one generation to the next. As a result, one of the best places for the international business communicator to seek out information on social organization is an unlikely source: material intended for children. Children's literature, television shows, and games are all rich sources of information about the values the members of a culture wish to impart to their children. On the most overt level, it is worthwhile to note what lessons these materials are intended to teach. In many cases, the lessons children are expected to learn from a fable or television show are summarized at the piece's conclusion. Moreover, because the material is intended for children, the lessons taught are often blatant.

To illustrate how cultural values are conveyed in children's tales, let us examine three variations on the theme of the lost child. A story of a little boy lost in the woods who finds his way home with the help of an assortment of grown-ups — the forest ranger, a police officer — teaches two primary lessons: to trust strangers and to trust those in authority. If in the same story, the little boy reaches home *unassisted* — by following the shadows cast by the sun and making a torch from a bundle of sticks to light his way at night — the lesson becomes the value of individualism and self-reliance. Finally, if the little boy simply stays put until his worried family, searching the forest, finds him and takes him back home, the moral concerns the value of kinship ties and the protective virtues of the family.

More subtle clues to the culture's social organization (especially in a heterogeneous culture) can be gathered from children's literature, television shows, and games by noting what elements of society are avoided or downplayed. Specific clues can be gleaned in the apparent class relations of the story characters; for example, one should note who plays the servant roles in the story and to what class does the protagonist belong. Similarly, you should note whether (and which) religion plays a role in material. Messages about religion can be overt — for instance, the children in the story attend a school taught by Catholic nuns, or subtle — for example, the story takes place at Christmas. Both these stories would reinforce Christianity as the norm around which society is organized.

You should also observe the importance of gender differences in children's literature. For example, the fact that the story described earlier featured a little boy rather than a little girl could be significant if, in that culture, most children's stories about self-reliance have boys as main characters while most stories about the protective virtues of the family focus on little girls. The distinction, if repeated often enough, would teach a lesson about gender roles. You can also assess the role of gender by observing the number of women or girls in the stories and the roles they play. Hofstede (1984, p. 199), for example, found a correlation between his masculinity index and a study, by Denmark and Waters (1977), of the number of times females were leading characters in the children's literature of five countries and the degree to which females were depicted in nontraditional roles. For example, Sweden frequently showed people of both genders in nontraditional roles (i.e., a boy as a baby-sitter) and was the only country Denmark and Waters surveyed in which there were more female leading characters than male; this finding corresponded with Hofstede's extreme *feminine* ranking of Sweden in his study.

You need not limit yourself to children's literature and television shows, although these might be the most accessible sources of instructive material for children. Watching people as they interact with their children in various public settings can also provide insights into the norms of a country's social organization.

The ideals of social organization, even when they vary from the practice, are still respected in most societies. Thus a South African businessman coming to the United States might, from his preparatory research, reach the conclusion that everyone he would meet there would adhere to the egalitarian principles embodied in that society's laws and institutions. He might be surprised to find that many U.S. businesspeople are prejudiced and even actively discriminate against minorities or women. If, however, the South African made a point of *not* discriminating or of praising the ideal of U.S. egalitarianism, he would likely be well received, even among those whose behavior was discriminatory.

Finally, because a culture's social organization results in part from the pressures exerted by that culture's ideals, business behavior may be influenced by those ideals likely to come under scrutiny even though the day-to-day practice may differ. For example, new-employee orientation manuals or speeches written for the CEO to deliver to the public may espouse principles that the company in reality does not practice as a matter of course. For business communication to be effective, certain issues of relatively minor importance to the company may have to be emphasized in order to conform to the pressures of society. Thus a company in a culture with an elitist educational system may feel the need to highlight those employees who are alumni of the culture's most prestigious universities, even though in practice it may not hire as many people from these schools as its public statements would indicate.

Businesspeople should remain aware of the way in which the values to which a culture adheres affect international communication. Social organization has an impact on all aspects of a culture. It is most likely to manifest itself in the workplace in the form of kinship and family structure, educational systems and ties, class systems and economic stratification, gender roles, the degree of individualism or collectivism people demonstrate, religion, attitudes toward occupational and recreational institutions, the nation's political and judicial system, and mobility. To the extent that international communicators stay abreast of these factors, their understanding of foreign cultures will be enhanced and the possibility that social organization will create a barrier to cross-cultural negotiations will be reduced.

Chapter
5

Issues of Contexting and Face-Saving in International Business Communication

CONTEXTING DEFINED

In the novels of Henry James, European characters run through lengthy internal monologues, filled with intense introspection and painstaking analysis of the simplest gestures and comments of others. Thus a Jamesian Briton or Frenchman will find significance in the passing of a teacup or the most casual inquiry into another's health. The reader must be attentive to the situation surrounding the conversation. Characters' emotions are often described in convoluted passages reflected in such constructions as "he thought that she thought that he thought that. . . ."

One source of tension in James's international novels is that few of his American characters share the penchant for analysis of inferred messages that his European characters engage in. The Americans seem surprised by the deeply refined sense of meaning the Europeans all seem to share. The Europeans, in turn, see the Americans as naive and easily victimized. James's Americans are constantly startled by turns of plot of which the European characters are already aware.

What James illustrated in his novels can be called *contexting*. We may define *contexting* as "the way in which one communicates and especially the circumstances surrounding that communication" (Borisoff and Victor, 1989, p. 140). Any communication relies on the context in which that communication takes place, as the British communication expert Ronald Wardhaugh has observed:

> If we were to attempt to say what any utterance in a conversation meant and, in doing so, ignored its context of use, we would be forced to conclude that its

meaning would be vague and ambiguous. It is just impossible to say what most utterances mean, or what their intent is, without having some knowledge of the situations in which they occur. That context includes not merely the linguistic one, that is, those utterance that precede and follow the utterance in question, but also the surrounding physical context, previous conversations between the participants, relevant aspects of their life histories, the general rules of behaviour the parties subscribe to, their assumptions about how the various bits and pieces of the world function, and so on. (1985, p. 101)

The greater the amount of knowledge and experience two communicators share, the less important it is for them to express directly what they wish to say or write. Conversely, the less these communicators share, the more necessary it is for them to convey their meaning through words and gestures — that is, the less they can assume to be understood. Indeed, as the German philosopher Jürgen Habermas argues, full comprehension in communication can take place only when both the message's receiver and sender are familiar with the context of the message:

In order to understand an utterance in the paradigm case of a speech act oriented to reaching understanding, the interpreter has to be familiar with the conditions of its validity; he has to know under what conditions the validity claim linked with it is acceptable, that is, would have to be acknowledged by a hearer. But where could the interpreter obtain this knowledge if not from the context of the observed communication or from comparable contexts? He can understand the meaning of communicative acts only because they are embedded in contexts of *actions* oriented to reaching understanding. (1984, p. 115)

Contexting is to a large extent culturally learned behavior. As the observations of Wardhaugh and Habermas indicate, members of the same culture need to be aware of a host of nuances; those nuances, however, are at least relatively familiar to the participants. Members of the same culture, therefore, select the interpretation of contexting cues in their communication from a limited menu of culturally determined acceptable behaviors.

As a result, members of the same culture (as compared to members of different cultures) rarely expend a great deal of conscious effort determining the appropriate level of contexting. For members of a particular culture, contexting comes as naturally as that nation's language. Indeed, language and contexting are closely linked, because people learn appropriate contexting behavior at the earliest stages of childhood language acquisition. Catherine Garvey, a child psychology professor specializing in language acquisition, has observed that people form their conception of speech as part of their understanding of dependent acts related to speech. This happens, she notes, because "as children are learning to talk, they are also learning the bases of social action and interaction" (1984, p. 8). In other words, children learn the contexting and language of their culture simultaneously.

As the contrast between James's Americans and Europeans reflects, however, the degree of contexting varies from culture to culture. Moreover, the degree of contexting itself reflects and affects attitudes toward another cross-cultural variable important to international business communication: face-saving, or the value attached to respect and status maintenance (discussed in more detail toward the end of this chapter).

HIGH AND LOW CONTEXTING

Contexting can be categorized as being either high or low. When individuals have considerable knowledge and experience in common, their communication is generally *highly contexted*. In the example above, the Europeans in James's novels communicate in a highly contexted manner. In highly contexted communication, what individuals choose *not* to put into words is essential to understanding the actual message intended.

In highly contexted interactions, the communicators commonly anticipate that what is not actually said is already understood. For example, a supplier and a purchasing agent who have conducted business for decades are likely to have developed a relationship of shared experiences and knowledge about each other. Differences in the purchasing agent's tone of voice, the pauses used, or even the choice of telephoning rather than writing a letter to request information would probably be recognized by the supplier as variations in the purchasing agent's normal communication style and work habits. The conclusions the supplier infers will affect their business dealings even if no verbal message is exchanged. Thus the supplier might detect a sense of urgency or displeasure even though the purchasing agent has not said anything to indicate annoyance. If the supplier modifies his or her own communication to respond to the agent's unspoken message, the supplier is acting in a high context manner.

When negotiators rely relatively little on shared knowledge and experience, their communication is called *low context*. Hints based on inferred messages between low context communicators are less apparent than between high context communicators. As a result, more information must be explicitly stated in low context exchanges than in high context ones. Emphasis is placed on verbal self-disclosure. For example, if the supplier and purchasing agent did *not* know each other well, the unspoken messages would not be obvious. To express displeasure, the purchasing agent would actually have to state his or her irritation before the supplier could be aware of it.

To the extent that members of low context cultures rely on verbal self-disclosure to communicate their primary message, they can be seen as *direct*; to the degree that members of high context cultures rely on means other than verbal self-disclosure to communicate their message, they can be seen as *indirect*. Moreover, in low context cultures, directness is often considered a virtue and indirect communication a waste of time or a strain on the receiver's patience. Most introductory business communication textbooks used in the United States, for example, stress the benefit of the so-called *direct plan* message, in which the content of a message is delivered early on.

By contrast, in high context cultures, directness is often considered rude and offensive, while indirect communication is recognized as a means to smooth over interpersonal differences and (as we will discuss later in this chapter) as a means to keep from losing face in conflict situations. Awareness of the two types can be crucial:

> Cultures differ in the extent to which people are direct or indirect, how requests are made, and more importantly, how requests are denied or refused. For instance, Philippine social interaction is based on what Peace Corps volunteers came to call "SIR," or "smooth interpersonal relationships." Yet Americans assigned to the Philippines were initially told to be perfectly frank in their dealings with the locals, which turned out to be a devastating piece of advice; the directness of the Americans was regarded as tactless and brutal, and totally contrary to the principles of SIR as practised in the Philippines (Furnham and Bochner, 1986, p. 205).

In this example, the directness characteristic of the low context U.S. culture of the Peace Corps volunteers was in direct contrast to the high context culture of the Filipinos with whom they interacted.

Edward Hall and Contexting

Edward T. Hall is the researcher who first coined the term *contexting* in the meaning indicated here. He has written several seminal works on contexting, particularly in cross-cultural situations (1959, 1966, 1976, 1983). In these works, Hall explains contexting in terms of the amount of information transmitted and the amount of information stored or assumed. He has diagrammed the relationship of information, context, and meaning in a pair of interlocking triangles. In the context triangle (see Figure 5.1), Hall indicates the amount of shared or stored information as a continuum ranging from little to a considerable amount. Low context communication is indicated at the bottom of the triangle. Since little information is stored, communicators must explicitly express their message—usually in words—and provide the information needed for full understanding. In high context communication, at the top of the triangle, a great deal of stored information is shared among communicators. Accordingly, much of a

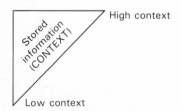

Figure 5.1 Edward Hall's context triangle

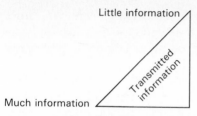

Figure 5.2 Edward Hall's transmitted information triangle

communicator's message is conveyed implicitly, and the unspoken or unwritten information may contain the essence of the message.

The second of Hall's triangles illustrates transmitted information (see Figure 5.2). This diagram shows a continuum of actual information explicitly sent in any communication. The top of the triangle represents little transmitted information; it reflects high context communication, in which the message relies largely on what is already understood. The bottom of the triangle suggests the low context communicator's reliance on transmitting much information explicitly.

Hall then combines the stored information triangle and the transmitted information triangle to form a communicated meaning square (see Figure 5.3).

Hall explains the significance of the newly created figure: "Combine the two [triangles] and it can be seen, as context is lost, information must be added if meaning is to remain constant. The complete relationship can be expressed in a single diagram; there can be no meaning without both information and context" (1983, p. 61).

Corporate Culture and Domestic Contexting Differences

The level of contexting depends on the degree of experience and information the communicators share. Absence of shared experience need not involve international cultural differences; subcultural groups (for instance, corporate cultures) may create contexting differences within a larger national culture. In our earlier example of the purchasing agent and the supplier, the degree of contexting did not depend on cultural vari-

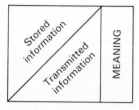

Figure 5.3 Communicated meaning square

ables but on shared knowledge and experience between communicators in the *same* culture. To the extent that people within society form subcultural units, creating in-groups and out-groups, variations in contexting within a culture can be marked.

Indeed, one difficulty in traditional approaches to many cultures' domestic business pedagogy is their common disregard for contextual issues in determining communication principles. Priscilla Rogers, in her study of U.S. dealer contact reports, suggests that forces of context result in "the disparity between company directives for report writing and actual management practice" (1988, p. 23). Thus, even in wholly domestic situations, the corporate culture provides a context, which acts as a bank of stored information for members of the corporation. It imposes on its members, in turn, a communication style that is likely to vary from that practiced in the national culture.

General business communication precepts, however, are subject only to what is considered good style in an abstract situation; they are constricted only by the national culture and the limitations of that nation's language. The rules of good business communication learned in the absence of a context (i.e., what is acceptable in a specific corporate setting) are thus only partially relevant in an actual (rather than hypothetical) business situation. As Brown and Herndl have observed, such contextless instruction "fights the culture — and always loses" (1986, p. 24). Shifts in contexting occur in domestic cross-cultural situations as a result of differences from one corporate culture to another and from one subgroup to another.

Contexting and International Cultural Differences

The most dramatic disparities in contexting are to be found between national cultures, far exceeding most variations among corporate cultures or other national subgroups.

The diversity in extent of contexting across cultures occurs for two reasons. First, members of a culture share an understanding of language, environment, technology, social organization, and the other variables discussed in this book. Their shared experiences allow for more highly contexted communication. Second, cultures vary in the level of contexting their members exhibit when they communicate with one another. It is this point to which Edward Hall returns again and again throughout his works. Hall notes that some cultures depend more heavily than others on inferences, or context, to convey their messages.

Thus an entire nation can be considered high context if it relies more on how a message is expressed than on what is actually said. Conversely, other cultures may be thought of as low context, because they emphasize the words used to communicate rather than the meanings inferred from the situation surrounding the communication. Indeed, the world, according to Hall, can be rank-ordered according to high and low context cultures:

> It appears that all cultures arrange their members and relationships along the context scale, and one of the great communication strategies, whether addressing a single person or an entire group, is to ascertain the correct level of contexting of one's communication. (1983, p. 61)

The German researchers Martin Rosch and Kay Segler combined Hall's communicated meaning square (described on p. 141) with the relative rank-ordering of context among major cultures (1987, p. 60). A modified version of Rosch and Segler's figure appears in Figure 5.4.

In Figure 5.4, those cultures with the lowest level of contexting appear at the bottom left. The German-speaking Swiss represent the culture with the lowest ranked contexting. Moving diagonally up the figure, Rosch and Segler place cultures with successively higher contexting in a continuum along the diagonal edge where the transmitted and stored information triangles meet. Thus, North American culture is generally more highly contexted than German-speaking Swiss culture. North American culture, which is relatively far down on the scale, is lower contexted than Italian culture, which, in turn, is lower contexted than Latin American cultures, and so on, with the Japanese representing the most highly contexted culture.

The differences in contexting are extremely important to international business communication. Assessing the degree of contexting in one culture allows the international business communicator to devise a strategy of either directness (relying on explicit information—low context) or nuance (relying on implied or understood information—high context).

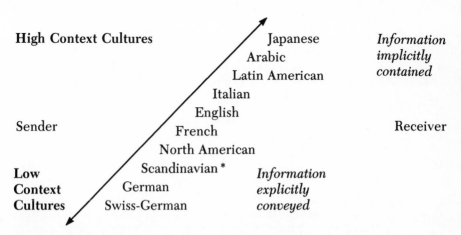

Figure 5.4 Context ranking of cultures. Based on Rosch and Segler (1987, p. 60). *Scandinavian category excludes Finland (Tirkkonen-Condit, 1987).

Stella Ting-Toomey summarizes the significance of this difference: "In the HCC [high context culture] system what is not said is sometimes more important than what is said. In contrast, in the LCC [low context culture] system words represent truth and power"(1985, p. 77).

It is, however, imprudent to stereotype members of any culture as automatically high or low context. The rank-ordering to which Hall, Rosch and Segler, and Ting-Toomey, among others, refer must be viewed as a rough guideline rather than absolute categories. Individuals within a society are likely to be higher or lower contexted than others within their culture (as our supplier and purchasing agent example earlier in the chapter illustrates). Hall himself warns that cultures in the midrange of contexting in particular may engage in a combination of high and low context communication. He notes, as an example, that

> French culture is a mixture, a melange, of high- and low-context institutions and situations. It is not always possible for the foreigner to predict in what proportions they will be found or in what order they occur. (1976, p. 109)

CONTEXTING DIFFERENCES IN CROSS-CULTURAL BUSINESS SITUATIONS

Differences in contexting across cultures lead to variations in actual behavior. These variations can result in differences in five main areas:

1. emphasis on personal relationships
2. belief in explicit communication, the law, and contracts
3. reliance on verbal communication
4. uncertainty avoidance variations
5. face-saving

Each of these areas will be discussed in the sections that follow.

Contexting and Cultural Differences in Personal Relationships

High context cultures in general place greater emphasis on the development of close interpersonal relationships than do low context cultures. Members of high context cultures depend on extensive amounts of stored or understood information to communicate their messages. The amount of information two strangers share remains an unknown to both parties. As a result, it is more important to members of a high context culture to establish a strong personal relationship with a stranger with whom they must communicate than it is to members of a low context culture. Only by getting to know the stranger can members of a high context culture determine the amount of information they share. In a low context culture, strangers would not need a context, or a bank of information understood by both parties. Since the low context culture relies on transmitted messages rather than on stored or understood information, any needed information could be explicitly provided.

John Paul Fieg, in his comparison of U.S. and Thai patterns of behavior, offers an illuminating contrast in the value placed on personal relationships in low and high context cultures. Although Fieg does not label the two nations as such, U.S. culture is classically low context; Thai culture, classically high context. Fieg notes that Thais look somewhat askance at U.S. business communication: "From the Thai perspective, Americans' preoccupation with persuasive speech, supporting facts, and quick arrival at the main issue causes them to overlook intangible, covert factors . . . such as human relationships, customs and timing" (1980, p. 74). For the Thais, the U.S. emphasis on specific evidence may allow for a quick arrival at the ostensible issue but may not provide the necessary trust to evaluate the meaning of any communication. Instead, the Thais consider it important to assess factors that are understood in the context of interactions:

> Of primary importance is the establishment of a good personal relationship based on trust and understanding. Rather than getting right down to business, the two parties will often have drinks or lunch together, search out their common interests, and perhaps meet later to share a favorite pastime. As the social relationship develops, business will be blended in; and eventually the specific point being negotiated, say the price of goods, will be resolved. (Fieg, 1980, p. 74)

Nor is the establishment of personal relationships as a prerequisite for successful business communication limited to Thailand. Similar attitudes are held in most high context cultures. Korea is a highly contexted culture that stresses the role of personal relationships:

> In Korea, as in many other Asian countries, business is a personal affair. The product, the profit, and everything else takes a backseat to personal relations. If you do not or cannot establish good personal relations with a large network of people, it is either difficult or impossible to do business in Korea. (DeMente, 1988, p. 20)

Similarly, in the highly contexted Arabic cultures, "Arabs mistrust people who do not appear to be sincere or who fail to demonstrate an interest in them personally" (Nydell, 1987, p. 61). As Gavin Kennedy indicates, this need in most Arabic cultures to show sincerity and demonstrate a personal interest (i.e., the construction of a foundation for high context communication) takes significantly more time than the direct, communication style of such cultures as the United States. Kennedy describes, for a U.S. audience, tactics for negotiating with Arabs:

> They do not like rushing into business subjects as soon as they meet you. It is bad manners to do so, and they will expect you to talk with them about social and other matters for some time — perhaps fifteen minutes or more on most occasions, though sometimes for several hours or, on special occasions, through several meetings. (1985, p. 100)

The way in which communication is used in high context cultures to establish a needed personal relationship has been described as a series of loops, in contrast to the image of a straight line that represents the explicit-information style of low context cultures:

> When Americans talk, they take the most direct route, one step at a time in a straight line to the finish. Not so the Arabs. They talk about other things before business. Then after they have talked about business for a while, they will loop off to talk about more social things, and eventually loop back to the business at hand. They will continue in this manner forever, and if forced by an impatient American to stay on what the American insists is the subject at hand, will become very frustrated. [George] Renwick says forcing our linear thinking on Arabs only "cuts off their loops," causing resentment and ultimately loss of productivity. (Copeland and Griggs, 1985, p. 103).

Because high context cultures tend to approach business communication in a more leisurely and indirect manner than their low context counterparts, the former emphasize broad objectives while the latter focus on specific details. Robert March, writing about the negotiating behavior of the high context Japanese, observes that "the Japanese are not accustomed to negotiating a contract or relationship in an item-by-item way. Usually, they seek a broad agreement first" (1988, p. 86). Similarly a Thai businessperson "begins negotiation not with a highly specific strategy but instead with a broad general objective" (Fieg, 1980, p. 74). The reason behind this in high context cultures is that, as Margaret Nydell writes regarding Arabs, "They evaluate the source of a statement or proposal as much as its content" (1987, p. 61).

The emphasis on personal relationships allows for certain strengths, such as flexibility to meet changing situations. It also contains certain weaknesses: in some cases deals may be concluded based on trust and personal ties rather than on ability to fulfill a commitment. While this happens rarely, such a situation led to one of the largest investment debacles of the late twentieth century. Kuwait was, in the early 1980s, the financial center of the Persian Gulf region. However, the Arabic culture's high context predilection for personal ties is not necessarily suited, without safeguards, to financial negotiation. Kuwaiti stock market traders' trust that investors were good for their commitments led to an overextension of credit that had disastrous consequences. John Train describes the situation:

> Well-established traders' postdated checks were accepted almost like cash. Legally, the payee could present a postdated check at any time, not only on the date written. But this was never done. It would have violated the old Kuwaiti tradition of trust, which also made it unthinkable that payment might not be made at all. A family simply had to make good on its commitments. There had, in fact, never been a bankruptcy. So when some stocks on the Souk al-Manakh began to jump 10 percent or 20 percent or even 50 percent a month, speculators rushed in to buy with postdated checks drawn on funds they did not have. They knew they could sell the shares to raise the cash when the checks came due. (1985, p. 18)

The result was a Kuwaiti market in postdated checks, leading to a boom; at its peak (in early 1981) some stocks advanced more than 100 percent a month. When in late August 1982, one holder of a postdated check presented it for payment before the date on the check, he showed a terrible breach of trust that ran counter to Kuwaiti culture. He also burst the investment bubble, since it was impossible to cash the check. The results were dramatic and rapid: "The balloon exploded. In no time hundreds of speculators were in default. Collapse followed. Gulf Medical, for example, plunged about 98 percent to a sixth of a dinar" (Train, 1985, pp. 20–21).

The behavior of high context cultures is often baffling to those in low context cultures. Yet serious misunderstandings are likely to arise even among cultures in which the degree of contexting is less extreme. This is because, while a type of behavior may occur in two cultures, it may have different meanings in those two societies. For example, as Raymonde Carroll (1988) has noted, the simple act of requesting information, which on the surface French and U.S. communicators do in the same manner, carries "profoundly different expectations" (p. 122):

> When I ask for information, I (an American) want to obtain as many particulars as possible, which I will combine to my liking, whereas I (a French person) prefer to express my wishes and let others provide me the information which will allow me to satisfy them. It now becomes clear that in the first case what I need most is correct information, whereas in the second what I need most is someone to count on. (1988, p. 122)

In other words, when the more highly contexted French ask for information, they are, "in a sense, delegating power" (Carroll, 1988, p. 116) in a way that their more low contexted U.S. counterparts are not. The French are thus more reluctant to ask for information of just anyone but tend to regard the act of requesting information as a means to build trust, friendship, or other bonds. Rather than ask a stranger in the street for directions (as someone from the United States would do), a French person will seek out a friend or go to an authority figure (a police officer in whom he or she has trust). Similarly, "a French person, as opposed to an American, is often reluctant to read the instructions . . . [but] prefers to ask someone close to him or her 'how it works'" (Carroll, 1988, p. 116). People in the United States, on the other hand, often first seek help only when they are unable to figure out accompanying instructions on their own. In short, the French person in seeking information is interested in establishing a personal relationship, whereas the U.S. questioner wants only to obtain information.

This contrast at first seems superficial but may actually lead to misunderstanding. In the United States, an inquiry can easily receive a response of "I don't know"; in France, such a response is generally unacceptable, since a personal relationship is at stake in the response:

> On asking for information from someone, I [as a French person] enter into a system of exchange of which we, the person I ask and myself, implicitly

[through context] know the rules. In asking my question, I make a choice, and, if only for a brief moment, the person I select becomes the chosen one, a special person. One could even say that I am honoring a person by asking this person for information, since I do not place my trust in just anyone. In asking for information, I affirm the existence of a relationship. In exchange, the person interrogated will do "everything possible" to answer, that is, to be deserving of my trust. Sometimes, my question may reverberate through a whole series of persons: if X, whom I have just asked for information, does not know the answer, X will not just tell me "I don't know" but, more often, "I don't know, but wait, I'll ask Y who must know." Y will ask Z, and so on; I may regret having asked the question, but I must keep still and await the answer, even if it ends up taking too much time. (Carroll, 1988, p. 117)

Explicit Communication, the Law, and Contracts

"A verbal contract isn't worth the paper it's written on," Sam Goldwyn, the Hollywood movie mogul and founder of Metro Goldwyn Mayer, supposedly said. Humor aside, Goldwyn's statement exemplifies the high emphasis placed on the written word in the United States and other low context cultures. In particular, low context cultures place great faith in explicit communication such as legal codes and contracts (see Table 5.1).

The emphasis on the written word results in a reliance on and respect for the law, the formal codification of a society's behavior. The law, in low context cultures, is rigidly adhered to and, significantly, provides a societal context independent of the context of a given interaction. The status of the law (which may be any set of rules, whether governmental regulations or official corporate policies) directly contrasts with the belief, in high context cultures, that individual interpretation of personal relations — the context of each person's interactions with others — is the primary governance of interpersonal behavior. In other words, in low context cultures the law governs people's interactions.

In low context cultures formal rules and laws are much more respected than in high context societies. The governance of behavior

Table 5.1 EXTREME HIGH AND LOW CONTEXT VARIATION REGARDING EXPLICIT COMMUNICATION

	High context	Low context
Emphasis on written word	Weak	Strong
Adherrence to law	Flexible	Rigid
Governance of interpersonal behavior	Governed by individual interpretation	Governed by external rules and regulations
Agreements based on personal promises	Binding	Not binding
Agreements based on written word (contracts)	Not binding	Binding

through abstract concepts is often confusing to those from high context cultures. For example, a visitor to the United States from Turkey, a relatively high context culture, was perplexed at the extent to which the law governs U.S. behavior: "Once . . . in a rural area in the middle of nowhere, we saw an American come to a stop sign. Though he could see in both directions for miles and no traffic was coming, he stopped!" (Kohls, 1981, p. 8). In Turkey, the law is able to bend to context. The Turk in the same situation would not have stopped because there was no need to do so. It is not that people disregard the law in Turkey, but that the context of the situation would override the law. The law is understood to govern behavior only in the context of its appropriate application. In low context (Turkey) and other cultures by contrast, the context is irrelevant; individuals must adhere to the law regardless of the specific situations. The law in low context cultures, as Edward Hall notes, "is so designed as to operate apart from the rest of life" (1976, p. 107).

The legal system in the United States provides a clear example of the low context emphasis on rules and regulations regardless of specific situations. In U.S. courts, contexting testimony (most notably hearsay evidence) is strictly inadmissible; only established facts are allowable. Answers to questions in court are frequently limited to "yes" or "no" responses; the context in which the information is set is essentially irrelevant to the fact itself. As Hall suggests, such practices "reveal the U.S. courts as the epitome of low-context systems. Those who are interested or well versed in the deeper significance of comparative law and who have a knack for recognizing patterns can get a feeling for other low-context systems by studying how the American legal system actually works" (1976, p. 107).

Contexting information *is*, to some extent, admissible in high context legal systems. For example, Italy and France both allow, in their civil law proceedings, two forms of nonevidentiary support: the decisory oath and the supplemental oath. In the decisory oath

> a party being unable to prove a disputed fact (let us call it fact X) in any other way, may "defer an oath" to his opponent, provided the truth concerning fact X can be assumed to be within the latter's personal knowledge. This is done by asking the opponent to affirm, under oath, the proposition that X is untrue. . . . If the party to whom the oath has been deferred, refuses or fails to take the oath at the time and place thus fixed, the truth of fact X is deemed conclusively established. If, on the other hand, he duly takes the oath, this is treated as conclusive proof of the untruth of fact X. (Schlesinger, 1970, p. 311)

In the supplemental oath, the court itself may intervene to provide greater contexting of a situation if insufficient evidence is available to prove a matter. The supplemental oath, unlike the decisory oath,

> is not "deferred" by a party, but authorized by the court on its own motion. The court can do this when there is some evidence tending to prove fact Y,

but the evidence is not quite sufficient. In such a case the court may permit the party asserting Y to affirm his assertion by a supplemental oath. (Schlesinger, 1970, p. 312)

In low context cultures, in general, the law (and the abstract principles it represents) govern daily life. As in the case of the U.S. driver stopped at the red light with no traffic for miles, members of low context cultures tend to follow regulations regardless of their relevance in the context of an applied situation. This is not the case in most high context cultures, where the law stands quite apart from what might be called an understanding of what is proper. Thus, Americans may have difficulty accepting or even understanding the so-called gentleman's agreement so common in relatively high context Britain. The tendency among lower context nations is to distrust the informal agreement, because the social forces of contexting are less binding than the authority inherent in written agreements or formal contracts.

The low context emphasis on the written word, particularly in the form of negotiated contracts, presents a major stumbling block in international business communication. Members of low context cultures in general believe that the written word is binding; members of high context cultures, by contrast, are more likely to believe that personal relationships are binding. A contract negotiated between a high and a low context party is likely to be viewed differently by the two parties.

To the low context party, the written word is binding, regardless of whether the two drafting parties remain the same or not. Thus *who* carries out the terms of the contract is irrelevant as long as the terms of the contract are followed. If the low context negotiator is, for instance, transferred to another division, this would in no way affect the legitimacy of the written agreement. His or her replacement would fulfill the contract terms, since personal relationships and identities are immaterial under the agreement. In contrast, to the high context party, the contract is a sign of good faith between the two individuals who drafted it; the relationship between the negotiators — not the contract itself — is what matters. The contract is a symbol of the bond between its drafters. As a result, the contract itself is less binding than the personal relationship of the negotiators.

Boye DeMente illustrates the difference with which cultures approach written agreements when he contrasts U.S. and Korean views toward contracts:

> Generally speaking, Koreans sign contracts with foreign businessmen to get the relationship started officially. Thereafter everything is subject to change and negotiation. Koreans do not regard the provisions of contracts as written in stone or as the fundamental basis of a business relationship. They regard the personal relationship and the desire for mutual benefits as the foundation of any business arrangement. A contract is essentially nothing more than a symbol of this relationship. (1988, p. 71)

DeMente elaborates:

> Being personal agreements rather than immutable laws, the terms of a partic-
> ular contract go out the door when the signers or the managers of a contract
> change. From this point, any contract is subject to the interpretations and
> expectations of the new managers, who devise a new set of unwritten terms to
> govern the relationship with the second party—and often implement these
> changes without informing the other side.
>
> This is a vital difference in the concept of a contract that the foreign
> businessman must understand. The essence is that when a Korean executive
> signs a contract with a foreign company, he is not necessarily obligating his
> own corporation to uphold the provisions of that contract. The corporation
> may not accept the obligation if it has any reason not to do so. It may be
> regarded as a personal matter between the managers who negotiated and
> signed the contract and the foreign party. (1988, p. 71)

Such differences in views arguably exist between any high and low context culture.

As noted already, the law, in high context nations, can bend according
to individual circumstances. In such cultures, the laws largely exist along-
side means for circumventing them when necessary. Informal social notions of what is considered proper are more influential than written regulations. Virtually no low context culture, for example, has a parallel to the
Japanese concept of *gyoseishido*, which roughly translated means "administrative guidance." It is through *gyoseishido* that the Japanese government ministries and central banks influence daily business interactions. A
government agency or a bank at the center of an important *keiretsu*
(trading alignment of companies) can intervene in a conflict between
companies to harmonize interests; they do so through *gyoseishido* in the
form of social pressure. No law is enforced or order given directly; rather,
the parties are brought into line through contexting, or informal under-
standings. As Steven Schloßstein observes, while such administrative
guidance

> may not have the *force* of law, it has the *effect* of law. It refers to the
> discretionary authority the Japanese bureaucracy has in administering legisla-
> tion, which is always created purposefully broad. This consists of suggestions,
> hints, threats, directives, and innuendoes that influence action in the desired
> direction. (1984, p. 214).

In this way *gyoseishido* acts as a connector of the official, legal guidelines
and the unofficial, unwritten guidelines of the culture's social order
(which often far surpasses the legal restraints). *Gyoseishido* is contexting
at its extreme: a highly individualized and flexible constraining force
acting "through an informal process of voluntary cooperation rather than
the time-consuming processes needed for legislation and prosecution of
offenders" (Lansing and Wechselblatt, 1983, p. 659).

In cultures in the middle level of contexting—neither particularly high nor particularly low—the conflict between informal and formal forces can be mixed. France is perhaps the best example. The French value the law and carefully codify behavior and, at the same time, provide informal means for getting around the law. John Ardagh, writing from a more highly contexted British viewpoint, has observed of the French that "their lives are spent devising ingenious rules and then finding equally cunning ways of evading them. Thus they are able to cut corners and circumvent some of the bureaucratic [restraints]. . . . That is, everyone, including officials, accepts that red tape can be tacitly ignored from time to time" (1987, p. 621).

High context cultures are not without formal regulations and law, but the law represents less of an absolute truth—at least in the codification of truths that the law represents—than in low context cultures. In a high context nation, truth is likely to be divided into what we might term a *public* truth and *real* truth. It is what the Japanese called *honne* (often translated as "essence" or "substance") and *tatemae*, or "form." This same distinction results in a greater concern in high context cultures for face-saving (maintaining outward appearances, or *tatemae*) than in low context cultures, in which form usually is substance and no distinction between *tatemae* and *honne* is outwardly recognized. While we discuss this dichotomy in the perception of truth in detail when we discuss face-saving later in this chapter, it is sufficient to observe here that an absolute notion of truth is less likely to exist in a high context culture than in a low context culture. In high context cultures, the truth is arguably circumstantial.

The Reliance on Verbal Communication

High and low context cultures often differ significantly in the degree to which they rely on verbal self-disclosure. Most high context cultures depend, as we have discussed, on a variety of factors—besides simply the words used—to decode the message they receive (see Table 5.2).

The way in which something is said, the past relationship between communicators, and the situation surrounding a communication exchange convey information in a high context culture that is either downplayed or ignored in a low context culture. Because, in low context cultures, verbal communication represents the primary means of communication, such cultures rely heavily on verbal communication. By contrast, high context cultures—where verbal communication is only one of many means of communication—do not depend in particular on verbal communication (a notable exception existing for most Arabic-speaking societies).

Differences in the stress placed on verbal communication are less noticeable in large groups, where individuals can remain relatively silent while others carry the brunt of the conversation. In business, however, most communication takes place in a small group or one-on-one setting: as a result, cross-cultural differences in the reliance on verbal communication is noticeable.

Table 5.2   VARIATION IN THE RELIANCE ON VERBAL COMMUNICATION BETWEEN
EXTREME HIGH AND LOW CONTEXT CULTURES

	High context	Low context
Reliance on words to communicate	Low	High
Reliance on nonverbal communication	High	Low
View of silence	Respected; communicative	Anxiety-producing; noncommunicative
Attention to detail	Low	High
Attention to intention	High	Low
Communication approach	Indirect; inferential	Direct; explicit
Literalness	Low literalness; interpretive	High literalness; noninterpretive

In low context cultures, people often dread silence. Because they feel uneasy when they have to interpret communication that does not rely on words, such individuals frequently speak simply to break the silence. In most high context cultures, on the other hand, people who are quick to jump into conversation for its own sake are considered weak and may be viewed with suspicion or even confusion.

One of the most highly contexted cultures is that of the Western Apache of the United States. A business communication exchange described by K. H. Basso in a study of the use of silence among Western Apaches exemplifies the avoidance of verbal self-disclosure in high context cultures. Basso describes the following incident (as it was related to him), in which two strangers find themselves part of a four-person round-up crew:

> One time, I was with A, B and X down at Gleason Flat working cattle. That man X was from East Fork (a community nearly forty miles from Cibecue) where B's wife was from. But he didn't know A, never knew him before, I guess. First day, I worked with X. At night, when we camped, we talked with B, but X and A didn't say anything to each other. Same way, second day. Same way, third. Then, at night on fourth day, we were sitting by the fire. Still, X and A didn't talk. Then A said: "Well, I know there is a stranger to me here, but I've been watching him and I know he is alright [sic]." After that, X and A talked a lot. . . . Those two men didn't know each other, so they took it easy at first (1972, p. 72).

A four-day silence in the face of uninterrupted living and working together represents an extreme example. Yet the reason for the men's hesitancy to speak is similar to that in other high context cultures. For the Western Apaches, Basso notes, strangers who "are quick to launch into conversation are frequently eyed with undisguised suspicion" (1972, p. 72), and "their willingness to violate convention is attributed to some urgent need which is likely to result in requests for money, labor or transportation" (p. 73).

The controlled use of silence is by no means limited to the Western Apaches of the United States. Active listening and communication by means other than words is a hallmark of several high context societies. Finland, for example, has been described as "a communication-reticent culture, in which silence is valued or at least tolerated to a greater extent than, say, English-speaking cultures" (Tirkkonen-Condit, 1988, p. 2). Similarly, it has been noted that "Africans also complain that Americans talk too much, especially in public places" (Copeland and Griggs, 1985, p. 103).

Perhaps the most notable use of communication through controlled silence in business and society takes place in Japan. "Speech, to many Japanese," according to Dean Barnlund, "is not a highly regarded form of communication. Words are often discounted or viewed with suspicion. Talk is disparaged" (1975, p. 89). "In Japan," Diana Rowland writes,

> silence is a virtue. It is during silent "meaningful intervals" that the famous belly language of Japan, the sensing of another's thoughts and feelings, goes on. Many Japanese proverbs proclaim the virtues of silence, a common one being, "Those who know do not speak—those who speak do not know." (1985, pp. 51–52)

In Japanese extraverbal communication is called *haragei*, which literally translates as "belly art." Both terms of the translation are instructive.

First, the Japanese conceive of *hara*, the "belly," as the center of one's being, like the English use of the word *heart*—that is, the seat of one's courage, caring, and higher feelings, but with the addition of intuitive understanding and tolerance acquired through experience. Thus when the Japanese speak of a person who has big *hara*, they do not mean an individual with a pot belly but a person with great intuitive knowledge, experience, and feeling.

The second part of the term *haragei* indicates that to be of big *hara* is an acquired "art." The Japanese, therefore, consider the mastery of *haragei*, or communication through intuition apart from words, to be an art. This is distinct from the attainment of logical knowledge. A common Japanese saying among experienced businesspeople reflects this distinction: "In your twenties, you must improve your mind, but in your thirties you must develop your *hara*." As Michihiro Matsumoto observes, "No remark, thus, is more insulting than: 'He has *atama* (head) but not *hara*,' because anyone who lacks *hara* is not in full control of himself" (1988, p. 37).

In Japanese business communication, *haragei* is used to resolve active conflict and prevent potential conflict. A form of silence and intuitive exchange, it takes the place that verbal communication holds in low context cultures:

> What argument is to Westerners, *haragei* is to Japanese. The former is verbal boxing, wherein strategy is what counts. Argument attempts to reach the

truth through conflict of opinions. The *haragei* way "stomachs" differences and avoids conflict. In contrast to logical argumentation, *haragei* may be termed extra-logical. *Haragei* can be an effective means of creating a favorable climate for reaching an agreement in principle, submerging differences, whereas debate can be an efficient means of crystallizing the differences before solving any problem. (Matsumoto, 1988, p. 43)

Haragei, however, is commonly misunderstood by business communicators of low context cultures. As we noted already, long silences usually make members of low context cultures uncomfortable. When the two attitudes toward silence meet in the workplace, unintentional and often disastrous messages may be communicated. For instance, a needless turn of direction occurred in the negotiations between a U.S. company and a Japanese corporation:

> At the point where the U.S. contingent laid out a series of proposed prices for the goods in question, the Japanese, as is culturally appropriate, were silent for some time. The Americans, uncomfortable with silence, interpreted this to mean the Japanese were unhappy with the prices quoted and immediately made a number of pricing concessions. The Japanese negotiators were both surprised and amused, since they really had no problem with the original prices (McCaffrey and Hafner, 1985, p. 29).

Most high context cultures withhold information in business communication to a greater degree than do low context cultures. It is possible to withhold information, however, and still use means to communicate other than silence. In France and Italy, for example, people slowly collect information as they think through ideas or proposals and construct personal relationships. But extraverbal communication does not supersede verbal communication. Although relatively little business information is likely to be exchanged in initial meetings in France and Italy, a mix of business and background — the contexting necessary to conduct business communication — is exchanged.

Thus Italian executives are less likely to discuss business over a meal than are their German or U.S. counterparts. Instead, they want to enjoy the food, share in social conversation, and — here and there — touch on a business topic or two.

Like the Italians, French businesspeople are often dismayed by what seems to be the extreme precision demanded by businesspeople from lower contexted cultures. This is borne out in the experiences of James McCaffrey (vice president of the U.S.-based Training Resources Group) and Craig Hafner (senior project officer with the U.S.-based corporation Camp, Dresser and McKee): "The French objected to what they perceived as the U.S. manager's obsession with detail and mundane practicalities at the expense of allowing a full exploration of the larger issues. The French tend to favor more rhetorical beginnings to meetings, more general talk and more room for disagreement" (1985, p. 27). Likewise, the Italian (Eiler and Victor, 1988) and French (Varner, 1988) business letters tend to reflect a higher degree of contexting than letters from such low context cultures as the United States. Both the French and Italian business writer is much more likely to pay attention to subtle messages embedded in a host of possible salutations, closings and sign-offs than are business-letter writers from low context cultures such as the United States. Italian business letters tend to provide pertinent information cumulatively, hinting at the central issues over a series of letters in which the subtleties are, in time, made clear. Similarly, with the exception of collection letters and negative messages, French business correspondence generally emphasizes formality and polite phrasing, with information provided in a "less action oriented format" (Varner, 1988, p. 64).

A third high context approach to verbal communication is that practiced in the Arab world. Contrasting U.S. and Arab styles, Copeland and Griggs have noted:

> With the Arabs, however, we struggle not with lack of information but with overexpression. Arabic is a poetic language conducive to exaggeration, fantastic metaphors, strings of adjectives, and repetitions which enhance the significance of what is said. In the Middle East, what one has to say is often outweighed by how one says it. Arab rhetoric makes it hard to interpret what is going on in the Middle East, not only for us but for other Arabs as well. The language allows for people to say things they don't mean, often with terrible results when what they say is taken seriously. During the Arab-Israeli skirmishes just before the Six-Day War, the Arab media threatened Israel with "We are going to burn your homes, rape your women and drive you into the sea." The Arabs were astonished when Israel took this literally as a declaration of war and retaliated accordingly (1985, p. 107).

In the Arabic form of high context communication, the task of message receivers differs from that of their counterparts in Japan. In the latter form, the receiver must interpret messages amid silence or when little verbal encoding takes place. Matsumoto says that low context "conversationalists listen to the words between pauses, whereas Japanese *haragei* practitioners listen more attentively to the pauses between the words and gestures" (1988, p. 51). Message receivers interacting within the Arabic form of high context communication face a different task. They must separate the central information from the peripheral—while keeping in mind that, as background for context, all peripheral information can, in time, come to the fore as central information.

In low context cultures, messages are communicated in a much more directly verbal way. Words are allowed to vary little in their meaning, regardless of the context in which they are written or spoken. This may make low context cultures seem rude in the eyes of higher context cultures.

For example, a sign observed by the author in the German-speaking portion of Switzerland was posted in three languages: German, English, and French. In German, the sign read *Walking on the grass is forbidden.* The directness of the phrasing reflected the extreme low context of German-speaking Switzerland. The English warning read: *Please do not walk on the grass.* The English version conveyed the same message, but the added nicety of "please" indicated the increased importance of politeness among the more highly contexted English speakers. More significantly, the shift to an individual decision ("do not walk") from the German version's external force ("is forbidden") seems to imply that a choice is possible, although the context of the sign precludes that as a real possibility. The English reader is as "forbidden" from walking as the German speaker; the message is simply less direct. The final message on the sign was in French. It read: *Those who respect their environment will avoid walking on the grass*. This message is even more highly contexted than the English version. It appears even more likely than in the English phrasing that the reader has the option of walking on the grass. Again, however, the context of the message prohibits walking on the grass just as effectively as the English and German messages. Nevertheless, a German who saw in translation the message for the French reader might well interpret that a *real* option for walking on the grass existed. In the literal reading of a low context culture, the French warning might appear to be a mere suggestion for environmentalists rather than a clear order.

Low context cultures may seem to be overly literal to members of high context cultures. They may demand, say, that a negotiating condition be stated explicitly even if all the parties understand the situation and even though, if the matter is stated overtly, one of the parties may lose face or be made to feel uncomfortable. The disastrous literalness of the Israelis in the pre–Six Day War example cited earlier may represent an extreme of the sort of conflict that can arise when a literal low context culture and an interpretive high context culture clash over the perceived meaning of a message. Day-to-day interactions in the world of international business are filled with less dramatic clashes deriving from the same source.

Members of most low context cultures have what seems to be — by the standards of high context cultures — an obsessive interest in data and explicit information. Hall has pointed out that this contrast is particularly noticeable in advertising. For example, he compares the approach used in German and comparatively higher contexted British automobile advertising in the U.S. market:

> Contrast the information in advertisements for the German-made Mercedes-Benz with those for the Rolls-Royce produced in England. The Rolls ad won't even tell the informed readers of automobile magazines such as *Road & Track* or *Car and Driver* the rated horsepower; Rolls representatives are known to have replied simply, "Enough," not sufficient answer for such informed readers, some of whom might even buy a Rolls. The Mercedes ad, on the other hand, has an abundance of data which is devoured by potential buyers. The readers of the above magazines expect a number for anything that can be measured, and horsepower is one of the first numbers they look for. (1983, p. 62)

One might extend Hall's example to certain Japanese advertising in the United States. The Japanese advertisers, even more highly contexted than the English, have in some instances not even directly mentioned their product.

For example, in the late 1980s Honda ran a series of television spots in the United States for their motorcycles. The commercials epitomized the lack of reliance on verbal communication in high context cultures. In one ad, the rock star Lou Reed appears in front of a graffiti-scrawled wall seated on a motorcycle. Reed says, "Take a walk on the wild side," referring to his well-known 1973 song playing in the background. After this message, Honda's name appears on the screen and the commercial ends. Reed is never identified; he is recognizable, to those who don't know what he looks like, by the context of the single line he says and his song in the background. Nothing is said either about the motorcycle or that—almost two decades earlier—the man sitting on the motorcycle laid the groundwork for what was to become punk and new-wave rock music. What the viewer is left with is a barrage of seemingly unrelated information to place in context. This is not a description of a motorcycle —but a bike placed amid images of the U.S. counterculture: a rough street, a now-classic song considered ahead of its time, and a man who, in the words of music critic David Gates, "sounds like the last guy in the world who'd lie to you—if only because he couldn't care less what you think" (1989, p. 68). The commercial—like many other Japanese ads in the United States—is quintessentially high context. Words are hardly used at all to communicate. Instead, the viewer is supposed to know the pertinent information before seeing the commercial; the television spot itself is just a means to reinforce a mood. Horsepower is never intended to be considered.

Uncertainty Avoidance

People in different cultures vary in uncertainty avoidance—that is, the degree to which they can tolerate ambiguity. This variance in the acceptance of uncertainty affects communication because the less one knows about another person, the more uncertainty is created.

Gudykunst (1983) has demonstrated a positive correlation between high context cultures and high uncertainty avoidance. Low context cultures are likely to have a greater tolerance for ambiguous communication (low uncertainty avoidance) than high context cultures. Members of high context cultures, therefore, are less likely to enter into communication with strangers or those they do not know well.

Clatterbuck (1979) observes that uncertainty diminishes as "information which is perceived as adequate for the making of necessary decisions within the interaction" (p. 148) increases. Uncertainty in itself is inherently disliked. Berger and Calabrese (1975) assert that "when strangers meet, their primary concern is one of uncertainty reduction or increasing predictability about the behavior of both themselves and others in the interaction" (p. 100).

The extent to which individuals tolerate uncertainty about the strangers they meet (and thus the lower the amount of information "perceived as adequate" to make decisions) influences the entire communication climate of the organization or culture to which they belong. For example, a Mexican executive — as a member of a high context culture — may feel uncomfortable doing business with a stranger. The Mexican will probably talk on nonbusiness matters for a while until the stranger's character can adequately be assessed. Knowing one's business partner is *central* to conducting business. As a member of a high context culture, the Mexican executive, for instance, might inquire about the stranger's views on issues unrelated to the business at hand. The executive may establish whether the two know someone in common or place great emphasis on the recommendation of a third party. Only if the Mexican feels that the stranger meets certain expectations as a person will business proceed smoothly. Uncertainty based on personal relations is not well tolerated.

A low context executive — one from the United States, for example — is less likely to make a personal assessment of a stranger; the executive is unlikely even to want to get to know the stranger personally. Such knowledge would be considered irrelevant to conducting business, and personal inquiries to be intrusive or, at the least, needless formalities. Instead, the U.S. executive would rely on written contracts to assure compliance. Uncertainty based on personal relations is more tolerated.

Hofstede (1984) has conducted the most extensive research on uncertainty avoidance, although he did not examine the correlation between high contexting and high uncertainty avoidance. Hofstede measured uncertainty avoidance in 40 countries as evidenced by cultural differences in the perception of three factors: (1) rule orientation, (2) employment stability, and (3) stress. Nations with *high* uncertainty avoidance adhered closely to rules, emphasized the importance of employment stability variables, and demonstrated high levels of anxiety, job stress, and worry about the future. Cultures *low* in uncertainty avoidance exhibited less adherence to rules, deemphasized employment stability variables, and showed lower levels of anxiety, job stress, and worry about the future than the other group. If the Gudykunst study (1983) mentioned above can be extended (although further testing is still needed), these attributes (adherence to rules, etc.) may also be seen to apply to high and low context cultures.

Face-Saving

No dimension of contexting is more important to international business communication than face-saving. We may define *face-saving* as the act of preserving one's prestige or outward dignity. People of all cultures, to a lesser or greater degree, are concerned with face-saving. Yet despite its universality, the importance attached to face-saving varies significantly from culture to culture. Moreover, the direction of that variability is

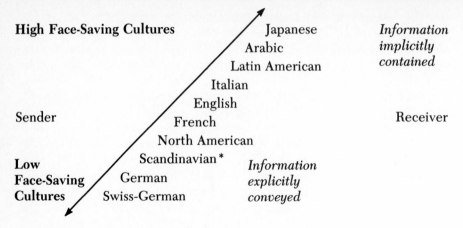

Figure 5.5 Face-saving ranking of cultures.
*Scandinavian category excludes Finland (Tirkkonen-Conduit, 1987).

predictable. The more highly contexted a culture is, the more importance its members attach to face-saving (see Figure 5.5).

Figure 5.5 describes the main traits of high and low face-saving cultures. For instance, low context cultures, as we have discussed, appear to those from high context cultures to be very direct. In large measure, the indirection employed by members of high context cultures is engaged in precisely to avoid even accidentally causing another person to lose face. The directness characteristic of low context cultures, on the other hand, is possible specifically because communicators are relatively less likely to feel that they have been affronted or that their prestige or dignity has been attacked (see Table 5.3).

Indirectness in high face-saving cultures is viewed as consideration for another's sense of dignity; in low face-saving cultures, indirectness is seen

Table 5.3   CHARACTERISTICS OF HIGH AND LOW FACE-SAVING CULTURES

	High face-saving	Low face-saving
Contexting	High	Low
Favored business communication approach	Politeness strategy; indirect plan	Confrontation strategy; direct plan
View of directness	Uncivil; inconsiderate; offensive	Honest; inoffensive
View of indirectness	Civil; considerate; honest	Dishonest; offensive
Amount of verbal self-disclosure	Low	High
Vagueness	Tolerated	Untolerated

as dishonesty. Honesty thus becomes culturally relative. The gulf in English between the terms *white lie* and *lie* illustrates the point. Whereas a white lie is a face-saving device in which contexting rather than verbal statement discloses the truth, a lie is an outright attempt to deceive. All cultures allow — to varying degrees — the use of white lies and other high context communication devices to allow individuals to save face. The more high context the communication of a culture is, the more its members use contexting to communicate. Relatedly, the more contexting the individuals in a culture use to communicate, the greater the likelihood that verbal disclosure will result in loss of face.

A society's emphasis on face-saving affects the way in which its members discuss business. Because members of low context cultures are generally less sensitive to face-saving issues, they often favor argumentation as a method of settling difficulties. Points are raised early and as clearly as possible. High context cultures, on the other hand, tend to favor what the Finnish researcher Sonja Tirkkonen-Condit (1988) calls a "politeness strategy," in which the central issues of an argument are expressed implicitly rather than explicitly. Finns use this strategy because, like members of other high context cultures, they are "prone to refraining from the face-threatening situation which argumentation necessarily involves" (p. 22).

Thus variation in face-saving does not rest, in low context cultures, on any cultural bias toward humiliating others or, in high context cultures, toward being intentionally vague. Rather, differences in the importance of face-saving derive from the way in which one is conditioned to allow others to save face. For example, John Condon describes the difference in face-saving practiced in the United States and in Mexico as a difference in the perception of

> the distance between what one thinks and what one says. Where "straight talk" is valued, the shortest distance is best. Lies of omission, for most Americans, seem less dishonest than those expressed. But where Americans north of the border may feel safe and honest with themselves by remarking ambiguously, "You don't know how much I've enjoyed this evening," Mexicans to the south would prefer to expound on their supreme enjoyment of such a magnificent occasion. (1985, p. 44)

Many Mexicans perceive their U.S. counterparts as lacking what Eva Kras refers to as the "personal sensitivity of Mexicans" (1988, p. 65). In other words, U.S. businesspeople are less likely to be as concerned with preserving face as are the more high context Mexicans. Kras warns that those from the United States particularly "need to resist saying outright, 'You are wrong.' The Mexican knows perfectly well when he has made a mistake, but verbalizing it puts him to shame and is liable to make him withdraw" (1988, p. 65). Kras makes an important point regarding the way in which Mexicans, and other highly contexted cultures, view verbalized face-losing matters. They are more likely to feel *shame*, whereas those from low context cultures are less likely to feel shame than *guilt*.

The distinction is reflected in (or possibly caused by) the nature of a society's communication and the related formulation of behavior into regulations and law. Deviance from behavior that is expected but not formally decreed is enforced by contexting through shaming the errant party. Deviance from behavior that is formally decreed is enforced by mandatory adherence to that society's governing rules and laws; when one breaks those rules and laws, one is guilty.

Therefore, guilt more than shame tends to govern behavior in low context cultures. As Glen Fisher has observed, "In North America and Northern Europe [i.e., low context cultures] culture tends, quite aside from law, to supply a *sin-and-guilt* control mechanism." He goes on: "In Southern Europe, the Middle East, and Latin America, on the other hand, *shame* tends to be the control mechanism of choice with one's relationship to other people and to the group the context for determining acceptable behavior" (1988, p. 110; Fisher's emphasis). Fisher makes a purely geographic distinction between face and shame, and indicates that "in the Orient the same motif is seen in ideas of 'face,' honor, dignity and obligation, all strong agents for controlling behavior irrespective of law (p. 111).

As a result, offenses in high context cultures may appear to be relatively slight to those from low context cultures. When members of a low context culture are told that they have done something wrong, they are likely to feel guilty, and it generally does not matter so much to them whether the reprimand occurs privately or publicly. In contrast, when members of a high context culture are shamed in private, they are still likely to feel affronted, but the affront is forgivable. Their major emotion is usually fear that the information will become public. And if the slight they experienced should become public, the affront becomes unbearable.

The intolerability of public loss of face has been discussed by communication experts regarding virtually every high context culture. "In Colombia," for example,

> and to some degree in all Hispanic countries, criticism of a person in front of friends is considered a serious affront to that person's dignity. Should such rude treatment occur, it is rarely taken lightly, and quick reprisal often follows. If a man does not defend his own honor and that of his family, he loses face, the worst of all social misfortunes. (Miller, Drayton, and Lyon, 1979, p. 22)

Similarly, Gavin Kennedy writes that Spaniards generally "lay great stress on personal honor, and you will find that contracts entered into by them are strictly filled." Indeed, the importance of saving face is so firmly entrenched that Spanish businesspeople "would rather take a loss than admit openly that they made a mistake" (1985, pp. 178–179). Writing of Arabic societies, Copeland and Griggs note that

> in America, children are taught, "Sticks and stones may break my bones, but words will never hurt me." The Arabs say the opposite: "A sharp tongue cuts deeper than the sword." Thus they attach great importance to compliments,

insults or indifference. Jerry Keneflick, an American executive with Whittaker Corporation in Saudi Arabia, found that affectionate mimicking of a favorite Saudi tennis instructor's efforts to say "Smash it," which came out "Smotch it," backfired. The Arab could not be convinced that he was not being ridiculed and was deeply hurt. (1985, pp. 107–108).

Most Pacific Rim cultures hold similar views. In Korea, this takes the form of *kibun*, often translated as "moods" or "feelings." "Koreans," Boye DeMente indicates, "are extraordinarily sensitive to slights and setbacks which damage their *kibun* and upset the harmony of their existence, and they go to what appears to Westerners to be extreme lengths to maintain their own *kibun* as well as that of everyone else" (1988, p. 26). This attitude has serious consequence for business in Korea (and other high context cultures). Fear of affronting others in whatever form — by causing a loss of face or damage to their *kibun* — may cause a serious breakdown in communication — particularly so when those from low context cultures are unable to interpret the information that is *not* put into words:

> The *kibun* factor often plays a decisive role in business because Koreans do not like to give anyone bad news, since such news will obviously damage the recipient's *kibun*. This results in a variety of reactions. Unpleasant news or information may be totally withheld, it may be delayed until near the end of the day to avoid spoiling the person's day, or it may be softened, sometimes to the point that it is misleading. (DeMente, 1988, pp. 26–27)

The aversion to bearing unpleasant news is evident throughout most of the Asian Pacific Rim nations. Relatedly, in most of these cultures, people have an aversion — for face-saving reasons — to saying "no" directly. Thus David Bonavia, in his thorough social analysis of the People's Republic of China, concludes that "what irritates most foreigners is the Chinese unwillingness to give a straight no in answer to an impractical or unwelcome request. Instead, it is *fuza* ('complicated'), or 'the responsible comrades are busy at the moment,' or 'perhaps there is some problem about this'" (1980, p. 127).

The refusal to say "no" directly is, perhaps, most fully developed in Japan. Indeed, so extreme is the penchant for avoiding a direct negative response that the Japan Export Trade Organization (JETRO) publishes a pamphlet on the subject to help foreigners understand the difference between a negative answer that seems to be a positive response and a truly positive answer. A Japanese businessperson who does not agree with what is said may choose to say nothing and, if pressed, may acquiesce even when no actual agreement is reached. To people from lower context cultures (and virtually all other cultures communicate in lower context than do the Japanese), this behavior can be confusing.

For example, if a U.S. executive were to ask a Japanese a direct yes-or-no question, arguably the *only* response possible in a traditional Japanese business setting would be to agree. Therefore, whatever the reality of the situation, the U.S. negotiator would receive a positive answer to the question "Can you finish this project by next month?" If the positive answer meant that the project could be finished in time, no difficulty would follow, although the Japanese might feel uncomfortable with so direct a question and might consider the U.S. businessperson to be rude. If, on the other hand, the "yes" answer was not realistic but—considering the context in which the question was asked—was the only face-saving reply possible, a great deal of conflict could follow. Not receiving the project in time, the U.S. participant would probably believe that the Japanese had lied. The Japanese would lose face in the eyes of his or her counterpart, while the U.S. businessperson would seem less worthy of respect to the Japanese for insisting on so obviously impossible a demand. Frequently, in high context cultures, those who cause others to lose face experience a loss of face themselves. Depriving others of their dignity disrupts the harmony high context communication attempts to maintain; the person who causes another to lose face thereby commits a transgression. As a result, both the person losing face and the person responsible for the contretemps may lose the respect of otherwise unaffected observers.

This does not mean that the Japanese (and several other Pacific Rim cultures) do not *in their own way* refuse requests. Instead, they allow context to communicate their refusal. Indeed, a myriad of ways to say "no" exist in Japan that are both face-saving and obvious to those attuned to them. "They may," Diana Rowland indicates, "simply apologize, keep quiet, ask you why you want to know, become vague, or answer with a euphemism for *no*" (1985, p. 47). Such euphemisms—often accompanied by pregnant pauses or nonverbal signals—can range from "I'll check and do what I can" (i.e., nothing) to "I'm not sure if this is possible" (because the answer is "no") to "This is very difficult" (which is as close to an actual refusal as usually possible without loss of face for one or both parties). The reason for so strong an aversion to saying "no" directly in Japan and similar cultures is tied to face-saving needs. "A blunt no," according to Rowland, "seems to the Japanese more as if you are saying 'no' to the person himself rather than to his idea, opinion, or request" (1985, p. 47). To some extent, *haragei*, discussed earlier in this chapter, is the practice of indirectly saying "no" taken to an art form.

Finally, people who attach great importance to maintaining face may seek revenge in some way against those responsible for their loss of face. This is especially evident in the most highly contexted cultures—those of the Pacific Rim, Latin America, and the Arab world. Arguably nowhere is this need for revenge more apparent than in Chinese culture:

> Face or *mianzi*, the regard in which one is held by others or the light in which one appears, is vitally important to the Chinese. Causing someone to lose face, through dressing someone down, failing to treat him or her with respect, or insulting someone, results in a loss of cooperation and often in retaliation. (Seligman, 1989, p. 56)

Boye DeMente has observed that, over the centuries, "the Chinese developed an often overriding need for revenge when their reputations were impugned or they suffered any injustice from anybody" (1989, p. 84). One method of revenge is open verbal attack, but such behavior — as we have seen — tends to lower the respect others have for the attacker. As a result, since

> active confrontation would also be viewed as unacceptable behavior on the part of the superior man, passive aggression is always fair game. . . . It can take different forms, but often appears as "inability" to accomplish something they know you wish to get done, or failure to show up at an appointed time with an obviously fabricated excuse. (Seligman, 1989, p. 49)

The need to settle the score plays a major role in almost all high context, face-conscious cultures.

ACCOMMODATING CONTEXTING AND FACE-SAVING DIFFERENCES IN INTERNATIONAL BUSINESS COMMUNICATION

To accommodate cross-cultural differences in contexting and face-saving, international business communicators should both anticipate how their messages are likely to be understood and remain alert to the actual — rather than merely the ostensible — meaning of the messages they receive.

Before you can effectively adjust your communication strategies, first determine where on the contexting scale the culture with which you interact is, relative to your own. While the scales devised by Hall and by Rosch and Segler (see Figures 5.4 and 5.5) may be helpful in making this determination, not many nations are included on the scales and, even then, variations within a larger culture may make unqualified use of the scales misleading. The easiest way to find out whether a culture uses high or low context communication is simply to observe and to listen carefully.

In dealing with lower contexted cultures than your own, keep five principles in mind: (1) the direct plan approach, (2) the relativity of blunt or rude behavior, (3) the importance of rules as abstract ideals, (4) reliance on explicit verbal communication, and (5) the distancing of personal relationships from business communication.

First, the lower the context of the other culture relative to your own, the more you should employ the direct plan approach to communication, since there will be a greater need to announce what you plan to discuss and less flexibility in the communication position you can adopt. In short, you are generally expected to state a position regardless of whether or not it is compatible with the views of the other parties.

Second, you should anticipate that a person from a lower context culture may seem blunt or even rude in stating positions but will probably be unaware of the bluntness or rudeness of his or her statements. This is precisely because, in most cases, such communication is *not* considered rude in that culture. It is important to recognize that, in low context cultures, communication in the form of persuasion and argumentation is distinctly separated from the individual. An attack on your position is not necessarily an attack on you. Thus a communicator who asserts that your idea is unworkable is probably more concerned about the feasibility of the idea and is not pointing out your foolishness in suggesting it. If you are not aware of this distinction, you may not be able to distinguish between communicators who actually are rude and those who, within the ground rules of their culture, would not be seen as offensive.

Third, you should recognize the importance of rules, regulations, and laws. The lower the contexting of a culture relative to your own, the more rigid its adherence to rules will appear. A person from a lower contexted culture will appear to be governed by rules which seem irrelevant or even counterproductive to you. Be aware that to members of a low context culture, the rules exist in the abstract; that is, there is a right way and a wrong way to do something. The actual situation matters less than the rules prescribed for the situation. Bending the rules in low context cultures is recognized, even by those who do so, as dishonest.

Fourth, the lower the context of the other culture, the more people in that society will seem to state the obvious and rely on explicit verbal communication to interpret what is meant. When dealing with such cultures, do not assume that anything not explicitly put into words will be understood. The people with whom you negotiate may seem excessively literal, obsessed with the precise meaning of a statement. They may also, in their intense interest in data and similar low context evidence, appear to be "number-crunchers" who value statistics more than humans.

Finally, low context cultures—while they may vary greatly from culture to culture in the friendliness of their people—generally separate business communication from the personal relationships of the communicators. Because they place more trust in rules, formal contracts, and other verbally based safeguards, they tend also to place less confidence in personal relationships, loyalty, and social ties. Business is usually conducted in a fairly cold manner. While there is no culture in which members base their decisions solely on the logic of benefit, the lower the context of a culture, the more its members will see such decision making as the ideal.

In dealing with more highly contexted cultures than your own, you should also keep five principles in mind: (1) the indirect plan approach, (2) the importance of face-saving, (3) the situational nature of rules, (4) reliance on implicit communication, and (5) the centrality of personal relationships in communication.

First, members of highly contexted societies will not feel comfortable committing themselves initially. Such people may seem intentionally vague when they are in fact establishing a background of information against which to place your message in context. It is generally advisable in conducting business with those from a more highly contexted culture to warm up the conversation with carefully chosen small talk that will give them an idea of the type of person you are. While it may not seem to you that they will get to the subject you consider important, they usually will if you are patient. Most high context cultures communicate in circular or spiral patterns of logic, rather than the direct line, from position to position, of lower contexted cultures. Consequently, once negotiators begin to discuss the matter of most concern to you, they may drift on and off the subject. Again, patience is helpful; forcing the issue may in fact be so offsetting that—if those with whom you are talking do not cut off the conversation altogether—they may feel the need to gather more background on you and prolong the discussion rather than speed it along.

Second, face-saving concerns tend to increase as the level of contexting increases. The higher the contexting, the more you must be conscious of how your message is received. Face-saving, moreover, is two-way. Embarrassing others through overly direct questions or stating things that will upset the other party may cause them to lose face. Just as likely, however, is that, through committing a faux pas, you may lose face yourself. It is therefore advisable to monitor carefully your behavior and your talk, to see your own actions in their worst light. The more highly contexted the culture is (relative to your own), the less likely that offenses you cause or mistakes you make will go unnoticed or be forgiven. You should also not confuse politeness with forgiveness or depth of feeling. The individuals you are dealing with will probably seem more polite than people in your home culture generally are. This has more to do with maintaining harmony and preventing loss of face than it does with the personal friendliness with which politeness is associated in lower contexted cultures. In high context cultures, your enemies may be as polite to you as your allies.

Third, be aware that, in high context cultures, a difference exists between surface truth and reality. Rules and formal law tend to govern behavior less than in low context cultures. Instead, situation rather than absolute principle seems to govern behavior:

> The Japanese use the terms *tatemae* and *honne* to describe these two standards which work in parallel, not in conflict. *Tatemae* is literally the outward structure of a building; the term refers to what is outwardly expressed, what appears on the surface. *Honne* is literally one's "true voice," and it refers to what one really thinks or feels. The Japanese assume that there may be a difference between what one says and what one thinks. . . . [People from low context cultures] are well advised to always consider the circumstances in which something is said. . . . the occasions, settings, "contexts" in Japan generally exert more influence on what is said or not said than is the case for [low context cultures]. Often circumstances dictate whether one can reveal

one's "true voice," or say what he is expected or constrained to say. One's true voice can be heard in a situation that allows for it. (Condon, 1984, pp. 25–27)

The concept of *tatemae* and *honne*, of course, is not limited to Japan. The same dichotomy holds true for most cultures that are more highly contexted than your own.

Fourth, the more highly contexted a culture, the more its members will seem to rely on *how* you express your message than on what you actually say. Thus you should be alert to *implied* information in what others say to you and to *inferences* that others may draw from what you say, even when you did not intend to convey such ideas. It is, in short, more necessary to read between the lines when dealing with such cultures.

Finally, most high context cultures rely on personal relationships to establish the trust and background information necessary for continuing communication. It is simply easier to communicate implicitly with those whom one knows well, Since high context communication *is*, by definition, implicit communication, those from high context cultures will certainly want to get to know you. Individuals with whom you deal will probably not limit business communication just to commercial exchanges. It is therefore advisable to build a personal relationship of trust and interests extending beyond business with such negotiators.

Chapter
6

Issues of Authority Conception in International Business Communications

*T*his chapter describes the effect that socially determined views of authority conception have on international business communication. In particular, the chapter examines the cross-cultural variability of two related manifestations of authority: power perception and leadership style.

AUTHORITY DEFINED

Authority itself is primarily symbolic in nature. In other words, authority does not exist in isolation but reflects instead the conception of organizational power and leadership common to an organization's members. Heller defines authority as "'shared beliefs' about the power or influence of an organization or an individual representing that organization. Authority is vested in an individual or an organization, accordingly, by the members of the organization or society for whom the individual or organization contains [represents] this shared meaning" (1985, p. 488). Since authority conception derives from the collective values of those who vest it, authority itself reflects the cultural values of the organization or society in which the authority is recognized.

The Elements of Authority

Authority, as the "shared beliefs" regarding power relationships of those who recognize it, is too broad to examine across cultures in any useful form for the average business situation. This is so because the "shared beliefs" about power relationships represent the entire culture's attitudes toward organizational structure and management in general. Consequently, it may prove valuable to examine differences toward the major components of authority: power and leadership style. These two elements represent aspects of authority that can be better isolated as cross-cultural variables. After examining these variables individually, we can combine the elements to obtain a fuller understanding of authority conception.

Since power and leadership style both represent facets of the conception of authority within an organization, it is somewhat misleading to divide them into separate categories. It is necessary to keep in mind that the two elements are interrelated and form an integrated whole in the conception of authority.

Power Defined   Authority and power are inseparable, as Heller's definition suggests. Authority is the *power* to direct the actions of others. For many, authority and power can be seen as synonymous. Claude George, whose textbook on supervisory management typifies the discussion of this issue, defines authority in terms of power: "Authority is the right to command or act and is the power you have over others. If you have authority, you can cause a person to do something that you want done" (1982, p. 265).

Leadership Style Defined   Authority extends beyond power to notions of leadership style. Leadership style can be seen as the symbolic context of actions through which persons in power cause others to do what they wish them to do. The research of Van Fleet and Al-Tuhaih (1979) has shown that leadership varies across cultures less in what leaders actually do than in the perceptions of their leadership among a culture's members. In other words, the functions of leadership are similar regardless of culture, but the attitudes toward leaders held by their followers shift markedly.

Power represents substantive action; leadership style is determined by symbolic action. Several authors (Peters, 1978; Pfeffer, 1981; Dandridge, 1985; Feldman, 1986) have recognized the difference between substantive action (power) and symbolic action (leadership). Both represent aspects of authority, but power deals with authority only in response to specific actions, while leadership style deals with the rationalization and legitimation of that authority. Pfeffer views symbolic action (leadership style) "in terms of rationalizing and legitimating action," but sees substantive action (power) as principally "the result of fundamental resource interdependencies and other environmental imperatives" (1981, p. 5). Leadership style, then, can be defined as that aspect of authority that places the application of power in its symbolic context.

The cross-cultural variability of the *perception* (as opposed to the reality) of leadership may be the result of the symbolic context in which the perception of leadership is embedded. Although power can be separated from its symbolic context, leadership cannot. Power as an element of authority deals only with substantive action while leadership deals with the meaning of the action involved.

Authority Conception and Cross-Cultural Communication

Views regarding power and leadership together shape the conception of authority within an organization. Yet because both these facets of authority conception differ drastically from culture to culture, authority itself is conceived of differently from society to society.

Differences in authority conception, in turn, directly influence the flow and effectiveness of communication in organizations and groups. The way members of a culture view authority affects many functions of communication. Authority conception helps determine, as well, the nature and frequency of upward and downward communication between subordinates and superiors. It also affects the degree of freedom to communicate with those outside the hierarchical structure of the organization. Finally, it lays the foundation for the importance of adherence to rules, the use of titles, and the acceptance of strangers.

POWER AND LEADERSHIP IN CROSS-CULTURAL TERMS

Power is legitimized through the conception of the authority of its holders. The way in which people legitimate power, however, differs across cultures. In cultures in which power is closely associated with those who hold it, leadership and power are essentially interchangeable concepts. In cultures where power is perceived as being independent from those who possess it, power and leadership are separate concepts.

Shils (1961) contends that authority conception derives from the attribution of charisma to those in power by their subordinates; Feldman (1986) asserts that the perception of the charisma of the power holder, in turn, both defines and is defined by the surrounding culture. Feldman observes that the

> process of attributing charisma to powerful offices contributes to defining the center of power. It also contributes to defining the center of the culture, because the exercise of power by leaders and the recognition of this power by individuals is what makes apparent the norms, beliefs, and ideals that are deemed important and serious by the organization. (1986, p. 214)

The relationship of power and leadership is, therefore, inseparable from the culture in which it is applied.

Cultures vary greatly in their understanding of power. In particular, differences exist regarding three points: the perception of power, power distance, and the function of the leader (or, in organizational terms, of the manager).

Power Perception

It is possible to view power according to two variables: (1) as either personal or universal or (2) as a means to make, or avoid making, decisions. Thus power can be perceived as either closely tied to or independent from its holder.

A great deal of consensus exists across cultures regarding the way in which power is perceived; indeed, most nations view culture in one of two ways. Yet the differences between these two conceptions of power are so great that societies holding one view frequently find the other view incomprehensible.

The two divergent notions of power fall into roughly geographic divisions — the Asian cultures and the Western (European, U.S., Canadian, and Australian). The most complete discussion of the differences between Western and Asian perceptions of power is, arguably, Lucian Pye's groundbreaking *Asian Power and Politics: The Cultural Dimensions of Authority* (1985). In this extensive study, Pye describes Western concepts of authority as a retreat from primitive (destructive) power, resulting in increasingly delineated and restricted forms of authority. By contrast Pye says, in Asia, power is the means to prevent a breakdown of the established authority, perceived as the bulwark against the reemergence of primitive power. Pye contrasts Asian and Western differences in authority conception in terms of culturally variant perceptions of power and leadership:

> Consistent with this view is the general acceptance by Asians of idealized authority even while they may dislike the practices of those currently in power. The greater Asian acknowledgement of the need for, and indeed the desirability of, authority, contrasts sharply with the Western enthusiasm for limiting authority, which is unaccompanied by any fear that the result could be the revival of primitive power. Most Asians respect authority too much to share the Western distrust of authority and power which was summarized in an editorial in the *Economist* in 1984: "the point about power is not who has it, but that nobody should have too much of it, because power is a bad thing." (p. 34).

At this point, we should repeat that it is dangerous to generalize in discussing intercultural communication. Indeed, this division does not account for whole groups of cultures (including most Latin American and African cultures) that do not easily fall into either camp. Moreover, it is untrue to claim that members of all Western cultures or all Asian cultures have the same attitudes toward power. Yet despite these differences, a framework can be constructed from the conceptual planks shared by most Asian societies, on the one hand, and by Western cultures, on the other hand. By contrast, the differences between traditional Asian and Western concepts of power are so great that they are — at least, for any practical business purpose — incompatible.

Western Concepts of Power   In the United States and Europe, most theorists traditionally have imbued power with two attributes: it is characterized by the ability to make and carry out significant decisions, and it exists as an abstract ideal. This dual definition of power has a strong foundation in modern European philosophy, rooted in the writings of Montesquieu, Adam Smith, John Stuart Mill, and Karl Marx. Since power is closely tied to conceptions of political dominance, European notions of power as the universal ideal historically were largely unquestioned. Indeed, European political imperialism rendered relatively meaningless any other concepts of power. The essentially Western understanding of power has generally been upheld for most of the twentieth century. The political and economic dominance of Great Britain and the United States, in particular, have led to the prominence of Anglo-American theorists in the conceptualization of power (Merriam, 1934, Russell, 1938; Lasswell and Kaplan, 1950; Dahl, 1961).

The Western conception of power is closely linked to decision making. Those perceived as having power have a twofold ability: first, they are able to make or participate in the making of significant decisions; second, they are able to implement these decisions.

This is not to say that all cultures in Europe and North America hold identical perceptions of power. Indeed, considerable evidence indicates otherwise. To cite but one example, the French researcher André Laurent (1983) divided the West into "Latin" (France and Italy) and "Northern" (the United States, Sweden, the Netherlands, Denmark, and Great Britain) countries and found that Latin managers were perceived as being considerably more motivated by obtaining power than were the Northern managers. In a later study, Laurent observed that French managers tend to "look at the organization as an authority network where the power to organize and control the actors stems from their positioning in the hierarchy," while British managers "view the organization primarily as a network of relationships between individuals who get things done by influencing each other through communicating and negotiating" (1986, p. 96). According to Laurent's studies, French managers are inclined to be more motivated by the goal of obtaining power and position in the organizational hierarchy than their British counterparts. In turn, British managers are more motivated by the achievement of objectives.

Moreover, such differences may be intensifying. As one article on changing views of authority conception in the United States put it, "More and more managers recognize that it's wrong to assume that authority is the source of results" (Pascarella, DiBianca, and Gioja, 1988, p. 41). In other words, in the United States, at least, managers may increasingly view authority less as power than as a means of attaining goals.

Still, despite such national differences, most European and North American cultures are more closely aligned with one another on perceptions of power than any one of them would be with the East Asian cultures discussed below. For example, in most European and North American cultures power is traditionally seen as an abstract ideal. Thus, in the Laurent (1986) study cited, individuals may either strive for power or seek to achieve objectives. In a cross-cultural survey of French and U.S. managers, such a choice still makes sense in both societies, despite differences between the two countries.

The concept of power as an abstract and absolute concept, however, makes no sense to many East Asian cultures. Like the perception of truth (discussed in Chapter 5), power in its traditional Western conception is not subject to circumstantial influences. People either hold absolute power (that is, they can fully implement what they decide to do), or they hold some fragment of power (that is, they can only decide on a restricted set of matters and/or they can only partially implement that which they decide to do).

As an ideal, power is traditionally seen as having two characteristics important to organizational communication: it is (a) independent of the person holding it and (b) universal. The notion of power as independent from the person who wields it at any give time is a major factor in business because it means that power is impersonal enough to transfer from person to person through title or position, quite apart from the personality of the individuals possessing that power.

Since it is seen as an abstract ideal, power is also viewed in the West as being universal. The Western notion of power — as the history of eighteenth- and nineteenth-century imperialism makes clear — has traditionally been considered universal. This is an important point in international business communication because it presupposes, on the part of most Europeans and North Americans, a belief that people everywhere, regardless of culture, will find the Western notion of power palatable, and so will *want* to participate in decision making and believe that power is independent of personality.

Asian Concepts of Power   The concepts of power in most Asian nations are diametrically opposed to those in Europe and the United States. In Asian cultures the powerful eschew decision making, and power is *not* an abstract ideal but instead is seen as circumstantial.

Asian power conception is characterized by a desire to *avoid* decision making (unlike the Western ideal of *participating* in decision making). As Lucien Pye has observed, in Asia traditionally, "to have power was to be spared the chore of decision-making" (1985, p. 21). In the West, power is demonstrated by the ability to override the dictates of social pressure. By contrast, in Asia, the social order is seen as designed for those in power, and thus power is enhanced as it adheres *to* — rather than overrides — that social order.

Asian power conception is embedded in its social setting. The widespread acceptance of consensus decision making in many Asian cultures may well result from this fact. At the least, the desire to be a part of a group rather than the leader is more noticeable in Asia than in the West. The effects of this view on leadership are illustrated in the observations of a pair of U.S. management trainers who attempted to train businesspeople in the People's Republic of China to use typical U.S. managerial techniques:

> Every group began their meetings with each member offering to be ranked last. This struggle for last place continued feverishly for approximately 15 minutes, which was one-half of the allotted meeting time. The student who had protested loudest and offered the most convincing argument for being the worst "won the honor" of lowest rank. Pleased with this victory, the lowest-ranked student relaxed into quiet contentment.
>
> Each group then nominated and ratified the assigned group leader as first in the ranking. Each group member offered support and evidence for the rightful designation of the group leader as deserving the highest rank. The group leader declined the nomination several times before modestly accepting. This procedure took about 15 minutes, using up the remaining discussion time. (Lindsay and Dempsey, 1985, p. 75)

The Chinese approach toward leadership and the technique for selecting first the *least* qualified person and then the leader surprised the trainers. Moreover, the procedure was consistent—"every group had behaved in exactly the same manner" (Lindsay and Dempsey, 1985, p. 75). To some extent, these differences reflect differences in face-saving (as discussed in Chapter 5). Still, they also represent real differences in the view of power and the relationship of the leader to the group to which he or she belongs.

Historically in China, Japan, Korea, Indonesia, and other parts of Asia, power was not related to choice—as it is in Europe and North America—but, rather, to the legitimation of the social order. In other words, status rather than freedom of choice was the primary manifestation of power. The historical equation of power with status carries over in the majority of Asian cultures in the form of the personalization of power. With the possible exception of Japan, Asian cultures conceive of power as resting in individuals rather than in the offices they hold.

Power in many Asian cultures, then, is not abstract but is, instead, directly tied to its possessor. This view manifests itself in various forms, all associated with a central patron or set of patrons, each of whom has his or her own set of client-subordinates. The workplace is itself transformed by this conception of authority, since the social organization that results links subordinates to their patrons—those with power—by intense bonds of obligation.

In Indonesia, for instance, the conception of authority legitimized through the personal assignation of power has led to *bapakism*, in which underlings are expected to be extremely loyal to their sponsoring superiors. The Indonesian workplace, in turn, is composed of several more or less self-contained hierarchical patronage circles, each centering on a paternal figure of exemplary charisma.

In Korea, several experts (Brandt, 1983; Pye, 1985; DeMente, 1988) have observed a similar phenomenon linking power to the perception of individual, personalized authority, with power emanating at least in part from family relationships and blood ties. "Family background . . . plays a vital role in both business and society" (DeMente, 1988, p. 29) and in the strictly hierarchical relationships of leading families reminiscent of the formal *Yangban* social system. In Japan, the *oyakobun* relationship ties the *oya* (senior) to his or her *ko* (junior) in a patronage network (*batsu*), in which the "*oya* is often responsible for the very success of his *ko*, or his protegé." This "bond tends to obligate the young person to an endless pledge of loyalties and respect to his senior benefactor" (Haglund, 1984, p. 72). Similarly, the direct link of power to the person who holds it has led to what Susan Shirk (1982) calls the "virtuocracy" of the People's Republic of China, where leaders are deserving of power because they are perceived to be (or at least are made to appear to be) more virtuous.

Most Asian cultures hold a power perception that is highly personal (compared to Western universal and abstract perceptions) and as a means to avoid (rather than control) decision-making.

Respect for Power and Communication Ritualization   Most societies ritualize communication to show respect for power, reinforcing the society's views regarding authority. This ritualization regularly appears in that society's business communication. For instance, we discussed at length in Chapter 2 the linguistic differences used between superiors and subordinates in such languages as Japanese.

Similarly, as discussed in Chapter 4, cultures differ in the perception of the relative importance of status. In business communication, accommodation of status differences becomes most evident in the formalization of address modes. The relative importance of title—whether inherited or earned through education or appointment—is a type of ritualized communication used to recognize status. The perceived significance of titles, however, varies from culture to culture.

Thus titles in business are relatively less important in the United States than in many other societies. An American business executive who received a letter with his or her title incorrectly worded is unlikely to become very upset. Even the president of a corporation is referred to simply as *Mr.* or *Ms.*, and Ph.D. degrees often go unacknowledged in common business address (although the use of *Dr.* for persons with a Ph.D. degree is more common in academic settings). Indeed. the closest parallel to titular affront in the United States would be the failure to use *Dr.* for dentists and physicians, and even this covers essentially only one profession.

In contrast, as one expert has written, "The Swedes themselves admit that they suffer from *titelsjuka*, by which they mean an unwholesome predilection for titles" (Lorenzen, 1964, p. 115). Until recently, Swedes listed most major occupational titles in the telephone book, with titles ranging from *a* and *advokat*, or lawyer, to *ö* and *ölutkorare*, or beer truck driver (*ö* being the last letter of the Swedish alphabet). To refer to a Swedish businessman who was director of his company simply as *Herr* (the Swedish equivalent to *Mr.*) rather than as *direktör* would fail to identify him with his status as an executive. Foreigners doing business with Swedes should, in both letters and oral communication, pay close attention to title. The task could prove to be a cross-cultural stumbling block for members of cultures that are more casual about titles. For example, U.S. business has no equivalent for such Swedish titles as *disponent* (manager of an industry) or *ingeniör* (engineer). Such positions exist, but not as titles attached to names.

Power Distance

In business, levels of power inherently differ. The way in which people of inequal power interact within an organization is called *power distance*. This variable was studied at length by the Dutch researcher Geert Hofstede. Hofstede, who coined the term, defines power distance as the "measure of the interpersonal power or influence between B [boss] and S [subordinate] as perceived by the least powerful of the two, S" (1984, pp. 70–71). Hofstede asserts that power distance between a boss and a subordinate in a hierarchy represents the extent to which either one can influence the other's behavior. He found, in a study of workers from 40 nations, that power distance "is to a considerable extent determined by . . . national culture" (1984, p. 72).

Through his research, Hofstede rank-ordered the 40 countries he surveyed on a 100-point PDI, or power distance index (see Table 6.1). Certain cultures were characterized as having a high power distance index, some as having a low power distance index, and many others as being somewhere in between. Countries ranked as having high power distance, such as the Philippines (94), Mexico and Venezuela (both 81), India (77), and Singapore (74), were characterized as having particular traits affecting business communication. Subordinates in these cultures were more likely to accept the fact that their superiors had greater power than they had and to believe that a superior was correct because that superior outranked them, whether the superior was in fact correct or not. Moreover, underlings often behave in a specific manner because their boss wants them to rather than because they themselves feel that the behavior is appropriate. In other words, the subordinates in high PDI cultures are unlikely to question authority and are less likely to initiate upward communication unless requested to do so.

Team interaction is also influenced among cultures ranked high on the power distance index. According to Rigby, "participants from high PDI backgrounds are unlikely to work well in team development exercises requiring face-to-face openness, frankness, and feedback concerning the impact of their own or others' behaviour on the group" (1987, p. 67).

At the other end of Hofstede's index are such countries as Austria

Table 6.1 POWER DISTANCE INDEX (PDI) VALUES BY COUNTRY BASED ON THE SCORES ON THREE ATTITUDE SURVEY QUESTIONS FOR A STRATIFIED SAMPLE OF SEVEN OCCUPATIONS AT TWO POINTS IN TIME*

Country	PDI Actual	PDI Predicted	Country	PDI Actual	PDI Predicted
Phillippines	94	73	South Africa	49	62
Mexico	81	70	Argentina	49	56
Venezuela	81	66	U.S.A.	40	42
India	77	78	Canada	39	36
Singapore	74	64	Netherlands	38	38
Brazil	69	72	Australia	36	44
Hong Kong	68	56	Germany (F.R.)	35	42
France	68	42	Great Britain	35	45
Colombia	67	75	Switzerland	34	32
Turkey	66	60	Finland	33	30
Belgium	65	36	Norway	31	27
Peru	64	69	Sweden	31	23
Thailand	64	74	Ireland	28	37
Chile	63	56	New Zealand	22	35
Portugal	63	53	Denmark	18	28
Greece	60	51	Israel	13	44
Iran	58	61	Austria	11	40
Taiwan	58	63			
Spain	57	56	Mean of 39 countries	51	52
Pakistan	55	74	(HERMES)		
Japan	54	57			
Italy	50	53	Yugoslavia (same industry)	76	53

*Actual values and values predicted on the basis of multiple regression on latitude, population size, and wealth.

Hofstede, 1984, p. 77.

(11), Israel (13), Denmark (18), New Zealand (22), Ireland (28), Sweden and Norway (both 31), and Finland (33). In these countries, rating low in power distance, subordinates are not so ready to accept the unequal distribution of power in the workplace. Instead of trusting a superior on the basis of position, underlings evaluated a superior's correctness on the way he or she responded to a problem. Subordinates were also less likely to behave in a particular manner because they were ordered to do so than because they (the subordinates) agreed with their boss that the behavior was appropriate. Moreover, as Rigby (1987) has noted, in work-team interaction, members of low PDI cultures were likely to be viewed by counterparts in high PDI nations as "being too open and confrontive with other team members" (p. 67).

Power distance, as it changes across cultures, alters the communication style between subordinate and superior. Superiors in all cultures expect their subordinates both to follow their orders and to show a degree of deference to them as authority figures. If judged by only one culture's power distance standards, serious misunderstandings can result. For instance, low PDI subordinates are likely to offend managers from higher PDI cultures. Similarly, managers in high PDI societies may fail to recognize the unspoken difficulties among subordinates from lower PDI cultures, precisely because they *are* unspoken.

Individualism, Collectivism, and Power Distance   In Chapter 4, we discussed the cross-cultural differences regarding individualism and collectivism as factors affecting international business communication. Such differences also influence the perception of authority. Indeed, several researchers (Campbell, 1975; Jaspers and Frazer, 1981; Douglas, 1986) have argued that the organizations to which one belongs determine one's views of institutional constraints. These views, in turn, reflect collective attitudes toward organizational authority.

As we discussed in Chapter 4, Hofstede (1984) ranked people according to their collectivism or individualism, finding that high individualism was negatively correlated with low power distance. Power distance and individualism are largely interrelated. Individualism in a culture, therefore, is likely to influence its members' authority perception.

Still, Hofstede noted that "although most high PDI [power distance index] countries are also low IDV [individualism] countries and vice versa, this is not always the case" (p. 157). He noted several disparities in such a correlation, though he provides only limited analysis of their source. For example, in Israel and Austria, there was a tendency toward "no strict authority but relative dependence on the collectivity," which he calls "independent collectivism." In contrast, he concluded that people in France, South Africa, and other countries have "a need for strict authority of hierarchical superiors, but *at the same time* stress their personal independence from any collectivity," which he calls "dependent individualism" (p. 157).

Leadership Style

Leadership style derives in large part from the culture to which the leader belongs. Subordinates are culturally taught to expect their leader to behave in certain ways and, in turn, those views shape the leader's behavior.

Leadership style directly affects the way in which people communicate in business. For example, leaders who employ a participative management style encourage communication with considerable egalitarianism and feedback. Those who do not, resist feedback and do not wish to have their orders questioned.

As the earlier discussions on power perception and power distance suggest, leaders (as the channels through which power passes) are perceived differently from culture to culture. Since, as we have discussed, the perception of the proper relationship between subordinates and their superiors varies across cultures, the complementary relationship of superiors to their subordinates (that is, leadership style) also changes to accommodate cultural differences in expected leadership behavior.

While this fact seems fairly straightforward, for the first three decades following World War II, leadership principles were viewed as being universally applicable. This erroneous assumption resulted in large part from an anomaly of history. After World War II, the United States was the only major industrialized nation left intact. The economies of Germany, Italy, Britain, Japan, France, the Soviet Union, the Netherlands, and other industrial powers were essentially bankrupt, and the means of production (from factories to available labor to capital) were seriously damaged or destroyed. The result was the economic dominance of the United States while these nations reindustrialized and recovered from the war.

The global position of the United States in the postwar period coincided with the development of a U.S. theory of management based on scientific and psychological principles of organizational behavior. In the 1950s and 1960s, many theories regarding workplace leadership and employee motivation were tested and accepted in the United States and disseminated abroad by U.S. managers, academics, and even government officials (in the form of such agencies as the Peace Corps). Many analysts considered these theories to be universal attributes of human behavior, particularly since no other industrial power existed in the aftermath of the war to suggest an alternative method of management.

Among these theories were Maslow's hierarchy of needs (1954); McGregor's Theory X and Theory Y (1960); McClelland's three motives of achievement, power, and affiliation (1961); and Herzberg et al.'s two-factor theory (1968). These theories describe U.S. workplace leadership and employee motivation admirably. However, they are *not* universal.

In the mid-1960s, with the major industrial powers nearly recovered from their postwar industrial nadir, the United States began to face competition from countries using different management and leadership styles. U.S. businesspeople and journalists were taken aback by the emergence of these competitors and spoke of them with surprise and disbelief as the Japanese, Italian, or German "economic miracles." The reemergence of these and other industrial powers seemed miraculous in large part because they reflected their own cultural approaches to leadership and management — rather than the reigning U.S. theories.

In response to these events, research was undertaken in earnest to test the cross-cultural validity of these theories. As a result, numerous researchers have either directly refuted or cast serious doubt on each of the then-dominant theories.

For example, Hines (1973) and Crabbs (1973) demonstrated outright the inapplicability of Herzberg's theories in non-U.S. settings. Similarly, Adler (1986) and Hofstede (1990) questioned the universality of McClelland's three motives, pointing out that his key term *achievement* is often untranslatable outside of English.

The leadership and motivation theories of Maslow and McGregor fared somewhat better in cross-cultural analyses. Yet researchers have consistently shown that even when the elements of these theories apply across cultures, they seem to do so for different reasons and in varying degrees. Numerous researchers have shown, for instance, that the components of Maslow's hierarchy motivate people in cultures other than the United States, but with significantly different weightings of needs or rank ordering. This is the case in India (Jaggi, 1979; Reddy, 1984), Mexico (Reitz and Graf, 1973), and Peru (Stephens, Kedia, and Ezell, 1979).

Similarly, research applying McGregor's theories has shown consistent dislike across cultures for Theory X leadership style, but with considerable variance from culture to culture regarding the degree of dislike (Haire, Ghiselli, and Porter, 1966; Hofstede, 1984). Even when people in different cultures have similar responses to Theory X and Theory Y leadership styles, their reasons for doing so stem from entirely different reasons. Thus the egalitarian principles of Theory Y have been shown in the People's Republic of China to align closely with the Maoist egalitarian philosophy, while Theory X represents the elitist leadership of the intellectual class (Oh, 1976).

More important from a business communication standpoint, the participative leadership style of Theory Y has within it a principle that may impede effective communication across cultures. Participative leadership styles promote the sharing of information and allow subordinates to know the truth of matters affecting them. The concept of truth as absolute, however, is itself a stumbling block. As we discussed in Chapter 5, some cultures—particularly those shaped by the tenets of Christianity, Judaism, and Islam—view truth as inflexible. There is no middle ground when dealing with principles of right and wrong. In many Eastern religions, which espouse harmony in surface relations (what the Japanese call *tatemae*, or outward structure), truth is more relative. For example, as Boye DeMente notes, "the moral implications of much of the business behavior in Korea today are blurred" (1988, p. 82).

Similarly, John Condon has written that

> the Japanese do not expect all people to be treated in the same way in all situations, nor do they think it is wise to always speak out what one believes. From a Japanese point of view this is not a matter of hypocrisy or deviousness. Rather it is a recognition that a "double standard" is necessary and practical. (1984, p. 25)

While this raises some questions regarding the international applicability of ethics, for our purposes it is simply enough to stress that the international businessperson should anticipate the possibility of such differences and the dangers in the application of participative leadership principles.

ACCOMMODATING DIFFERENCES IN AUTHORITY CONCEPTION

Awareness of differences across cultures in authority conception is probably the best means for accommodating potential difficulties. The businessperson abroad should pay particular attention to how others react to shows of power and to how they treat their leaders. Whether sources of power are group-based or individually based, and whether power is centralized in individuals or decentralized throughout groups, are issues of concern for the international businessperson.

Once again, the study of the children's literature of a culture may prove enlightening. Considerable understanding of how power is perceived and leaders are treated can be derived from the social guidelines laid out in teaching young people how to behave toward those in power and whether or not they have the right to question authority.

In dealing with cultures in which power distance is higher ranked than in your own, you should give clear orders and not demand participative feedback. Generally, underlings in such cultures question the legitimacy of the manager who asks their opinion regarding a command, since they believe that superiors are in their positions because they are supposed to know more than subordinates. Conversely, in communicating with power distance cultures lower-ranked than one's own, you will want to provide feedback. Generally, managers in low PDI cultures are sincere in their desire to hear the opinions of their subordinates, even if that opinion contradicts the manager's. You should be careful, nevertheless, not to interpret requests for participation in decision making or feedback as indications of diminished power. Indeed, the more powerful the leader in low PDI cultures, the more open to feedback the leader should be.

Before conducting business with members of different cultures, talk with others who have experience in working with that culture. People who have hands-on experience are most likely to be aware of the more subtle signs of power, such as the use or lack of use of appropriate titles.

Finally, in no other area of business communication is it more necessary to update your knowledge than in the area of authority conception. Since the reigning theories of leadership of the 1950s and 1960s have been challenged in cross-cultural situations, it is important to remain flexible toward differences in leadership style.

Chapter
7

Issues of Nonverbal Communication and International Business Communication

*A*s Macbeth and his wife plan the murder of their guest King Duncan in the first act of William Shakespeare's great play, Lady Macbeth warns her reluctant husband to take care to hide the uneasiness his nonverbal actions betray. "Your face, my thane," she warns him, "is a book where men may read strange matters."

Shakespeare, with his keen insight into human behavior, observed the importance of unspoken messages in communication hundreds of years before psychologists, anthropologists, and other social scientists began seriously to study the importance of unspoken, or nonverbal, communication.

In our own century, communication researchers have confirmed what Shakespeare intuited. Indeed, the amount of information people communicate nonverbally exceeds what they communicate by using words. Roy L. Birdwhistell, in a groundbreaking, systematic study, suggests that as much as 65 percent of a message's meaning is transmitted through the sender's nonverbal communication (1970). Thus even in an exchange that takes place entirely among members of the same culture, it is possible for individuals who ignore nonverbal cues to misunderstand over half of the message they receive.

Moreover, in certain situations different cultures may rely more heavily on nonverbal (versus verbal) communication. One particularly dramatic contrast can be seen between 'Aina Pumehana (native Hawaiians) and Caucasian Hawaiians. In one study, Caucasian Hawaiian school children sought help *verbally* 93 percent of the time (with boys doing so 86 percent and girls 100 percent of the time). In the same study, 'Aina Pumehana children sought help verbally only 19 percent of the time (boys did so 35 percent of the time and girls *never* did). The 'Aina Pumehana asked for help, but they did so nonverbally by, among other means, increasing eye contact with or standing near the helpgiver (Gallimore, Boggs, and Jordan, 1974, pp. 211, 215–216). While this example is drawn from the schoolroom instead of the workplace, it is instructive because of the extreme degree of cross-cultural variance in reliance on nonverbal behavior it illustrates (admittedly not all cross-cultural differences regarding this factor are so dramatic). The example is also useful to the international businessperson because the function the study tested (manner of help-seeking) is central to managerial communication in the workplace.

Information communicated nonverbally should indeed be viewed as subject to sociocultural differences. People from different cultures are likely to express themselves nonverbally in different ways. It is important, however, to note that one major exception exists in the area of facial expressions to show emotion (or affect display). Considerable research has been conducted (Ekman, Sorenson, and Friesen, 1969; Izard, 1971, 1980; Ekman, Friesen, et al., 1987; Shaver, Schwartz, Kirson, and O'Connor, 1987) that indicates high agreement across cultures in the display of specific emotions in facial expressions. Nevertheless, even regarding facial expression, as one expert observes, "although the expression and inner experiences that characterize the fundamental emotions are innate and universal, there are numerous cultural differences in attitudes toward the emotions and their expression" (Izard, 1980, p. 216). To a large extent the nonverbal message sent through facial expression is universal, but the degree to which individuals are taught to mask those facial expressions remains a cross-cultural variable. In other words, it is more permissible in some cultures to show emotion than in others. Moreover, while considerable accuracy in interpreting universal facial expressions exists across cultures, researchers have suggested that members of one culture may be better able to pick up messages signaled by facial expressions in some foreign societies than in others (Rosenthal, Hall, DiMatteo, Rogers, and Archer, 1979; Ekman, Friesen, et al., 1987). In short, the

> differences in accuracy . . . appear to be a function of cultural dissimilarity, that is, the most accurate judgments were made by respondents in cultures highly similar . . . and the least accurate judgments in cultures highly dissimilar. (Gudykunst and Ting-Toomey, 1988, pp. 385–386)

Consequently, nonverbal behavior, even in its most universal aspects, is very likely to be subject to misinterpretation across cultures.

Nonverbal behavior reflects the historical development of a nation in a manner parallel to the etymology of that culture's language. Historical differences across cultures, consequently, may result in marked contrasts not only in language but in nonverbal behavior as well. Mary Douglas, in several seminal works on the cross-cultural interpretation of nonverbal communication (1970, 1971, 1973) asserts that a person's body itself acts as an analog of his or her social system:

> The body, as a vehicle of communication, is misunderstood if it is treated as a signal-box, a static framework emitting and receiving strictly coded messages. The body communicates information for and from the social system in which it is a part. (Douglas, 1971, p. 387)

The interpretation of the messages implicit in nonverbal behavior grows even more problematic in cross-cultural situations, because the chances of misinterpretation increase when people from different societies attempt to communicate. A harmless or friendly gesture in one culture may be understood as threatening or antagonistic in another.

DEFINITION

Before going on, it is important to acknowledge that a great deal of debate has taken place regarding exactly what the term *nonverbal communication* means. The lack of agreement is due, in large part, to the close association of verbal and nonverbal communication. A nonword utterance, for example, is arguably nonverbal communication. Yet a nonword utterance used often enough in place of a word or as a modulator of a word becomes in time a sort of word and therefore a form of verbal communication. For instance, among the British upper classes, it is common to utter a throat-clearing noise to indicate hesitancy. If a throat-clearing noise accompanies an intemperate word, it serves to moderate what is said, much as the word *somewhat* might do. An educated Englishman might legitimately use a throat-clearing noise as a synonym for the word *somewhat* . . . in the phrase "the news could be viewed as *somewhat* damaging." The noise, filling in as it does for a word, begins to take on the attributes of verbal communication.

To the extent that the theoretical details of this debate, although important, remain only tangentially related to business communication, we can agree for our purposes to choose one of the many existing definitions as a starting point. Nonverbal communication expert Randall Harrison's (1974) definition seems sufficiently accurate. He defines nonverbal communication as "the exchange of information through nonlinguistic signs." In turn, Harrison defines *signs* as "a stimulus which, for some communicator, stands for something else"; *nonlinguistic* as "nonword signs"; and *exchange* as "more than one communicator linked in some way so that at least one of them can respond to the signs produced by the other" (p. 25).

Harrison's definition of *signs* eliminates stimuli that neither sender nor receiver perceive to communicate anything. His definition of *nonlinguistic* precludes nonauditory verbal communication such as sign language for the deaf. Finally, the definition of *exchange* includes only two-way linkage, which excludes, for example, gestures a sighted person might make in speaking to a blind person.

To Harrison's definition we must add a relevance to *business* to remain within the realm of international business communication. Narrowing the focus in this way eliminates several areas of nonverbal communication. For example, music and other fine arts represent a form of nonverbal communication. Most listeners can interpret the opening lines of Beethoven's Fifth Symphony as suggesting death, but the subject material and the way in which it is communicated is far removed, of course, from the world of business.

International nonverbal business communication, therefore, may be defined as the exchange among members of different nations of business-related information through nonlinguistic signs.

ACTIVE AND PASSIVE NONVERBAL COMMUNICATION

Generally speaking, nonverbal business communication may be divided into two categories, which we may term *active* and *passive*. Active nonverbal communication may be defined as nonverbal behavior the communicator can consciously modulate. For example, speakers who wave their arms a great deal in their home culture are capable of controlling or reducing such behavior when they enter a culture whose members gesture less frequently.

Passive nonverbal communication may be defined as nonverbal communication over which the sender has less control. For example, in one culture the color green may be viewed as very positive; in another culture, very negative; and in yet another, a patriotic symbol whose meaning depends on the individual's political sentiments. The nonverbal message communicated by the color green—in the form of a waving banner at a rally, for instance—is generally received passively. The choice of color may itself be a deliberate one; the cover of a stockholders' annual report say, falls to its designer's conscious selection and so is sender-generated. Still, passive nonverbal cues are more often receiver-generated. In other words, the message's receivers—rather than its senders—must adjust for cross-cultural differences in their interpretation of the unspoken messages.

For our purposes, active nonverbal communication falls into six main categories that are likely to be important in international business communication:

1. Kinesics, or movement
2. Appearance
3. Oculesics, or eye behavior
4. Haptics, tacesics, or touching behavior
5. Proxemics, or space usage
6. Paralanguage

Passive nonverbal communication, in turn, can be divided into four main groupings that tend to differ, in business communication, across cultures:

1. Color
2. Numerals and counting indicators
3. Nonkinesic emblems
4. Olfactory communication, or smell

KINESICS

Definition

In 1970, Julius Fast published a best-selling book called *Body Language*, which did much to advance public interest in how people communicate through movement. Social scientists collectively categorize all communicative body movements under the general rubric of *kinesics*. The term *kinesics* itself comes from the Greek word *kinein* ("to move"), and covers a broad range of nonverbal activity, including facial expressions, pacing and other leg movement, body posture and gestures of the hands, arms, head, and torso.

Forces Affecting Kinesics

Four major forces affect kinesic behavior: (1) personal idiosyncracies, (2) situational factors, (3) gender differences, and (4) cultural differences.

Personal idiosyncracies follow little pattern and are difficult to generalize. They range from consciously used but unique hand gestures to uncontrollable tics or twitches. Since personal idiosyncracies are by nature personal, they do not help the business communicator in any but the most specific cases.

Situational factors, such as timing or size, come to bear on the appropriateness of a gesture. For example, preachers addressing crowds in a stadium or large auditorium may raise their arms high over their head and hold up one finger, saying that there is but "one way to God." In the setting of a stadium, this otherwise dramatic motion would seem less extraordinary because the size of the audience would demand an exaggerated gesture for mere visibility's sake. A less grand gesture, such as holding up a finger in a small motion in front of the chest, would be lost on all but the front rows of the audience. The same low-key gesture at a small gathering of followers in an office would seem *situationally* more appropriate than shooting a hand over the head, which would, in that setting, seem overly dramatic.

Gender plays an enormous role in kinesics in two ways. First, researchers have indicated that men and women differ in the types of kinesics they use (Henley, 1977; Borisoff and Merrill, 1987). The psychologist Judith Hall (1984) suggests that these differences have developed because of one gender's (usually women's) subordinate position relative to the other in any given culture. Second, men and women appear to differ in their learned ability to interpret kinesics (Rosenthal et al., 1974; Henley, 1977; Rosenthal and DePaulo, 1979; Borisoff and Merrill, 1985; Borisoff and Victor, 1989).

The last element affecting kinesics is culture. Most kinesic behavior is learned. The specific types of body movement an individual grows to recognize as desirable are closely tied to the kinesic behavior of those around that individual — that is, members of his or her culture. The relative expansiveness, frequency, and speed of body movement, as well as specific gestures themselves, are often rooted in historical influences on a specific culture. Although culture is the most important area of concern here, the four factors do not occur in isolation. Cultures vary in the role that personal, situational, and gender differences play in acceptable kinesics.

Thus in a culture that condemns signs of nervousness, a personal idiosyncrasy such as a twitch will be more of an irritant than in a society less critical of nervousness. In a culture in which arm movement during communication is not common a preacher's sweeping gesture might be inappropriate in *all* situations, including a rally in a stadium. Finally, just as sex roles change from culture to culture, so do the gender-based restrictions each culture sets on its members. For example, in the United States it is customarily acceptable for a woman to sit either with her legs together or crossed, while a man can sit with his legs apart. Such kinesic behavior is culturally learned; in many Asian and European nations, sitting with the legs spread apart is often considered inappropriate for both men and women.

Unlike verbal communication, kinesics has no dictionary of meanings and must be carefully evaluated in each communication exchange. Still, individuals remain relatively straightforward in their kinesic messages (at least in comparison to their verbal communication) once the receiver of the message is made aware of them. And because cultures tend to emphasize certain kinesic behavior that is relatively distinctive, the influence of a culture is more far-reaching than the effects of personal idiosyncrasies, situational factors, and even gender. Cultural differences in kinesics may therefore be easier to learn and detect than other kinesic factors.

Kinesic Classifications

Paul Ekman and Wallace Friesen, in a series of seminal works (1969, 1972, 1974), have classified kinesics into five categories based on the purposes each body movement serves: (1) emblems, (2) illustrators, (3) affect displays, (4) regulators, and (5) adaptors. Each of these kinesic types are subject to change across culture.

Emblems   Emblems are nonverbal messages that have a direct verbal counterpart. They are usually deliberate signals used in place of a verbal message or accompanied by a verbal equivalent.

Perhaps more than any other kinesic classification, emblems are highly variable from one society to another. For example, the ring gesture is among the most common of all emblems (see Figure 7.1). Consisting of the thumb and forefinger touching, it is subject to a bevy of interpretations (Morris, Collett, Marsh, and O'Shaughnessy, 1979). In the United States and Canada, the gesture which indicates agreement or acceptance, represents the letters *OK* a common figure of speech for over a century (its origins are often attributed to the political campaign of President Martin Van Buren, whose nickname was Old Kinderhook). In Tunisia and several other nations, the same gesture is considered an insult, representing the number zero and implying that the person to whom it is shown is worth nothing in the sender's estimation. In yet another interpretation, the gesture may be seen — as it is in several Mediterranean countries — as obscene. The reading of the ring symbol as a body orifice has a lengthy tradition, dating back to ancient Greece.

Similarly, the tapping of the nose as a gesture is a widespread emblem with marked differences in interpretation. The gesture itself ranges from touching the side of the nose (Figure 7.2) to touching the tip of the nose (Figure 7.2b). Morris, Collett, Marsh, and O'Shaughnessy (1979) found six different meanings for the emblem in Europe alone, four of which were relatively common. The most frequent interpretation, suggesting complicity, appeared in south England, Scotland, northern Ireland, and Sardinia. A second meaning, common to south and central Italy but almost entirely unrecognized elsewhere in Europe, was as a warning for another person to be alert; whereas in Belgium and, on occasion, in parts of Scotland, the same gesture would indicate that the *speaker* was alert. Finally, an interpretation of the tapped nose gesture in Wales, although used to a lesser extent throughout Great Britain and Ireland, was that the receiver of the message was "nosey."

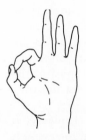

Figure 7.1 "OK" emblem.

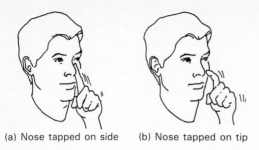

(a) Nose tapped on side   (b) Nose tapped on tip

Figure 7.2 Nose-tapping emblem. (a) Nose tapped on side. (b) Nose tapped on tip.

Emblems, as overt symbols, are relatively easy to detect. When a Tunisian expresses anger at an "OK" sign flashed by a Canadian counterpart, the misinterpretation can be identified without much trouble. Cross-cultural difficulties in the reading of emblems are, in this way, akin to the problems a speaker with limited fluency in a second language may have.

A misused emblem, if recognized as such, is little different from a misused word in a foreign language. For example, a North American in Greece might respond with either an indication of agreement or an obscenity to the question "What do you think of this?" The reaction of a North American with limited fluency in Greek who accidentally uses a verbal obscenity at a point in the conversation where it makes sense (although a different sense from the intended) is like a North American who flashes the ring emblem in Greece when either the meaning of "OK" or an obscenity would make sense. Cross-cultural differences in the understanding of emblems leads more often to embarrassment than to serious misunderstanding.

A dramatic misinterpretation of an emblem took place at the time of Nikita Khrushchev's visit to the United States during the height of the cold war. As the Soviet leader walked down the stairway of his airplane, he turned toward the reporters, film crews, and photographers awaiting him on the runway and, smiling, employed a common Russian kinesic emblem. He clasped his hands above him and deliberately shook them first over one shoulder, then over the other shoulder. The U.S. news media covered Khrushchev's gesture widely, and his clasped hands appeared as front-page material in newspapers and the lead story on television news broadcasts across the country. The reporters (and most of the people of the United States) had misinterpreted the Soviet leader's gesture.

In the United States, the kinesic emblem Khrushchev displayed is most commonly used by boxers and represents the emotion a boxer feels following a decisive victory. For most people in the United States, therefore, Khrushchev's clasped hands seemed to indicate a gloating confidence that the Soviet Union would be victorious over the United States. The Soviet leader, in turn, had no idea that his gesture had been so damagingly misinterpreted. He had intended the gesture to communicate its common Russian meaning of two people embracing each other in friendship. A similar gesture was visible to U.S. audiences decades later in the film of the 1987 Leningrad concert of the musician Billy Joel. As Joel sang, he faced a concert hall filled with Russians clasping their hands above them to communicate their appreciation of the diminishing hostility between United States and the Soviet Union that the concert symbolized.

Another difficulty in the use of emblems derives from cross-cultural prejudices — particularly among nations that border each other or have a history of rivalry. In such cases, the member of one culture may recognize and correctly interpret a foreign emblem but look down on it as representative of the other society:

> Sometimes two adjoining cultures develop a prejudice against one another's customs. If, for instance, there has been a long-standing rivalry between two neighbouring states or nations, the gestures of one may be shunned by the other. To adopt the foreign gesture would be disloyal, or would smack of affectation. Some Englishmen, asked if they ever kiss their fingertips, might reply that "only Continentals do that," for example. This is not a case of the Englishmen being ignorant of the gesture but rather that they consider it un-British and therefore to be avoided. (Morris, Collett, Marsh, and O'Shaughnessy, 1979, pp. 263–264)

Similarly, many people from the United States consider European gestures as being, in the words of one U.S. management writer, "too 'European,' effete, 'effeminate' in the pejorative sense, and un-American" because "our anti-aristocratic, democratic ideology pits us solidly against too much refinement" (Miller, 1987, p. 57).

Many gestures are directly tied to language. For example, the English expression *on the other hand* is often accompanied by the palm of the hand extended up to the side. The same concept exists among French speakers as *de l'autre côté* and among German speakers as *andererseits*, literally "on the other *side*." Their accompanying gesture, therefore, deals less with the *hand*, as it does among English speakers, than it does with the *side*.

Some languages (as we have seen in Chapter 2) have expressions with virtually no equivalent in another tongue. The accompanying kinesic emblems to such gestures, as a result, are even more far afield than the words. Thus in a negotiation between English and French speakers, an interpreter can readily translate the French expression *Ça t'a passé sous le nez*, as "You missed your opportunity." The interpreter would probably make little sense of the French speaker's emblem of passing the hand beneath his or her nose. This emblem, which to English speakers would seem bizarre, makes sense only in the context of the expression's French rendering, which literally means *That passed under your nose*.

The world is filled with differences in interpretations of emblems. Using the left hand in most Arab cultures is offensive. Sprawling or leaning back in a chair in the United States is a sign of feeling comfortable with others (rather than the more universal suggestion of disrespect). The relative deepness of bows in Japan reflects an elaborate system of interrelated messages.

The key point here is *not* to memorize a list of customs and taboos around the world. Such a list would reduce cross-cultural nonverbal communication to either a bewildering array of unintelligible practices or a collection of quaint "do's and dont's." Instead, international business communicators should be aware of different kinesic emblems in order to recognize them as they occur, expanding knowledge of them as one does the words in a language.

Illustrators   Illustrators consist of body movements that act in tandem with verbal communication to reinforce, describe or emphasize the speaker's message. Illustrators are considerably less deliberate than emblems, but they remain gestures of which the user is quite consciously aware.

Illustrators appear to be more universal than emblems, but it is important to note that, as Birdwhistell has indicated, "no gesture or body motion . . . has the same social meaning in all societies" (1970, p. 81). Thus most cultures have the illustrator of pointing, to accompany a verbal message that an object is "over there." The relative broadness of the gesture or the way in which the hand is held at the end of the arm (e.g., with one finger extended, two fingers extended, or the hand open) varies from culture to culture.

While the use of illustrators is fairly universal, the choice tends to be culturally unique. Genelle Morain (1987) conducted a study of old newsreels of a highly popular mayor of New York, Fiorello La Guardia. The son of an Italian-speaking father and a Yiddish-speaking mother brought up in the United States, Mayor La Guardia was perfectly fluent in the three languages most commonly spoken in the polyglot city during his administration in the 1930s and 1940s: English, Italian, and Yiddish. Morain showed the films with the soundtrack turned off and asked viewers to identify the language La Guardia was speaking. Native speakers of the three languages were able to identify the language he used based solely on the kinesics — primarily illustrators — he employed. His English gestures were relatively infrequent and small-scale; his Italian gestures were broad and symmetrical; and his Yiddish gestures were one-handed, choppy, and kept close to the body.

Affect Displays   Affect displays, Ekman and Friesen's third class of kinesic behavior, are nonverbal messages of the body and especially of the face that convey emotion (that is, affective states). Without uttering a word, people can communicate a wide variety of moods or feelings. Indeed, researchers have isolated ten major categories of facial affective displays: happiness, surprise, fear, anger, sadness, disgust, contempt, interest, bewilderment, and determination (Ekman, Friesen, and Ellsworth, 1972; Leathers, 1976). Moreover, the ability to recognize affect displays is among the earliest of all learned communication behaviors. Clinical studies have shown that infants are capable of distinguishing different affect displays in pictures by their sixth month (Charlesworth and Kreutzer, 1973; Stern, 1977).

Significantly, affect displays are remarkably universal. Studies of people from widely different cultures have demonstrated that individuals can consistently associate pictures of facial expressions with the corresponding emotion (Ekman, Friesen, and Ellsworth, 1972; Boucher and Carlson, 1980; Izard, 1980)

Yet while the principle affect displays are innate to human nature, considerable differences occur across cultures regarding the degree to which each society permits its members to display these emotions. Many southern European, Latin American, and Middle Eastern cultures, for example, allow considerably more affective display of emotion than do northern European, anglophone North American, or Pacific Rim nations.

Still, it is dangerous to generalize about people's expected affective displays according to their culture. The U.S. perception of Japanese control over emotional expression as somehow inscrutable or of the often satirized reserve of the British upper classes can serve as a communication barrier through stereotyping. Similarly, the U.S. perception of Italians and Brazilians as ebullient and hot-tempered, based on the comparatively greater degree of freedom their cultures afford them in affective displays, is equally misleading. Such superficial analysis does not allow the U.S. international businessperson to distinguish the Japanese, Briton, Italian, or Brazilian whose behavior truly is extraordinary. To assume that particular Italians are enthusiastic or excitable because they have been conditioned to let their emotions be expressed in affect displays prevents the observer from distinguishing them from any other Italian. The non-Italian businessperson cannot identify which Italians are reserved and which *are*, in fact, hot-tempered or extremely friendly.

The dangerous division of cultures into emotional and nonemotional categories misinterprets the degree to which a society permits its members to express emotion through affect displays *as* the emotion itself. Regardless of the degree to which emotion is allowed to show, the emotions most likely still exist. A Japanese businessman who is angry but does not display that anger kinesically is still angry. Although an Argentine businesswoman in the same situation would probably express through affective display her anger, her feelings are not necessarily more intense merely because she did not hide them. Such a comparison demonstrates only that it is culturally acceptable in Argentina to show anger through an affect display, whereas it is unacceptable in Japan to show anger through such an affect display. The emotion is universal; only its kinesic representation is culturally limited.

It is important to note that affect displays are often gender-linked.

According to Roy Birdwhistell (1970), such differences may have a biological basis. He suggests that socially learned gender differences in kinesic behavior evolved precisely because humans are—biologically speaking—weakly dimorphic (that is, human males and females do not differ anatomically as much as many other species). As a result, sexual characteristics are often learned social-behavioral patterns. Birdwhistell observes that in all the cultures he examined (Chinese, middle- and upper-class British, Kutenai, Shushwap, Hopi, Parisian French, and U.S.), both men and women distinguished not only male and female kinesic patterns but also effeminate male and masculine female patterns. He is careful to emphasize, however, that no kinesic behavior is innately masculine or feminine. The interpretation of any specific kinesic behavior is learned and, therefore, is culturally specific.

Kinesic behaviors that are most noticeably gender-linked are affect displays. For example, in the United States, men are taught that they must maintain more reserve than women. While it is generally unacceptable for a man or a woman to display sadness in any business situation in the United States, men encounter stronger disapproval for doing so. A businesswoman who cried in a confrontive situation would be considered unprofessional, but her inappropriate affect display might sometimes be forgiven as "feminine." If a man in the same situation cried, his behavior would generally be considered unforgivable. Conversely, a U.S. businessman who displayed anger might be condemned as overly assertive but forgiven as a male, whereas a U.S. businesswoman's show of anger in the same situation would be considered aggressive and too masculine. However, in at least one Middle Eastern nation, the emotions associated with men and with women are opposite those of men and women in the United States: "In Iran, men traditionally display emotions that Americans consider feminine. Men are acceptably emotional. . . . They weep easily and are given to impulsive behavior. Women, on the other hand, are expected to maintain control and remain practical" (Vargas, 1986, pp. 43–44).

Finally, stereotyping according to variations in the amount of affect display considered appropriate from culture to culture is dangerous because each culture differs in which emotions may and may not be expressed. A culture that permits its members to express one emotion freely may restrict affect displays for another emotion. For example, Brazilians are often noted by those from the United States as being—by comparison—emotional; yet as protocol expert Sandra Snowden observes, Brazilians generally make a strong effort to "hide their annoyance" (1986, p. 325). Brazilians' relatively greater use of affect display than their U.S. counterparts might cause the latter to generalize such expressiveness to include all emotions. As a result, U.S. businesspeople might overlook a Brazilian's annoyance because the kinesic expression of this emotion might be expressed more subtly than other emotions.

Still, the international business communicator should not ignore cultural differences in the acceptability of expressing emotions through affect display. The communicator who approaches the use of affect displays with an open mind may find that they provide a useful indicator of a culture's expectations toward the expression of particular emotions. More important, the communicator should be flexible in interpreting affect displays among those from other cultures. The displays themselves may be universal, but the learned response of accepting or rejecting their use is culturally bound.

Regulators   When people listen to someone speak to them, they respond with a broad range of nonverbal signals to indicate that they are paying attention. This nonverbal feedback serves to monitor and control what the speaker says to the listener; they enable the speaker to know, among other things, when a point needs to be clarified, when the listener would like to say something, and when the listener would like the speaker to continue. These cues are known as regulators.

Many regulators cross cultural boundaries, but frequently the finer points of their interpretation do not. For example, head nodding is widely recognized as a favorable regulator. (An exception to this is Bulgaria, where the gesture indicates negation.) Yet when Canadian listeners nod, they generally signal agreement; when Japanese listeners nod, they indicate only that they have understood. Thus Canadian executives conducting negotiations in Japan might be surprised to find their counterparts disagreeing with points to which the Japanese had seemingly nodded assent. If the Canadian speakers had interpreted the Japanese head-nodding as, instead, a positive regulator (that is, a regulator indicating that they should continue speaking), they would have been correct. Most regulators are similar enough to indicate to speakers across cultures whether to continue speaking or to allow the listener a turn in the conversation. Neither a Canadian nor a Japanese would interpret a head nod as a signal to *stop* speaking. What *is* most subject to change is the source of positive gesture (in this case, whether the head nod indicates agreement or merely comprehension).

The frequency and size of regulators are also subject to cross-cultural differences. One often-noted difference between subcultures in the United States relates to variations along racial lines in the use of regulators. While exceptions exist, research seems to indicate that many African Americans use more subtle regulators than Americans of European descent. Marjorie Fink Vargas notes that

> American students from black communities have frequently complained that white American teachers, counselors, and employers insult them by talking down to them. Harvard professor Frederick Erickson investigated the problem and offered this explanation: Because the black students do not give a speaker the same nonverbal feedback that white students do, white teachers think that they don't understand. While receiving instruction, a white student will nod emphatically and murmur "uh-huh." Blacks nod almost imperceptibly or say "mhm," seldom both. As a result of this difference in feedback, speakers from purely white American cultures tend to overexplain to blacks,

thereby insulting them by treating them as seeming incapable of understanding the first time. (1986, pp. 47–48)

Many regulators go beyond kinesics to include eye movement or brief verbal responses. These nonkinesic regulators are more likely to reflect cross-cultural differences. While eye contact is discussed in more detail below in the section on oculesics, the subject merits brief mention here, since some eye contact extends beyond the mere use of the eyes. For example, in most cultures, face-to-face head nodding and eye contact are the norm. In other cultures it is customary for the listener to look away from the speaker and to nod; the intention of the listener is to present his or her *ear* to the speaker, since the ear (and not the eye) is the logical sensory organ for receiving speech. Eye contact is therefore made peripherally. Members of cultures in which face-to-face eye contact and head nodding are customary are, in turn, likely to misinterpret the proffered ear of their listener—despite his or her accompanying head nods—as a kinesic regulator expressing disrespect or lack of interest.

Adaptors   Adaptors are the last category of kinesics Ekman and Friesen identified. Adaptors occur on a very low level of awareness and represent those kinesics people use to fill some personal need.

Some adaptors are employed to resolve a specific physical function. Scratching, and squirming in a seat, for example, are adaptors filling the personal need to stop an itch or to settle more comfortably in a chair. Other adaptors are used as a means of mental rather physical release. For example, chewing on a pencil is an outlet for intense concentration, and jiggling a knee up and down is an outlet for nervousness. In all cases, people develop adaptors early in life and remain relatively unaware of them. Thus, as Mark Knapp observes, "Adaptors are not intended for use in communication, but they may be triggered by verbal behavior in a given situation associated with conditions occurring when the adaptive habit was first learned" (1980, p. 9).

Much was made, in the popular psychology books of the early 1970s of reading people's secrets through understanding their adaptors. Thus books like Fast's *Body Language* (1970) and Nierenberg and Calero's *How to Read a Person Like a Book* (1971) claimed to allow people to have insight into others' thoughts through interpreting such adaptors as the way they crossed their legs or arms. To a large extent, this approach to adaptors is misleading and imparts to adaptors far more significance than they warrant. It is true that an individual exhibiting signs of nervousness through adaptors is likely to be nervous, but the variety of adaptors indicating nervousness are so numerous and overlap with so many adaptors used to satisfy other physical or mental needs that their value as an interpretive tool in business communication is virtually nil.

What does merit attention regarding adaptors in a discussion of international business communication is that an essentially meaningless adaptor in one culture can take on emblematic significance in another. We alluded to this earlier, pointing out that what serves as an emblem in one society may have no counterpart elsewhere. In the United States, showing the bottom of one's shoe may be an adaptor to make the sitter more comfortable, while in Indonesia the same gesture might be viewed as a deliberate emblem reflecting disrespect.

Certain emblems carry a meaning only in some countries and have no meaning in other cultures, where they may serve merely as adaptors. Thus a clear nonverbal message can be sent of which a receiver remains wholly ignorant. In particular, adaptors involving posture and arm position take on different meanings across cultures. The gesture of crossing one's arms in front of one's chest in the United States is essentially meaningless, although it may be an adaptor to offset a feeling of uneasiness or defensiveness. In Fiji, by contrast, the same motion is a distinct emblem indicating that the listener has respect for the speaker.

Similarly, some emblems are considered adaptors (or entirely inappropriate emblems) unless shared among those with whom one is close. Smiling, for instance, is often ignored as unintended unless it occurs among friends. This was evident when McDonald's opened its 3-story, 27-cash register, 900-seat restaurant in Moscow's Pushkin Square. While the 20,000 Soviet customers served broke McDonald's opening-day world record (Moskowitz, Levering, and Katz, 1990, p. 66), it was not the result of the nonverbal communication training McDonald's gave its Russian workers:

> Training employees hit a real glitch when they tried to teach them to smile at customers. The problem was resolved when the automatic social behavior was identified. "The Russians insisted they were a very friendly people; the problem was friendliness didn't include smiling at strangers. In Russia you only smile at people you know." (Decker, 1990, p. 23; internal quoted words are by Marija Dixon)

Sometimes adaptors that remain essentially meaningless in one culture can take on highly offensive emblematic significance. An example is the forearm jerk, a gesture in which one hand is placed in the crook of the other arm, which is then bent upward ending in a fist (see Figure 7.3).

Figure 7.3 Forearm jerk.

This gesture carries little meaning in English-speaking North America. The same gesture, however, is highly obscene in Italy (and is relatively common in several other nations). An Italian making this gesture to a North American communicates nothing, unless the North American is aware of the gesture through its context (and English-speaking North Americans belong to very low context cultures). Conversely, North Americans may at times make the gesture before resting their head on their fist and nodding, a movement that in both North America and Italy communicates pensiveness. To an Italian observer, reaching that pensive emblem by using an obscene gesture may seem an intentional show of contempt, tempered by the situation.

Such miscommunication can occur in domestic settings as well. For example, in the United States, a raised middle finger is equivalent to the Italian emblem described above. If, during a yawn, a U.S. speaker accidentally extends the middle finger, his or her U.S. audience might consider this movement intentional. No *initial* difference exists between the accidental nonverbal *domestic* exchange and the U.S.-Italian accidental nonverbal exchange. Instead, the difference is in the reaction that *follows* miscommunication. The U.S. speaker who accidentally communicates an obscene gesture to an Italian audience remains unaware of the source of the Italian reaction precisely because that source—the unshared emblem—is a mystery to the speaker. But the U.S. speaker who accidentally communicates an obscene gesture to a U.S. audience can trace the source of the misunderstanding.

While the strongest reaction to adaptors in cross-cultural business communication may result from the unrecognized imitation of foreign emblems considered obscene in other cultures, most misinterpreted adaptors are decidedly not obscene. Indeed, unintentional obscene emblems, because of their forcefulness, are likely to be the easiest to identify.

More insidious are adaptors that, while meaningless in one culture, convey an acceptable (or at least nonobscene) meaning elsewhere. For example, in most of the Arab world and such countries as Indonesia, (as noted earlier) showing the sole of one's foot is considered offensive, though not obscene. It is a sign of contempt or lack of respect.

This emblem, if used at all, is generally delivered subtly in a fashion that distinguishes it little from the European and American adaptor of crossing one's legs. Thus, a Belgian executive who crosses his or her legs in Saudi Arabia may unknowingly be expressing a lack of respect in a manner that is nonetheless quite understandable to the Saudi. The Saudi is unlikely to respond with a shock recognizable to the Belgian, as might be the case if the emblem were obscene or delivered in an unusual manner. Consequently, the Belgian will not only have unwittingly offended the Saudi, but will have no way of recognizing the source of the offense. The Saudi will judge the emblem by his own standards particularly if he had reason to believe that the Belgian had a fairly thorough understanding of

Saudi culture (e.g., if the Belgian spoke Arabic or had visited Saudi Arabia before).

Finally, adaptors that might be overlooked in one culture may be viewed as rude in others, even when they are still understood to be adaptors and not emblems. For instance, in many Western cultures, a jiggling leg is an adaptor, usually to relieve nervousness, and is often overlooked. In many Pacific Rim societies, most notably in Taiwan, the same jiggling leg, though still seen as an adaptor for nervousness, is not readily overlooked. Instead, it acts more as an affect display, since the expression of nervousness is generally less acceptable.

Raymond Gorden (1974) studied the reaction of Colombian host families and the U.S. foreign exchange students living in their homes. Gorden found notable opposition to the U.S. students based on the adaptors the exchange students used. They unknowingly sent nonverbal messages through their use of what to them were adaptors but to their hosts were overt nonverbal taboos. In particular, Gorden observed the strong irritation the Colombian hosts felt when the students placed their shod feet on furniture. The students, in turn, felt shocked at their hosts' reactions, often defending themselves by pointing out that they did not place their shoes on the furniture frequently or did so in their own rooms. This rift in perception is illuminating. A tendency exists among those whose adaptors are offensive to another culture (but not their own) to recognize but downplay the importance of the cross-cultural communication barrier. In the case of the U.S. students in Colombia, Gorden notes:

> They seemed to think it strange that the señora's reaction was out of proportion to the frequency with which they committed the act. The point that is missed is that, if a certain action is taboo, a person needs to do it only once (like standing on the altar of a church during communion) to be immediately put into a special category as a type of deviant who is capable of such an act. (1974, p. 130)

For the Colombians, the feet on the furniture represented such an act. The hosts did not interpret the posture as a harmless adaptor used as a means to stretch out and become more comfortable. Rather, they viewed the gesture as an indicator of disrespect, even though they did not associate it with an overt emblem. To the Colombians, "this act was clearly interpreted as an act to assert one's superiority" (p. 130).

APPEARANCE

An individual's general appearance is a strong nonverbal communicator both within a culture and across cultures. Numerous researchers have demonstrated that an individual's overall appearance in the workplace has an impact on how others evaluate that person's work-related behavior (Landy and Sigall, 1974; Cash, Gillen, and Burns, 1977; Shrout and Fiske, 1981; De Meuse, 1987).

Appearance can be divided into inherent biological differences (such as skin color) and acquired nonbiological differences (such as dress).

Biological Differences

Biologically, people do not look alike. They are subject to a host of differences. People differ in the color and the shape of their eyes. People vary in the color, amount, and texture of their body and facial hair. People vary in their relative stature and body structure.

None of these physical differences inherently communicates anything. Nevertheless, members of a given culture learn to value certain physical characteristics. Thus a culture that is homogeneous in physical traits may learn to view either unfavorably or favorably the physical characteristics of foreigners who differ physically from them. In cultures that are heterogeneous in physical attributes, people are generally taught to favor certain physical characteristics over others. For instance, empirical studies have demonstrated that the rating process in performance appraisals and other work-related evaluations is affected by rater stereotypes regarding a variety of immutable physical variables, including racial and ethnic group (Crooks, 1972; Huck and Bray, 1976; Schmitt and Lappin, 1980; Wendelken and Inn, 1981); gender (Rosen and Jerdee, 1973; Schmitt and Hill, 1977; Schneier and Beusse, 1980; Gupta, Beehr, and Jenkins, 1980); and age (Schwab and Heneman, 1978; Cleveland and Landy, 1983).

As discussed in Chapter 4, businesspeople conducting business in other cultures need not (and, on an ethical level, arguably ought not to) accept these cultural biases. Nevertheless, it would be foolhardy to ignore such differences. Businesspeople who, for example, are unaware of racial distinctions under the South African apartheid system are unlikely to conduct successful communication in that country. If, on the other hand, businesspeople are aware of the values attached to race in South Africa but choose to ignore those racially based distinctions, they are in a better position to face the opposition that their behavior will elicit than those who remain ignorant of those distinctions.

In any case, it is improbable that any one individual will change the values a culture places on biological differences. In effective international business communication, values placed on such factors as race can only be viewed as different, not inherently wrong. Only within the ethical framework of his or her own society can the international business communicator pass such judgment.

Dress and Adornment

Not all differences in appearance are biological, of course. Rather, people can alter their appearance by their selection of dress and adornment. The choices people make regarding how they clothe and groom themselves communicates powerfully on a nonverbal level. Moreover, several re-searchers have observed a direct correlation between an individual's mode of dress and the way in which others evaluate that individual in the workplace (Gibbons, 1969; Schneider, 1973; Rosenfeld and Plax, 1977; De Meuse, 1987).

In some cases, an individual's mode of dress can even be used to offset biological differences in appearance. Thus, the uniform worn by officers in the armed forces communicates something about the rank and relative power of the wearer, regardless of prejudice for or against the officers' race, gender, or other immutable physical characteristics. Although an officer's uniform is assigned, choices in mode of dress are often less straightforward and may be carefully chosen by the wearer. For example, when J. Walter Thompson, the U.S.-based advertising giant, first began placing women in major executive positions in the late 1920s and 1930s, "the more important women at JWT wore hats in the office, to distinguish themselves from unhatted secretaries and subordinates." (Fox, 1985, p. 289) In effect, the women at JWT used mode of dress to overcome sexist prejudices by creating a uniform of sorts. The hat of the female executives, in effect, communicated a difference in rank that required among others the suspension of socially acquired prejudices common at the time.

Many people believe that their manner of dress and adornment communicate a *personal* statement. The nature of that personal statement is shaped by the individual's relationship to his or her culture as a whole, but appearance and dress also convey an individual's group identity. The type of dress or the style of hair or beard an individual wears thus carries a series of messages regarding the particular community, class, nation, religion, or even political group to which that person belongs. Often the cultural differences in business dress are marked and convey a strong message. The Mobutu suit of Zaire and the Mao jacket and cap in the People's Republic of China represent not only cultural statements but overt messages regarding the politics of their wearers. Similarly, the *chadors* of many Muslim societies and the turbans of Indian Sikhs have both a cultural as well as a religious implication.

Each culture or subculture to which an individual belongs has its own conventions of dress. In Europe and the Americas, for example, a man wearing a formal dinner suit (tuxedo) makes an impression different from a counterpart in a three-piece suit and tie or in jeans and a T-shirt. Although certain situations demand specific styles of dress within a culture, the association of a given setting with a particular mode of dress is a learned cultural value and is not itself universal. For example, the distinctions among formal wear, business suits, and jeans are widespread across cultures. Thus, the American and European cultures who adhere to these classifications of dress have a perspective that — even if it does not unite them — at least separates them from cultures with different standards of attire. The very fact that such modes of dress are so prevalent, however, may easily lead to cultural ethnocentrism. The Tanzanian policy in the 1960s to force Masai males to wear trousers represented a kind of cultural imperialism. As Ali Mazrui notes, "The whole Tanzanian policy of seeking to 'civilize the Masai' by getting them to wear trousers seemed to be a direct attack on the most significant aspect of the cultural identity of the Masai" (1978, p. 203).

Despite the widespread adoption of Western business dress among cultures to whom it had previously been foreign, it is still dangerous to assume that the idea of differentiating cultures by the way they dress is antiquated. Distinctions in dress and appearances based on culture are numerous. Indeed, international communicators who assume that all business dress should match the conventional Western wardrobe make a serious error. For example, while most Saudis would generally consider Western attire to be acceptable for an American or a European conducting business in Saudi Arabia, it is not necessarily true that a Saudi businessman would wear such an outfit. He would be more likely to wear a *ghutra* (head cloth) and *thobe* (a traditional Arabic white, flowing robe). International communicators who view such modes of dress as unbusinesslike make a harmful ethnocentric assumption. First, if their disdain is expressed, they are likely to offend the Saudis to whom a *ghutra* and *thobe* are perfectly proper business attire. Second, they may be unable to distinguish the Saudi businessman who is appropriately dressed from one who is not.

Many messages regarding workplace dress are more subtle than that between a *thobe* and a three-piece wool suit. Although Saudis accept foreigners in Western business attire, they would find tight-fitting clothing or (especially for businesswomen) short sleeves offensive, even though such outfits are acceptable variations of Western business attire in Europe or the Americas. Such sensitivity remains an issue not only in the clothing one wears but in the advertising and other support material one brings to a presentation. For example, one international business adviser has recounted:

> "Beauty shots" of sexy models displaying your product can seriously offend the Arab sense of female propriety. . . . A Detroit auto maker found himself in trouble in Abu Dhabi when he presented ads featuring curvaceous women clad in outfits that, while acceptable by U.S. standards, outraged his Muslim customers. (Chesanow, 1985, p. 131).

Differences may also occur among cultures that share conventional standards of business dress. North and South Americans, have both adopted the Western suit as the wardrobe of the workplace. Yet Gorden (1974) found that Colombians were dismayed by the fact that U.S. males tended to polish their shoes less frequently than Colombian males. A Colombian might judge a U.S. male with unpolished shoes as slovenly; yet those who judged U.S. males by Colombian rather than U.S. standards would not be able to differentiate between the truly slovenly North

American and the well-groomed one who — reflecting his own cultural standard of dress — simply did not polish his shoes as often as Colombians do. In turn, the U.S. businessman in Bogotá would do well to polish his shoes to maintain a favorable impression in Colombian society. Thus, even among those cultures that share the same choices of clothing, the way in which they handle and wear their clothing differs according to cultural values.

It is possible to argue that attention to such minute details of appearance are trivial. Still, foreign business communicators are at a disadvantage when their domestic counterparts can read the nonverbal messages based on appearance and they cannot. The mode of dress is a form of language that communicates clearly to those who have learned it. Indeed, the French semiotician Roland Barthes, in his seminal study *Système de la mode* (1967), equates the type of dress or costume with language. Equated with speech is *clothing*, or the way in which garments are worn (choice and relative size, coordination of pieces, cleanliness and length of wear, personal quirks). *Costume*, or the language of dress, is dictated by broad cultural values, while clothing — the way in which that dress is worn — is determined by the individual application of those values.

Appearance and mode of dress, as we have already indicated, serve to indicate group identity. In relatively homogeneous cultures, clothing is arguably also fairly homogeneous. This makes learning the language of dress easier for the foreigner entering a homogeneous society than for the foreigner entering a heterogeneous society. The more subgroups to which a member of a culture may belong, the more modes of appearance and dress its members are likely to adopt. This is particularly evident in such culturally diverse nations as India, Israel, and the United States. The U.S. semiotician Jack Solomon describes the effect of such diversity on wardrobe in the United States:

> The complexity of the dress code in America, the astonishing range of styles that are available to us in our choice of clothing signs, directly reflects the cultural diversity of our country. Americans are differentiated by ethnic, regional, religious, and racial differences that are all expressed in the clothing they wear. Age differences, political differences, class differences and differences in personal tastes further divide us into finer and finer subcultures that maintain, and even assert, their sense of distinct identity through their characteristic clothing. From the severe black suits of the Amish to the safety-pinned T-shirts and chains of punk culture, Americans tell one another who they are through the articles of their dress. (1988, p. 170)

The Dress for Success Wardrobe

Even among culturally diverse nations such as the United States, a substantial degree of conformity to the standard business mode of dress exists. Throughout the late 1970s and the 1980s, the global business community directed considerable attention toward wardrobe engineering, clearly manifested in a host of books and articles that focused on wardrobe not as a fashion statement but as a means of nonverbal business communication. We might label the attire promoted by the wardrobe engineers as the dress for success wardrobe, after the most popular of these works, John T. Molloy's *Dress for Success* (1975) and *The Woman's Dress for Success Book* (1977).

Molloy asserted that certain colors and styles of dress convey messages of power and success to others in the workplace. He based his advice on a number of studies of people's reactions to identical presentations delivered in different outfits. Audiences responded most receptively to presentations in which the presenters wore certain types of outfits. Molloy's message, echoed by dozens of authors after him, was clear: the ambitious businessperson should dress for success according to Molloy's advice.

The suggestions Molloy and other wardrobe engineers made are remarkably widespread across cultures. This has less to do with the innate universality of the mode of dress described as with economic power of the West. As Ali Mazrui notes:

> Perhaps the most successful cultural bequest from the West to the rest of the world has in fact been precisely Western dress. Mankind is getting rapidly homogenized by the sheer acquisition of the Western shirt and the Western trousers. The Japanese businessman, the Arab minister, the Indian lawyer, the African civil servant have all found a common denominator in the Western suit. (1978, p. 202)

Nevertheless, the advice of Molloy and his colleagues exhibits a strong cultural bias. While it is true that the dress for success wardrobe has gained global acceptance, Molloy and others claim that certain styles of appearance (dark wool suits, short hair) impress others in the workplace. These wardrobe advisors popularized the intended message of the outfits they recommend. They do not, however, explain why such dress is accepted as such.

Solomon (1988) suggests that the dress for success wardrobe dates back to the Puritan tradition in America and England and the belief in a severe dress code. With the rise of Oliver Cromwell's heirs in Britain and their Puritan descendants in North America, a strict dress code, according to Solomon, became emblematic of a bourgeois mentality. The code grew in acceptance as bourgeois elements in Britain gained power in the eighteenth and nineteenth centuries and as the Northern puritan tradition in America prevailed after the fall of the aristocratic Confederacy.

The wardrobe, in turn, became a symbol of success because of the political and religiosocial dominance of the Protestant work ethic, as communicated by those who wore such clothing; nothing in the wardrobe is any more natural or proper than any other sort of outfit. Indeed, the Puritans and Cromwellians, Solomon notes, adopted the wardrobe at least in part to separate themselves from the colorful dress, long hair, and luxurious fabrics of the royalty and the Cavalier tradition of the English aristocracy. The ascendancy of U.S. and British economic and political power in the last two centuries has, in turn, done much to disseminate this style of dress throughout cultures for whom it carries no traditional value at all. Its use merely reflects, as does the widespread use of English as a universal language for business (see Chapter 2), the dominance of British and U.S. political and economic power. Nothing about the dress for success wardrobe is innately universal or innately businesslike.

OCULESICS

Oculesics is the term used to describe the way in which people use their eyes in a communication exchange. Often such behavior is referred to as *eye contact*, which popularly refers to a mutual interlocking of eyes.

Most researchers, however, reject the term *eye contact* as too limiting. Eye behavior extends beyond simply looking into another person's eyes. When people look at one another, they look at the entire face, an act social scientists refer to as *mutual gaze*.

Yet eye behavior extends even beyond mutual gaze. A person still communicates through eye behavior — for example, when he or she decides not to look at another individual's face. Similarly, when an individual looks at another's body (for example, at someone's legs), a message is communicated that does not include mutual gaze. Even when, as is customary in many cultures, one stares at the floor or ceiling when riding an elevator rather than looking at the other passengers, a message is sent. Finally, the kinesic activity associated with eye behavior (e.g., squinting, winking, fluttering eyelids, eyebrow movement) affects how others understand eye behavior, regardless of any mutual gaze. The term inclusive of such activities for this broad sense of communicative eye behavior is *oculesics*.

Oculesics are, regardless of culture, among the most powerful of all nonverbal communicators, probably because eye behavior is the first learned mode of two-way communication. During the first three months of life, infants can see only about eight inches; this distance, researchers have shown positions an infant's eyes exactly eight inches from its mother's eyes when she is breastfeeding or when she holds the baby in the most frequently used bottle-feeding positions (Robson, 1967; Stern, 1977). Moreover, mothers spend about 70 percent of the time during feeding directly gazing into their child's eyes (Stern, 1977). Since feeding in this position is the primary waking activity among infants regardless of culture,

> the arrangement of anatomy, normal positioning and visual competence dictated by natural design all point to the mother's face as an initial focal point of importance for the infant's early construction of his salient visual world, and a starting point for the formation of his early human relatedness. (Stern, 1977, p. 36)

Oculesic interaction is the first true form of communication infants develop. People in all cultures are inherently longest-practiced and best-versed in oculesics among all forms of communication. Children, regardless of culture, learn to engage an adult's attention oculesically long before they learn to speak.

Cross-Cultural Differences in Oculesics

Despite the universal early *learning* of oculesics as a means of communication, the *way* in which oculesics are used varies from culture to culture. Variations in the sort of oculesics used can lead to dangerous assumptions. An individual may interpret a foreigner's oculesics as either too direct or not direct enough according to that individual's own (rather than the foreigner's) cultural expectations. That people expect others — whether from a different culture or the same culture — to behave alike oculesically was indicated in a survey of North Americans' perception of categories of intercultural communication, conducted by Judith Martin and Mitchell Hammer (1989). Martin and Hammer found that respondents selected direct eye contact and attentive listening as the most frequently mentioned (and, therefore, arguably the most important) nonverbal behaviors for both speaker and listener, regardless of whether the interaction was an American–American, American–Japanese, or American–German exchange.

While the frequency with which Martin and Hammer's respondents cited eye behavior as key to intercultural communication reflects the importance of oculesics, the fact that the North Americans surveyed specified *direct eye contact* as the *type* of oculesics illustrates the difficulty likely to arise in cross-cultural interactions. Direct eye contact, the dominant form of oculesics in the United States to indicate listening (the other most frequently cited behavior among Martin and Hammer's survey), is *not* a universally acceptable indicator of listening. Whereas the untrained communicator from the United States or Canada might make direct eye contact to indicate attentiveness, a foreign counterpart could easily interpret such direct eye contact in a different way.

For example, the North Americans Martin and Hammer surveyed indicated that they would engage in direct eye contact when speaking to Japanese and that they would expect the Japanese to do so as well. The Japanese, however, would probably respond unfavorably to direct eye contact and would (without cross-cultural training) be even less likely to use the kind of direct eye contact the North Americans expected. Indeed, as Edward Hall and Mildred Reed Hall have observed, the Japanese "are made uncomfortable by Americans who look at them directly; they choose to look down or at the corner of the room" (1987, p. 122).

In several Asian cultures, direct eye contact is seen as insulting. Cambodians believe that directly meeting the gaze of another person is "something akin to invading one's privacy" (Dodd, 1982, p. 265). If the North

American respondents in Martin and Hammer's survey behaved in such nations according to their assumptions about oculesics, they would have inadvertently sent a nonverbal message exactly opposite what they had intended.

Moreover, the degree of appropriate mutual gaze is only weakly defined by the word *direct*. The respondents who emphasized the need for direct eye contact may well find that their perception of *direct* differs from what other cultures consider a forthright gaze. Most U.S. listeners, for example, are taught to shift their gaze occasionally (e.g., by nodding). By contrast, says J. Vernon Jensen, "the educated Briton considers it a part of good listening to stare at his conversationalist and to indicate his understanding by blinking his eyes, whereas we Americans nod our head or emit some sort of grunt, and are taught from childhood not to stare at people" (1982, p. 265). Similarly, Edward Hall notes that, in most cases, "Arabs look each other in the eye when talking with an intensity that makes Americans highly uncomfortable" (1966, p. 151). The question then arises as to how direct is direct eye contact and to what extent other oculesic activities play a role in mutual gaze.

Cultural variations in oculesics are not limited to international settings. For example, differences among ethnic groups within such polyglot countries as the United States may create difficulties in communication. Many minority groups are unaccustomed to the direct mutual gaze characteristic of mainstream U.S. social interaction. James Doyle, assistant superintendent of the Troy School District in Michigan, related the following incident illustrating cultural differences between the Native Americans and non-Native Americans in his school:

> I made a major cultural error. While disciplining an American Indian student for skipping school, he took his eyes off me and put his head down. I said, "When I'm talking to you, pick up your head and look me straight in the eye."
>
> Later, from the father, I discovered it was a sign of respect when an American Indian responds by lowering his eyes. It meant he was accepting this responsibility in this situation. When I forced him to look me in the eye, it went against his cultural and historical customs.
>
> I created a situation of confusion and probably hostility (1989, p. 17).

Frequently, direct eye contact as an acceptable form of oculesic communication is linked to attitudes regarding age or rank. In many societies, it is appropriate only among those equal in rank and age, a situation that is a relative rarity in the workplace. The role of age and status is evident (although with some exceptions) in much of sub-Saharan Africa, Spain, and Latin America (Burgoon and Saine, 1978; Vargas, 1986). Studies have shown that in the United States, however, direct eye contact as an acceptable form of oculesic has less to do with age or rank (Ellsworth and Ludwig, 1972; Beebe, 1974) than with a person's sense of credibility and belonging.

Gender and Intercultural Differences in Oculesics

In many cultures, gender plays a role in the nature of oculesics. Studies in the United States, for example, have found that women spend as much as 15 percent more time gazing at their partners (Exline, 1963; Vargas, 1986) but that women are considerably less likely than men to sustain direct eye contact (Henley, 1977; Borisoff and Merrill, 1987). Such sex-linked distinctions in oculesics may be universal; however, the degree of distinction is culture-specific. For instance, while a Norwegian woman may make less direct eye contact and more indirect oculesic contact with her male counterpart, she probably makes more direct eye contact with men than the typical U.S. woman does. This was illustrated in the comments of the linguist and former U.S. senator S. I. Hayakawa:

> In American cities if you look at a girl whom you do not know, she promptly averts her eyes. It was both a surprise and a pleasure to me, when I visited Norway, to find that when I looked at a pretty girl in the street, she would look right back — not provocatively or impudently, but simply in curiosity, like a child. (1979, p. 76)

Hayakawa's anecdote is instructive for five reasons. First, his comments demonstrate the difference between Norwegian and U.S. standards of direct eye contact. Second, his observations reflect how oculesics nonverbally reinforces sexism (the only "girls" he looks at are "pretty"; their return eye contact is to him "a pleasure"). Third, the passage indicates the greater degree of freedom men in his culture are allowed in staring at women than vice versa, since he implies that a U.S. woman staring back at him directly would do so "provocatively or impudently." Fourth, Hayakawa seems to have misinterpreted the oculesic message of the Norwegian recipients of his staring. To him, their direct gaze made them seem to him curious, "like a child." This interpretation reflects a sexual stereotyping, reinforced by U.S. culture, that women are more innocent than men and thus more childlike. It is unlikely, for example, that the former senator would have interpreted the oculesic message he received from "a pretty girl" in the same way if the stare had been delivered by an ugly man. In other words, he read into the oculesic exchange the sexual overtones that would have been present in such an incident in the United States but were probably absent in Norway. Finally, it is worthwhile to note that the entire exchange between Senator Hayakawa and the Norwegian women on the street occurred solely through oculesics.

Because Hayakawa presumably found the direct gaze of the Norwegian women to be flattering, it did not present a significant cross-cultural stumbling block for him. Indeed, he indicated that the cross-cultural oculesic difference was pleasurable. Quite the opposite cross-cultural effect, however, remains possible. For instance, French and Italian men tend to look more prolongedly at women than U.S. men do. Their stares are often unsettling to U.S. women who interpret such oculesics by U.S. standards. As Marjorie Fink Vargas notes:

When American women visit Italy or France, they are sometimes upset by the way men look at them. Instead of taking them in with a glance the way American men do, Italians and Frenchmen look for embarrassingly long periods of time, examining their body inch by inch. French and Italian girls, accustomed to such looks, must think American men are extremely cold. (1986, p. 63)

HAPTICS

Haptics is the way in which people communicate through their touching behavior. Handshaking, backslapping, kissing, and hugging are all types of haptics that are common in the workplace in some cultures but uncommon in others.

To some extent, all cultures communicate through touching behavior. The frequency of haptic exchanges and the amount of physical contact customary, however, is subject to great variability. Dean Barnlund observes in his analysis of U.S. and Japanese communication styles that "there is a wide discrepancy in the extent of physical contact preferred by Japanese and Americans during conversation. Americans reported two to three times greater physical contact with parents and twice greater contact with friends than the Japanese" (1989, p. 35). This contrast is even more illuminating when we consider that, in the United States, touching behavior in public is generally less common than in most other cultures. Another important point in Barnlund's contrast of U.S. and Japanese haptics is that physical contact in either culture increased with familiarity or intimacy. "Japanese and Americans both," he notes, "were more physically demonstrative with people they felt close to than those they felt to be more distant psychologically" (p. 34).

With the exception of hostile haptic behavior (i.e., punching or kicking), people in all cultures touch to increase the degree of intimacy. Five major types of haptics have been identified, each representing progressively greater degrees of intimacy (Heslin, 1974):

1. functional/professional
2. social/polite
3. friendship/warmth
4. love/intimacy
5. sexual arousal

For all practical purposes, only the first three categories are relevant to *business* communication.

The boundaries between each category even within the same culture are somewhat blurred so that it is often difficult to determine when touching has, for example, increased from merely polite haptics to the level of friendship. It may prove useful to examine the handshake, a relatively widespread haptic exchange. Canada is used as the example culture because Canadians tend to shake at the midrange grip and number of pumps among common handshaking behavior.

It is customary for Canadian businesspeople to shake hands when meeting. Such an interaction would normally represent a first-level (functional/professional) or a second-level (social/polite) haptic exchange. A Canadian businessperson who refused to shake a colleagues' hand would be considered impolite. The nature of the handshake, however, varies widely within the three categories. A brief and perfunctory, level-one handshake (hardly a handshake at all) would be interpreted as nearer a nonhaptic interaction and—though not rude—would suggest a lack of warmth. Most Canadian businesspeople would shake firmly and for several pumps of the hand; in other words, the handshake would be a second-level interchange, indicating neither unreceptivity nor receptivity. As the conventional haptic response, its use would be neutral. An extended and firm handshake, in turn, would exceed the expected response, pushing the handshake near or into the third level (friendship/warmth). Most Canadian businesspeople would expect such an extended handshake only from close associates and would interpret it as a sign of receptivity.

The difficulty in the use of haptics occurs when people from different cultures apply different standards to distinguish between levels of familiarity. For example, Japanese are considerably less haptic than Canadians; it is not customary for Japanese in Japan to shake hands at all. As a result, Japanese in Canada—while they are likely to know that they should shake hands—may be inexperienced in determining exactly how much pressure to exert and how long to extend their handshakes. They may shake their Canadian counterparts' hands too weakly or for too short a period. Such a "failed" attempt at a standard handshake would unintentionally convey the same message as a Canadian's perfunctory handshake; it would be interpreted as unreceptive. The message a Canadian would intend a handshake to send would, in turn, be lost on the Japanese. A short or a long handshake would be the same to the Japanese, who would—unless trained to recognize such haptic signals—interpret any type of handshake as a Canadian custom that probably is somewhat unpleasant for the typically less demonstrative Japanese.

Differences occur, as well, even when both parties *are* familiar with handshaking but have learned to shake hands with different degrees of intensity. For example, handshaking is common in both Spain and Canada, yet because members of these two cultures shake hands with different degrees of intensity, each party would interpret the other's handshake differently.

Spanish businesspeople customarily shake hands both with more firmness and for a longer time than their Canadian counterparts. The Spaniard in Canada might, without foreknowledge of Canadian behavior, interpret a Canadian's neutral, level-two handshake as a level-one, perfunctory gesture. The Spaniard would justifiably construe the Canadian's comparatively milder grasp as a sign of unreceptivity and coldness. To the Canadian, in turn, the Spaniard's level-two handshake would have the firmness and warmth of a level-three handshake.

Moreover, when Spaniards *do* wish to indicate a receptive, friendly, or warm (level-three) handshake, they clasp the forearm of the other party's shaking hand, forming a double handshake. Since such haptic behavior is virtually nonexistent in Canada, the untrained Canadian experiencing a true level-three handshake from a Spaniard would probably grow extremely uncomfortable. The Spaniard would have exceeded what is allowable in Canada as businesslike haptic behavior, extending into the realm of a level-four exchange reserved for love or intimacy. This is not because Canadian lovers shake hands in the Spanish level-three fashion. They do not; indeed, this sort of double handshake is more or less unknown in Canada. Rather, it is that, in Canada, the touching of any part of the arm is considered intrusive, except in a level-four relationship. Businesspeople in Canada simply never touch each other on the arm above the hand; Spanish businesspeople who are on particularly good terms do.

The example used here is not limited only to handshaking or only to Canada. The continuum it illustrates suggests the way in which cross-cultural differences in haptics can create barriers to effective international business communication. The example could apply to any haptic behavior, from backslapping to embracing, that is common to any given culture's business communication.

PROXEMICS

Proxemics refers to the way in which people structure the space around them. We have already discussed the proxemics of environment in Chapter 3. The relative size of offices, use of doors or walls for privacy, and distance between desks in shared rooms are examples of environmental proxemics in the workplace. What most concerns us here is the use of proxemics among people in interpersonal communication exchanges.

"Spatial changes," Edward Hall notes, "give a tone to communication, accent it, and at times even override the spoken word" (1959, p. 160). All people maintain a sphere of space around them for comfort. If another person intrudes into that space, the individual feels that the other person is invading his or her space and is too close. Depending on the context of the intrusion, the intruder may be thought of as overly aggressive or overly intimate. The usual response to such a situation is an almost instinctive retreat to the acceptable distance. By contrast, if someone engaging in conversation stands considerably outside an individual's sphere of space, the individual is likely to feel that the other person is too far away. Such a person is often viewed as overly formal. The physical distance may, in fact, be attributed to personality traits, described in such telling figures of speech as *stand-offishness* or being *too distant*.

In interpersonal communication, how distant is *too* distant and how near is *too* near is almost universal *among members of the same cultures.* The exact converse is also true. The distance considered acceptable in interpersonal communication is rarely the same from one culture to the next. For example, Copeland and Griggs have observed that "[North] Americans are most comfortable when standing a little over an arm's length apart" (1985, p. 17). By contrast, people from most Latin American, Middle Eastern, and southern European countries prefer to stand considerably closer. Similarly, several other cultures, most notably the Japanese, prefer to stand somewhat farther apart.

It should be noted that the categorization by culture is broad here. Robert Shuter (1976) found considerable difference in the comfortable speaking distance observed among people in Latin America. People in Costa Rica "interact significantly closer than do individuals from the two Latino cultures [Panama and Colombia] to the south" (p. 50). Thus it is somewhat misleading to characterize all three cultures as "Latin American" in proxemics. Nonetheless, individuals in those three nations — as Latin American in proxemic behavior despite their disparity — would, when speaking to one another, stand closer together than most people in the United States and Canada.

Proxemics have a strong parallel to haptics. Like haptics, the use of proxemics reflects degrees of intimacy. Just as Heslin (1974) divided touching behavior into predictable categories of progressively more intimate behavior, a decrease in the space between individuals has been demonstrated to indicate a parallel increase in their intimacy.

Edward Hall (1966) categorized the use of personal space around the body into four proxemic divisions, each representing progressively weaker degrees of intimacy:

1. intimate
2. casual-personal
3. social-consultative
4. public

Intimate space is reserved for those with whom one has the closest relationships, while an individual's casual-personal space is ordinarily approached only by friends and relatives. The social-consultative space is the proxemic distance most likely to be encountered in the workplace; it represents the sphere of surrounding space in which the individual feels comfortable among mild acquaintances or strangers. Finally, public space is usually limited in the workplace to public speaking or oral presentations. Of these four categories, only the first would be totally unacceptable in a normal business exchange. However, as with Heslin's categories of haptic acceptability, the boundaries of these categories shift from culture to culture.

To illustrate this point, we can examine the social-consultative (i.e., the standard business conversational) distance in Vermont, as a contrast to other cultures. Vermont was selected not because the United States is midrange in proxemics (it is, in fact, proxemically a bit more distant than most cultures) but because it was against the northeastern United States that Hall measured his proxemic categories.

In a typical conversation between two Vermont businesspeople who were not well acquainted, the social-consultative distance would be between 4 and 12 feet. In a conversation between a Vermont and a Qatari businessperson, however, the Qatari would likely feel that a distance of 4 to 12 feet represented public space. The Qatari, in fact, would probably move at least into the Vermonter's casual-personal area (between 1½ to 4 feet) and even into what would be considered intimate space in Vermont (about 1½ feet).

In such a situation, the usual reaction would be for the Vermonter to back up a step or two to reenter the social-consultative space acceptable in Vermont. The Qatari would interpret this as a sign of rejection, because the Vermonter would, in the Qatari's interpretation, be maintaining a purposefully public distance. In an attempt to clear up the apparent confusion in the desired level of friendliness, the Qatari would probably again move closer. If the pattern continued, the U.S. businessperson would again step backward, and the process would be repeated until the Vermonter had literally been backed up against the wall.

The reverse situation would be likely to occur in an interaction between a Japanese and a Vermonter. The space customary between two Japanese speakers would seem too distant in a U.S.–Japanese exchange. A particularly friendly U.S. businessperson might attempt to move closer to demonstrate his or her friendliness and enter what in the United States would be the casual-personal space, reserved for friends. Because that space represents the Japanese intimate space, the Japanese would back away, just as the Vermonter did when talking to the Qatari.

PARALANGUAGE

Paralanguage represents all sounds that people produce with their voices that are not words. Among the first researchers to study paralanguage closely was George Trager (1958). Although Trager examined numerous aspects of paralanguage, he divided it into the three broad categories: *voice quality*, *vocalization*, and *vocal qualifiers*. These three classifications remain the fundamental building blocks of paralanguage research.

Voice Quality

Voice quality comprises such factors as pitch, resonance, pace, articulation and enunciation, and rhythm control. Although it is possible to modulate voice quality to mimic another's voice, the voice quality of any individual is distinctive.

Certain types of voice quality carry culturally ingrained stereotypes.

Thus in the United States, a woman with a high-pitched, strident voice may be judged as discontent, while a woman with a low-pitched, breathy voice may be judged as sexy. Neither assessment may be accurate, yet communicators have been taught to make such associations. As misleading as such associations are in domestic exchanges, they may prove especially dangerous in international business communication because no evidence exists to indicate that they are universal.

Some aspects of voice quality interpretation, however, are both accurate and fairly universal. In particular, several researchers have demonstrated that listeners can interpret honesty, emotional state, rank, and general attitudes based primarily on voice quality (Kramer, 1963; Davitz, 1964; Addington, 1968; Williams, 1970; Zuckerman et al., 1982). Evidence also exists indicating that culture does not provide an impediment to the interpretation of such attributes. Beier and Zautra (1972), for example, found that subjects in Poland, Japan, and the United States were equally accurate in identifying the vocal communication of emotions through voice quality.

Vocalization

The other primary category of paralanguage is vocalization, nonword noise that accompanies speech. Vocalization includes vocal segregates (tongue-clicking, *um*'s, sniffs, *harrumphs*, and similar noises) and vocal characteristics (sounds associated with such behavior as giggling, moaning, yelling, snickering, whining, crying, and groaning).

Vocalizations are fairly universal. When exceptions occur, they tend to be minor and readily interpreted across cultures. Thus, U.S. business communicators may punctuate their speech with *uh*'s, the French with *eh*'s, and the upper-class British with *er*'s, but all three are of similar vocal duration, placement, and use and consequently can be easily understood across cultures.

Vocalizations, however, do represent a potential communication barrier in international business, because cultures differ in the degree to which they consider the use of vocalizations acceptable. While the interpretation of vocalizations is relatively clear from one nation to another, their use and misuse are subject to cultural norms regarding the expression of the emotions they communicate.

Vocal Qualifiers

Vocal qualifiers represent the range of attributes regarding relative volume (soft to loud), pitch height (low to high), and extent (word elongation or clipping). George Trager (who identified these categories) actually included vocal qualifiers as a subset of vocalizations. For our purposes, however, it is more useful to place vocal qualifiers in their own category, since they are much more subject to cross-cultural differences than are other vocalizations.

Each language has its own acceptable ranges of vocal qualifiers. Moreover, many cultures that speak the same language differ in the range of acceptable vocal qualifiers, and such variations can represent substantial sources of miscommunication. For example, as one observer has noted, "loudness in the Arab world conveys a message of strength and sincerity" (Vargas, 1986, p. 68). That same degree of loudness might strike a businessperson from the United States as irritating or aggressive. In turn, the standard decibel level of most U.S. speech is considerably higher than in most north European societies. Thus U.S. businesspeople may find that their normal level of speech is as annoying to a Norwegian as the normal range of speech for a Saudi is to them. Moreover, a Saudi businessperson addressing superiors customarily lowers the voice as a sign of respect, but when U.S. businesspeople lower their voices, the act may communicate a variety of messages ranging from calm strength to uncertainty. Respect and humility would rarely be among the suggestions the U.S. businessperson lowering the voice would have intended to convey.

PASSIVE NONVERBAL COMMUNICATION

Near the opening of this chapter, we indicated that nonverbal communication could be divided into two types: active and passive. To this point, we have described active nonverbal communication (nonverbal behavior for which the speaker is more or less directly the cause). While kinesics, oculesics, haptics, and the other nonverbal communication practices we have discussed represent the primary focus of most nonverbal communication studies, they are not the only nonverbal messages that have an influence in business.

Passive communication, the perception of signs submerged in the environment, has three defining features. First, it is not specifically interpersonal; second, it is ubiquitous (everything communicates some message); third, and in part related to its ubiquity, it is perceived in a manner of which the receiver is only partially aware or even entirely ignorant. We will examine the first two of these topics in detail.

Suprapersonality

Passive nonverbal communication is not interpersonal; rather, it is *suprapersonal* and is essentially unaffected by the interpersonal aspects of a communication exchange. In other words, passive nonverbal communication influences the reception of messages independent of any action that the sender of a message performs. Because of this, it plays a much greater role in written communication than does active nonverbal communication, which is more prominent in spoken exchange.

Instead, while the perception of passive nonverbal communication may influence interpersonal exchanges, that influence is only secondary.

A person is most apt to respond to the passive nonverbal communication in the environment when no one else is present, and even when (in a natural setting) no other person has had an influence. When passive nonverbal communication surfaces in an interpersonal exchange, the message conveyed goes beyond the people involved. The process is unlike the active nonverbal communication we have described, in which each person's actions—ranging from handshaking to eye movement—idiosyncratically emphasize his or her individual communication style.

Ubiquity

Passive nonverbal clues are everywhere. That all things convey some sort of message is the premise of the science called *semiotics*. Semiotics was developed in the first two decades of the twentieth century by two men independently (both of whose works were published in full only posthumously): the Swiss psycholinguist Ferdinand de Saussure (1915, 1983) and the U.S. logician Charles Sanders Peirce (1931–1966). Saussure and Peirce asserted that all objects act as signs, which correspond not to the object itself but to a network of culturally learned concepts. Thus, when we classify a green bean and a yellow squash as different because of their colors, we categorize them according to our concept of color. It is a learned attribute that yellow and green *are* separate colors, rather than merely different shades of the same color. After all, in the spectrum of visible light, yellow and green run together as neighboring parts of a continuum.

Four Major Elements of Passive Nonverbal Communication

Passive nonverbal communication might include any number of elements. For our purposes, we shall examine (because of their frequency in business communication) only four of these elements:

1. color
2. numerals and counting indicators
3. nonkinesic emblems or symbols
4. olfactory messages or smell

Color   In the years following World War II and well into the 1960s, the Swiss psychologist Max Lüscher published a series of groundbreaking works (1948, 1949, 1955, 1959, 1961) on his research into the use of color as a diagnostic tool in psychoanalysis. Lüscher demonstrated through a series of stringent clinical tests that an individual's psychological makeup could be assessed at least in part through that person's preference for and rejection of specific colors. He tested people's reactions to 73 specific colors and later developed a "Quick Test" of less exactness using shades of eight colors: gray, dark blue, green, red-orange, yellow, violet, brown (a darkened yellow-red), and black. Lüscher found a great deal of similarity among the Europeans he tested regarding the correlation of color preference with predictable psychological behavior. For example, he determined that most subjects found dark-blue calming, which he attributed to associations with nighttime and sleep.

Lüscher made commercially important observations as well, noting that blue was more often associated with sweetness, while green was generally associated with astringency. On the basis of these findings, he suggested that manufacturers of sweeteners should avoid green packaging and might profit by adopting blue packages. Many European and U.S. manufacturers successfully followed Lüscher's advice in determining questions of color in painting work environments as well as in marketing and packaging products. Consultants used Lüscher's color test to screen job applicants for companies. In the late 1950s a series of books popularized the principles of color research and consumer preference, applying the studies of Lüscher and others to the U.S. market (Cheskin, 1957; Packard, 1957; Ketcham, 1958). These works shared the results of studies of consumer preference for packaging colors of products ranging from detergents to coffee, tobacco, and beans. Chief among the successes cited was General Mills' adoption of bright red for its Betty Crocker line of cake mixes, a move that was shown to have quadrupled sales in just two years (Cheskin, 1957). Lüscher himself acted as a color consultant for pharmaceutical companies, automobile makers, advertising firms, architects, and flooring manufacturers.

Yet for all the success of the Lüscher color test in business application among various European countries, little work has been conducted to validate Lüscher's test for non-Europeans or Americans of European origin. Indeed, at least one study using the Lüscher color test to assess reintegration difficulties of Europeans returning from developing nations (Klar, 1968) did not fully consider the possibility that immersion in non-European societies might have modified standard cultural attachments to specific colors.

Despite the lack of formal testing, considerable evidence exists that color preferences and rejections are not universal. First, several early researchers (Heider, 1932; Duncker, 1939; Bruner, 1973) indicate that perception of color is linked to expectation of color. Thus Duncker (1939) found that a green felt leaf shown in a red light was more often guessed as being green than was a green felt donkey held in the same light. As many as 50 percent of the subjects — depending on the color and the object involved (Bruner, 1973) — undergo a compromise reaction (guessing the wrong color of an item on the basis of expectation). Since compromise reactions are primarily the result of guesses according to what one has learned within one's culture, the perception of culture itself is, arguably, culturally linked.

Color symbolism is also highly subject to cultural variation. Lüscher argues that dark blue is associated with nighttime and sleep, universal experiences for all societies. Yet for the Hopis of the U.S. Southwest, the dark blue of corn has a religious significance and serves, as well, as one of the four Hopi directional colors. These associations are lost outside the Hopi community.

One not need refer to so small a group as the Hopis to recognize international differences in the perceptual associations of colors. Since 1971, following the passage in the United States of the Occupational Safety and Health Act (OSHA), blue has been legislated to symbolize equipment for preventing and reducing hazards. Similarly, OSHA has made widespread, in the United States, the association of yellow with physical danger and the need for caution. A cautionary meaning attached to yellow—though probably based on the color's ease of visibility—is not without precedent in Europe, where yellow was used, in the Middle Ages, to mark off heretics and the quarantine victims of the plague, and which has several modern parallels in the twentieth century. Still, this interpretation of yellow was not dominant in the United States until the OSHA rulings.

By contrast, throughout much of Europe, Canada, Australia, and New Zealand, yellow carries (as it did in the United States before the OSHA rulings) more positive associations. This accords with Lüscher's findings regarding perceptions of yellow, which he links to associations with sunshine, the aspirational halo around the Holy Grail, and, thus, happiness. Indeed, the art historian George Ferguson, in his comprehensive *Signs and Symbols in Christian Art* (1954, rev. ed. 1976), while acknowledging yellow's negative meanings, records that in the traditional symbology used in European paintings, "yellow is the emblem of the sun, and of divinity. . . . St. Peter wears a yellow mantle because yellow is the symbol of revealed truth" (p. 153). It is for this reason that the papal flag is yellow and white. Yellow communicates a more positive feeling in packaging, advertising, and the work environment in most other Western countries than in the United States.

Yet people in the United States, whose majority culture has deep European roots, are primarily subject to most of the findings of Lüscher and his followers. To a large extent, U.S. color perception is derived from European values and traditions. This is much less the case in non-Western cultures.

The annals of international business are filled with costly errors based on presumed similarities in color preferences. For example, the U.S. and European association of black with death is not universal. Such symbolism has its origins in the Old Testament (Job 30:30) and the Church's use of black as a liturgical color for death and mourning. Connotations for white —the liturgical color for purity, faith, virginity, and innocence—also have direct biblical origins (Psalms 51:7, Matthew 17:2, Matthew 28:3). Its use in the predominately Christian West has therefore come to be associated with the purity of such products as soap and detergent, as well as with the innocence and virginity of bridal wear.

By contrast, in countries outside the Judeo-Christian tradition, such associations are wholly absent. Indeed, in Japan and many Asian countries, white is the symbol of mourning. Black, on the other hand, has few negative connotations and is more commonly associated with high technology products (the origin, ironically, may have been Henry Ford's restriction of all Model T automobiles to black).

As we noted, yellow is an upbeat and positive color, according to Lüscher; this finding has been reinforced by the successful use of yellow in U.S. and European advertising. Yet, as Neil Chesanow has discussed regarding China, yellow, as "the color of emperors, won't be well-received in the now Communist People's Republic" (1985, p. 223). In Europe and the Middle East, by contrast, purple is the color of royalty. The tradition has its origins in ancient Phoenicia, where purple dye, rare in nature, was extracted from the shell of the Mediterranean murex to color the clothes of the wealthy. When the murex was nearly made extinct, its value as a dye increased to the point that only royalty could afford (or in many cases even legally be allowed) to wear purple. China, culturally isolated from this tradition, developed entirely different associations with purple, which to them "denotes a barbarian" (Chesanow, p. 223).

Other symbolic uses of color are more directly tied to political history. Many nations, for example, are associated with a specific color. Green has come to represent Ireland throughout that country and in Great Britain, as well as in nations with large Irish immigrant populations such as the United States, Canada, and Australia. Elsewhere, however, green may suggest quite different images. Cultural disparities in a color's symbolism may have direct relevance to business communication. David Ricks recounts that

> at least two different firms encountered problems in their Hong Kong marketing efforts when they decided to use green hats in commercials. One company attempted to sell its beer using the message that the beer was so good that even the Irish like it. The Irishman, of course, wore a green hat while drinking his beer. The other firm marketed cleaning agents and in its commercial featured individuals tossing hats at a male model. A green hat eventually landed on the man. In both cases, the color chosen was not appropriate; the green hat is a Chinese symbol used to identify a man as a cuckold. Understandably, both products were avoided. (1983, p. 68)

Similarly, in China, Burma, (Myanmar) and other Asian countries occupied by Japan in World War II, the use of red, particularly in the form of a circle, still carries connotations of the Rising Sun and Japanese military aggression. This symbol is well recognized not only by those countries formerly occupied but by Japan itself. This association, however, is almost entirely absent in Europe and the Americas, where a red circle has been used successfully in advertising.

Some color associations reflect differences in behavior. For example, in the United States people are expected to want *white* teeth, while in much of Southeast Asia, *black* teeth represent status, denoting that one is wealthy enough to be able to chew betel nuts leisurely (betel nuts are almost unknown in the United States). Ricks describes how significant this difference in preferred dental color was for one U.S. toothpaste manufacturer:

> Pepsodent reportedly tried to sell its toothpaste in regions of Southeast Asia through a promotion which stressed that the toothpaste helped enhance white teeth. In this area, where some local people deliberately chewed betel nut to achieve the social prestige of darkly stained teeth, such an ad was understandably less than effective. The slogan "wonder where the yellow went" was also viewed by many as a racial slur. (1983, p. 65)

It would be impossible here to list all the colors and their symbolic messages from culture to culture. However, the sensitive businessperson should be aware of the possibility of such associations.

Numerals and Counting Indicators   Counting is universal to all cultures. The number systems used are not, although the Arabic, or Western, system of enumeration is understood almost everywhere in international business. Arabic numerals are arguably the closest we come to a universal system of communication.

Ironically, the system of enumeration known as the Arabic is not (and has never been) in any easily recognizable form widely used in Arabic-speaking countries, except in formal documents. The numerals we call Arabic actually come from India, where they were developed by Hindu traders around 300 B.C. These Hindu traders, in turn, brought their enumeration system to the Arab world, from where it was brought to Europe. With the collapse of the Roman Empire — and with it the abandonment of Roman numerals in commerce — the system of numbers shared among Hindu and Arab traders was extended to Europe. Since the system reached Europe via the Middle East and North Africa, Europeans called it Arabic.

The nearly universal use of Arabic numerals, however, does not extend to all aspects of enumeration — especially in the case of the decimal notation. For example, in the United States and Canada, it is customary to divide the fractional portion of a decimal from the whole number with a period, while thousands are separated from hundreds by a comma. Thus four thousand, three hundred eleven, and fifty-two hundredths would be expressed as *4,311.52*. In European decimal notation, the use of comma and period is precisely the reverse of the North American notation practice: commas separate decimal fractions from whole numbers, while periods separate thousands from hundreds. The European rendering of the same number would be *4.311,52*.

Similar differences exist regarding the way people express numbers by counting on their fingers. For example, in the United States and many other countries, people customarily begin counting with their index finger and proceed to their middle finger, ring finger, pinky, and conclude on their thumb (see Figure 7.4a). By contrast, in other countries—most notably in northern Europe—people begin counting on their thumb, moving to their index finger, their middle finger, and so forth (see Figure 7.4b). This distinction can pose some minor difficulties of which the businessperson abroad should be aware.

For example, a Michiganian who, in speaking, employed a kinesic emblem emphasizing the number 2 would hold up what would appear to be a *V* symbol to his or her European counterparts. Since *V* itself has many meanings varying from culture to culture, the European audience might read the gesture as signifying something other than the number 2. Moreover, differences in counting on the fingers carry over into verbal messages describing the nonverbal behavior. Thus a set of directions accompanying a product in the United States might indicate holding a wire between the *first* (index) and *second* (middle) fingers. The same set of directions would not be acceptable if the product were exported from the United States to the German market. In Germany, the *first* and *second* fingers would refer to the thumb and index finger; the intended message would be to hold the wire between the second and third fingers.

A more important caveat regarding numbers, however, rests less in their expression than in the symbolism people of different cultures attach to specific numerals. Such associations are distinctly *not* universal. Like colors, numbers often carry symbolic overtones that vary from culture to culture. While this point need not concern businesspeople excessively, the careful negotiator should be aware of the more important symbolic connotations that might represent an extreme rejection or attachment to a given number.

For example, in most Christian countries the number *13* has strong negative associations. While the dislike for *13* has its origins in the 13 attendants at the Last Supper, most Europeans, Americans, and Australians do not make this link so obviously; for them, the number is merely unlucky. The distaste for *13* is so intense that some people actually fear the number. This phobia is widespread enough that architects often skip

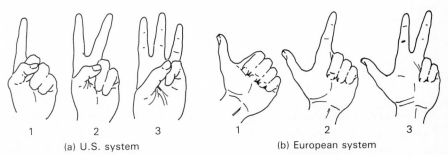

| 1 | 2 | 3 | 1 | 2 | 3 |

(a) U.S. system   (b) European system

Figure 7.4 Counting to three on the hand. (a) U.S. system. (b) European system.

the thirteenth floor of an office building or hotel, going straight from 12 to 14.

The aversion to *13*, however, is by no means universal. In most non-Western cultures, the number is symbolically meaningless and has interest if at all as an oddity to point out regarding Europeans, Americans, and Australians. Indeed, since the Jewish Talmud teaches that God has 13 attributes, Jews in non-Christian countries may even consider the number to convey a positive message.

Nonkinesic Emblems or Symbols   All cultures use symbols. *Symbols* may be defined as emblems, tokens, signs, or even musical passages that represent some otherwise unrelated item (often a concept or abstract idea). What the symbols represent varies a great deal. We have already discussed two subsets of symbols: the culturally learned associations people have toward both colors and numbers. Even clothes and other aspects of appearance act as symbols. Other symbols range from flags to figures.

The symbol itself has its own intrinsic meaning as well as its symbolic connotation. Thus the hammer superimposed on a sickle is simultaneously a set of work tools and a concrete representation of the Soviet Union.

Some symbols may be inherently universal. The German ethnologist Adolph Bastian first brought this position into prominence in the mid-nineteenth century in his theory of elementary ideas. Influenced by Bastian, other major theorists, most notably the psychologist Carl Jung and the anthropologist Bronislaw Malinowski, have carried this belief into other fields, pointing toward the striking similarity of certain archetypal elements in myths, beliefs, religions, cultural traits, and folklore. A circle, for example, has been shown to represent unity and wholeness in such diverse cultures as the ancient Aztecs, early Christians, Tibetan Buddhists, and modern Native American rites.

Our interest, however, is less with the archetypical symbol than with those symbols intentionally created to be universally recognized. The international businessperson is likely to be less affected by the symbolic importance of a circle representing unity than by the recognition value of a specific type of circle.

Thus a circle with a diagonal line through it is a universal symbol of negation. If such a symbol encloses a picture of a burning cigarette, the international businessperson (and everybody else) should be able to determine that it is the universal symbol for "No smoking." Such symbols are important in international business, where linguistic barriers preclude verbal descriptions.

Such universal symbols as the "No smoking" sign, although they are important in conducting international business, carry little emotional importance. Ignorance of the universal "No smoking" symbol may lead to damaged goods or an unexpected sounding of a smoke detecting alarm, but are unlikely to create cross-cultural barriers to communication. This, however, is distinctly not the case with all universal symbols. Many arouse intense emotional responses.

For example, a red circle centered on a green background is the officially recognized symbol for Bangladesh. It identifies ships and embassies anywhere in the world as being Bangladeshi, and no other nation— by international agreement—can adopt as its own the red circle on a green background. As with most universal symbols (the archetypical symbols identified by Bastian and Jung excepted), symbols are more important to those whom they most affect. Thus a Bangladeshi is more likely to feel strongly about the Bangladeshi flag than would, say, a Canadian. The difficulty the international businessperson encounters is in giving appropriate respect to such a universal symbol or even—in many cases—in recognizing it.

A Bangladeshi businessman in Canada may feel affronted when his hosts fail to recognize the Bangladeshi flag. Considering the relative economic importance of Canada in proportion to Bangladesh, he is likely to feel that Canadians who do not recognize the Bangladeshi flag feel that Bangladesh is unimportant and by extension that they think *he* is unimportant. This situation is worsened when the Bangladeshi himself *is* aware of the red maple leaf and other symbols of Canada.

The degree of affront is likely to increase with the importance a culture places on its symbols. In the situation just described, the Bangladeshi may with reason consider the Canadians in question arrogant, but he may rationalize the lack of recognition in Canada of his nation's symbols precisely because Bangladesh does *not* conduct a large amount of trade with Canada. Similarly, he may realize that, because his country is relatively new, its flag may not yet be as well known as a nation of its importance merits.

This would not be the case were the Canadians unable to recognize the French tricolor. A French businessperson would be less likely to indulge in such rationalizations. Indeed, the reaction to the offense might be just the opposite, since the French businessperson would consider France (whether correctly or not) to be more important both in commerce and in world affairs than Canada. At the very least, the French businessperson would expect such recognition based on the fact that France *is* among the leading trading powers and has strong ties to Canada. In such a case, failure to recognize the flag might be interpreted by the French businessperson as a sign of the Canadians' stupidity rather than of Canadian arrogance.

Such offenses may derive not from lack of recognition of symbols but from ignorance of the role they play in a culture. An advertiser who is aware of the importance of holy symbols in most Muslim countries may, out of recognition, attempt to incorporate these symbols in promotional material, only to find that the use of Islamic symbols in advertising is either prohibited or considered disrespectful. One famous example of the use of nationalistic emblems in a promotional campaign ended disastrously:

> Dow Breweries introduced a new beer, Kebec, in 1963. To highlight the French-Canadian national overtones for the beer, an advertising campaign

was especially planned for such emphasis. But in its broad and liberal use of French-Canadian symbols, certain nationalistic emblems were inappropriately included. Loud protests from the public denouncing the company's "profane" use of sacred symbols forced Dow to withdraw the campaign within fifteen days. The error was unintentional, yet the drastic consumer reaction proved very costly to Dow. (Ricks, Fu, and Arpan, 1974, p. 15)

Other symbols intended to be universal are neither as neutral as the "No smoking" sign nor as emotion-laden as a national flag. Most corporate logos fall into this category. Thus recognizing the stylized tortoise-shell logo of Kikkoman (actually the Japanese character *man*—meaning 10,000 years—placed inside a hexagon) is likely to please Kikkoman employees with whom one conducts business. Not recognizing this well-known corporate logo may not win favor with these people but probably will not evoke the sort of intense reaction that not identifying a national symbol might.

Not all symbols are intended to be universal. Symbols of many fraternal organizations, for example, are deliberately kept secret from outsiders. Recognition of the symbol, in turn, indicates a group member and may lead to preferential treatment.

Some symbols, such as those with religious or political meaning, may be viewed with differing intensity. Difficulties in international business are likely to occur in two ways. First, people from homogeneous cultures may not be sensitive to the fact that others may find such symbols offensive. Second, people from cultures highly tolerant of others may not anticipate intolerance among members of cultures less accepting of societal differences. Thus, a Christian businessperson wearing a cross on a chain may well go unnoticed in a primarily Christian country, such as Portugal, or in a country relatively tolerant of religious differences, such as India. The cross worn in many North African and Middle Eastern countries, however, is less likely to go unnoticed. Instead, as one international business advisor warns, wearing a cross "will cause offense and in some countries it's against the law to wear Western religious objects" (Chesanow, 1985, p. 127).

Olfactory Messages, or Smells   In the Americas, northern Europe, Japan, Australia, and New Zealand, smell is not considered a major source of messages in business communication. These nations may be called nonolfactory cultures. The absence of olfactory messages is very much expected in nonolfactory cultures. The presence of natural odors on one's breath, under one's arms, or in any other way associated with the body is considered offensive. The negative message communicated through body odor can be so intrusive that it may interrupt communication altogether.

Such an aversion to natural body smells is not universal. Many cultures do not mask odors but instead interpret their presence as olfactory messages. We may call these olfactory cultures. For instance, most Arabic societies, as Edward Hall (1966) observes, recognize that natural body smells may be positive: "By stressing olfaction, Arabs do not try to elimi-nate all the body's odors, only to enhance them and use them in building human relationships" (p. 160). Such smells communicate emotions rang-ing from fear and tension to relaxed friendliness. Many African and south-ern European cultures similarly recognize olfactory messages.

In the nonolfactory cultures, while people are aware of the role of body odors as an indicator of distress or other emotions, they are cultur-ally taught to eliminate or mask these odors. People use deodorants, mouth washes, and other products expressly to neutralize any olfactory message. To the extent that ignoring these messages prevents them from receiving information about the emotional state of those with whom they communicate, they are at a disadvantage when dealing with members of cultures in which interpreting olfactory messages is commonplace.

More problematic, however, is the cultural attitude toward masking or not masking body odors. Aversion to body odors in nonolfactory cul-tures, as mentioned earlier, is very marked, and the desensitization to olfactory messages results in a tendency to look with dismay on those who do not mask body odors. The objects of the disdain, however, may be entirely unaware of the response they have aroused among members of nonolfactory cultures.

This potential cross-cultural communication barrier is compounded as olfactory cultures recognize body odors as something positive or at least as generally inoffensive and perfectly natural. Indeed, masking body odors may have negative implications as effete or even dishonest. On the other hand, since the aversion among members of nonolfactory cultures may be so powerful that they may break off communication, it may represent a major impediment in international business communication.

ACCOMMODATING INTERCULTURAL DIFFERENCES IN NONVERBAL BEHAVIOR

As with other cross-cultural matters discussed in this book, awareness of differences in nonverbal communication will aid the international busi-nessperson. While first-hand observation is the best way to acquire this awareness, personal experience need not be the only means to do so. Indeed, those who wait until a business meeting abroad to familiarize themselves with foreign nonverbal communication practices may feel so uncomfortable or may make so many faux pas that by the time they acquire the necessary awareness, they may have seriously undermined their business relationship with their foreign counterparts.

One of the richest sources of information on other cultures' nonverbal communication behavior is as close as the local videotape store or movie theater. In our increasingly integrated world economy, motion pictures from a wide range of cultures are becoming more easily available. The same is true, though possibly with less variety of cultures, for television shows. Even when films are not readily available where you live, you can import films and television shows from most European countries, the United States, Canada, Australia, Japan, India, Taiwan, the Middle East, and, increasingly, many South American and African countries. Viewing foreign films and television shows—even if you do not speak the language—can familiarize you with the kinesics, oculesics, haptics, and other nonverbal communication behavior of a culture. Once you are abroad, it is advisable when possible to request a television in your room for the same reason.

Illustrated news and business magazines are another source of information on nonverbal business communication. By studying photographs (including advertisements) of prominent business and political figures, you can assemble a composite picture of how members of a culture expect businesspeople to dress or how closely to each other they are expected to stand.

Government protocol guides, etiquette books for natives, and business handbooks for foreigners may also prove useful if you do not follow them too strictly. Even foreign novels and nonfiction accounts that describe nonverbal behavior, though often misleading or exaggerated for dramatic effect, may provide some clues for a visitor.

Finally, interacting with those from the culture in question in advance of your own business trip is always advisable. Whether as a tourist or in meetings with foreigners who are visiting or living in your own country, it is useful to interact with others in a situation less pressured than a business encounter, so that you have the luxury to observe and to make mistakes.

Few intercultural differences are as difficult to accommodate as those that are nonverbal in nature. So much of our nonverbal behavior is patterned at so early an age—well before the acquisition of verbal skills—that a great deal of our nonverbal behavior takes place without our full awareness. Simply being aware of differences may not be enough to offset the discomfort or irritation that stems from misunderstanding nonverbal clues (nonverbal symbols that have close verbal equivalents such as the interpretation of symbols or kinesic emblems may be less troublesome). Thus it is not easy to interpret as friendly someone who stands farther away from us in talking than we expect or who shakes our hand too weakly. It is difficult not to make eye contact with someone whom in our own culture we would normally look straight in the eye.

It is even harder to handle invasive behavior. Most people find it extremely distressing not to step back when a person moves to a point we have learned is too close to us. Many people from less haptic cultures find it nearly impossible not to cringe when someone shakes their hand or accompanies the shake with an unexpected clasp of the upper arm. It is hard to avoid feeling offended when a subordinate looks us steadily in the eye when we have been raised to associate eye contact with signs of respect.

Because of this, the most important advice with which to arm yourself when going abroad to conduct business is to remain flexible. It may take years to adjust your own nonverbal behavior to that of the members of another country. As with many persons' experiences in acquiring second languages, it may be that you never fully come to use or even recognize all the subtle nuances of the silent language of foreign nonverbal communication. Still, you can remain open to accept differences. It may be best, at first, not to trust your initial reactions abroad to nonverbal cues; they *are* often incorrect. Close observation and flexibility in your own nonverbal communicative behavior, however, will go a long way to mitigating the barriers such cross-cultural differences present.

Chapter
8

Issues of Temporal Conception in International Business Communication

TIME AS A MEDIUM OF COMMUNICATION

The perception of the way time is used is a medium of communication. "The value of an activity," Leonard Doob (1971) explains, "is positively correlated with its temporal priority, the objective time devoted to it, and the frequency with which its duration is judged" (p. 63). The use and perception of time, in accordance with Doob's three areas, represent a means to convey specific information.

Doob's first area, the temporal priority one sets (that is, in what chronological order one undertakes a series of tasks) communicates how important a task is in business situations. For instance, if a manager enters her office and finds two memoranda both marked URGENT waiting for her on the desk, she must decide on which of the two pressing situations she must respond to first. All other factors being equal, the choice she makes tells all affected parties which situation she considers more important. In other words, she assigns a temporal priority to one memorandum over the other.

Doob's second area, the relative time assigned to an activity, also communicates information. This applies to both social communication (whether a telephone conversation is, in view of one or both parties, too long or short for a friendly call) and business communication (whether it is too long or short for a business call confirming an afternoon meeting). Similarly, how much time an individual develops to prepare for a business meeting, how long a company allows an advertising campaign to continue, and how much time is allocated to a host of other projects all indicate the relative importance assigned to the activity compared with other activities.

Finally, Doob's third area, how frequently one passes judgment on time, communicates a message. In Doob's words:

> The frequency with which temporal judgment is passed also provides a clue to the value of an activity. . . . When the activity considered significant is the passing of time itself—the "time-is-money" approach under special circumstances—then temporal judgments must be frequently made; otherwise the precious commodity might be wasted or improperly allocated. (1971, pp. 64–65)

The application of Doob's principle is common in many business interactions. For example, accountants who are paid by the hour are advised to refrain from constantly glancing at their wristwatches. On the other hand, it is understandable that their clients—those who are *paying* for the time—do frequently look at the clock.

THE RELATIVIST PERCEPTION OF TIME

Time is among the most indefinable of concepts. Philosophers from Augustine and the Platonists, in the fifth century A.D., to Ludwig Wittgenstein, in the twentieth, have grappled with the nature and meaning of time.

Indeed, considerable debate exists even regarding the ability to measure time *as* a physical reality. The way in which scientists understand physical reality—time included—has been revolutionized in our own era. The belief in the constant nature of time has been thrown aside in favor of a notion of time as governed by general relativity and the uncertainty principle, concepts that Werner Heisenberg, Max Planck, Kurt Godel, Hermann Minkowski, and Albert Einstein developed in varying degrees early in this century and that the British physicist Stephen Hawkings (1988) popularized in the late 1980s.

The perception among physical scientists of the general relativity of time has been mirrored in the last quarter-century in the work of several major social scientists who have developed a time-geographic model of time (Hägerstrand, 1970, 1972; Bullock, Dickens, Shapcott, and Steadman, 1974; Ellegard, Hägerstrand, and Lenntorp, 1977; Shapcott and Steadman, 1978; Winston, 1982). This model, often called the Lund Approach (after Lund University in Sweden, where Hägerstrand developed it), measures *social* (rather than the physical) variability of time. Time as measured in physics, therefore, represents only one dimension of the understanding of time in general.

INDIVIDUAL RELATIVITY OF TIME

The importance of the Lund Approach in organizational behavior in general and business communication in particular is that the time-geographic model of time recognizes the *individual* nature of time. Just as the theories of general relativity and the uncertainty principle in physics, in the late twentieth century, have pointed toward an understanding of physical as well as relative time, Hägerstrand and other theorists using the Lund Approach in the social sciences have demonstrated that the social conception of time is equally unfixed. Using the Lund Approach, it is possible to formulate the individual's temporal constraints in the physical terms of "location in space, areal extension, and duration in time" (Hägerstrand, 1970, p. 11) to predict likely patterns of organizational behavior.

Temporal conception, at least in the field of business communication, therefore, is just as important as any physical definition of time. *Temporal conception* may be defined as the way in which individuals understand and use time. While people can measure time with at least reasonable objectivity using, for example, a clock or a calendar, the relationship between time as physically measured and time as perceived by the individual varies.

Nevertheless, the Lund Approach deals almost entirely with the perception of time in terms of the relationship between the physical time of the material environment (i.e., clock or calendar time) and the use of time by individuals (i.e., scheduling and time-space relationships). The time-geographic conception of the Lund Approach, in short, leaves out the important aspect of time as a *culturally* variable entity. Rose (1977) queries: "In brief, the question is, will the time-geographic model provide us with a credible isomorph of human experience of time?" (p. 43). The implied answer to Rose's question is *no,* precisely because the human experience of time is affected by the *individual* experiences of any given man or woman. As the Australian theorists Parkes and Thrift have observed:

> Too often in human geography, space-time behaviour has been studied only in terms of the interaction between the material environment (world one) and the subjective environment (world two). An intermediary is needed—a third world which mediates between world one and world two. This is the world of objective knowledge, a cultural product. (1980, pp. 231–132)

In other words, to the extent that certain biological conditions universally affect all people, certain aspects of the subjective environment of the individual (world two) can be predicted according to material records of physical time (world one). Yet, as we will discuss later, to the extent that the subjective perception of time is *culturally* derived, the perception of physical time as a factor in the individual's subjective environment is itself a culturally changing variable.

Much of the variance between physical and perceived time is individual in origin. According to Brian Holly, "Since no two individuals view time . . . in exactly the same way we must speak of relative time . . . when investigating behavioural outcomes of human decision-making processes" (1978, p. 7). In business communication, in particular, relativity in the perception of time is readily apparent in the different individual perceptions of arguably static time. For example, the person giving a speech before a condemnatory or unfriendly audience may perceive an hour-long presentation as stretching out considerably longer than the clock indicates. The same speaker presenting before a highly receptive audience may be surprised to find that the time allotted for the speech passed much more quickly than expected.

The origin of this divergence between the physical measure and the individual perception of time was explained by Immanuel Kant, the eighteenth-century German philosopher. Kant asserted that time is not an objectively comprehensible phenomenon but rather a sensible intuition. As the example of the public speaker shows, the sources of Kant's notion of a sensible intuition of temporal conception may derive from the individual situation of the perceiver. In this regard, no two people can ever view any specific passage of time in the same way. The individual situations *of* the individuals—being innately different—create different temporal conceptions.

Yet individual situations do not result only in *divergent* conceptions of time. *Shared* individual experiences may result in shared temporal conception. Whole groups of people, while having somewhat different individual influences on their perceptions of time, still can view the passage of time in similar ways. On the simplest level, this can be illustrated in the relationship between the listeners and the speaker in a business presentation. A consultant may view the time elapsed in a presentation entirely differently from the businesspeople listening to the lecture because of the major difference in their individual situations. But the common act of listening that the members of the audience share is likely to make each member's conception of the time involved—even if still individually divergent—more similar to those of the other members than to the consultant's conception of the same period of time. This is because the consultant's behavior (speaker rather than listener) in relation to the businesspeople attending the lecture is more divergent than the individual members of the audience's relationship to one another.

This shared conception of time deriving from shared individual experience, in turn, can be extended to larger arenas of shared experience. To some extent, as biological creatures, all people share a common biological conception of time, which has some direct effects on the work environment. For example, biological temporal considerations influence how long a worker can go without sleep or even how long an employee will be healthy enough to work.

Yet shared conception of time goes far beyond merely biological considerations. Such factors as type of activity (as illustrated in the contrast between speaker and listener), degree of motivation, and the relative age of individuals all affect the perception not so much of time itself but of the duration between events that serve as markers of time.

TEMPORAL CONCEPTION AND CULTURE

The marker of time that concerns us most in this discussion, however, is cultural patterning. While much individual variance in temporal conceptions rests in personality differences, much of the variance also rests in that individual's culturally learned behavior. Each culture indoctrinates its members with socially reinforced principles regarding time.

Time is, as the title of Edward Hall's seminal work (1959) on the subject reflects, the "silent language" of cross-cultural communication. Many anthropologists (Sorokin and Merton, 1937; Kroeber, 1948; De Grazia, 1964; Lévi-Strauss, 1967; Maxwell, 1972; Hall, 1983) interested in the cross-cultural variability of temporal conception have concluded that nothing intrinsic in the human condition or nature at large leads people automatically to understand time in terms of clock or calendar units. Instead, as Doob (1971) points out, "Each society provides appropriate information for passing temporal judgment" (p. 60).

J. T. Fraser, founder of the International Society for the Study of Time, goes so far as to assert that to "become and remain a tribe, society or civilization, it was necessary for each to create and continuously maintain its *social present*. A carefully kept sequence of social presents is called a *schedule*" (1987, p. 190). Accepting Fraser's observation as essentially sound, we can see that scheduling and culture are inextricably intertwined, with one defining the other. As Fraser observes, this relationship is directly linked to communication:

> A group of people is able to form a tribe, a nation, or a civilization only if they can cooperate in some ways and share certain values. These conditions can only be met if there exists a social present maintained through communication. (1987, p. 196)

It is perhaps prudent to note that while some empirical evidence (particularly from the 1960s and early 1970s) exists to support cultural variability in the perception of time (Schwitzgebel, 1962; Melikian, 1969; Meade and Singh, 1970; Deręgowski, 1970; Doob, 1971), the most convincing and thorough treatments of temporal conception rest on anecdotal and nonempirical observation. While a need exists for more complete empirical study, the reasons for the predominance of nonempirical research may well rest in the difficulty in accurately describing time. As Jan Deręgowski (1980) has observed:

> A precise interpretation of data obtained in the course of [time] estimation experiments is difficult. A cross-cultural difference might under such circum-

stances arise out of any one or more of the following: (1) different attitude to time, (2) difference in familiarity with units of time (e.g., a minute may not have any specific meaning to the subject), and (3) differences in familiarity with numbers (e.g., a subject may say "100" whenever he means a large number). (p. 79)

Nevertheless, cultural patterning, as the individual perception of time shared by groups of people subject to the same influences, remains apparent in business communication.

For instance, in our earlier example, the members of the audience, as listeners, share a common individual experience regarding the time the lecture takes. Consequently, both audience member and consultant are likely to have a common conception of the amount of time that is allowable for the lecture.

If we accept Fraser's notion of culture as the product, at least in part, of a societally imposed social present maintained through communication, "the width of the social present is determined by the time necessary to make people take concerted action" (1987, p. 196). This conception of time is culturally learned. Time is compartmentalized according to cultural patterning, and that patterning differs from culture to culture.

For example, in the United States, both the consultant giving a lecture and businesspeople listening to the lecture probably expect that if the presentation is scheduled to last an hour, it will last an hour of physical time, even if the perception of the passing of that physical time differs. The lecture may even end five minutes sooner without notice.

If, however, the hour-long lecture ends after 65 minutes rather than the allotted 60 minutes, virtually all the audience members are likely to become irritated. If the lecture extends to 70 or 75 minutes, the speaker may be asked to finish, or audience members may leave to attend other appointments, even though the lecture is not over. Indeed, in the United States, audience members are likely to leave a speech that has gone 15 minutes over the scheduled time even if they believe that the information provided in the presentation will benefit them more than their next appointment. U.S. businesspeople may leave a speech that has extended an additional 15 minutes even if they do not have another commitment. Scheduled time, in the United States, is more important than the time actually needed to complete a given task.

Such a reaction to a presentation that extends beyond the allotted time is not universal. In Saudi Arabia, for example, scheduled time is *less* important than the time needed to complete a task. A lecture in Saudi Arabia scheduled for 60 minutes is allowed to go on for 75 minutes if the members of the audience believe that they will benefit more from listening to the speaker than from going to their next appointment. Predetermined schedules are usually more flexible in that country than in the United States. The difference in the U.S. and Saudi reaction to the lecture reflects a fundamental difference in the way members of a culture are conditioned to view time. The United States holds to the view of closely scheduled time, whereas Saudi Arabia has a looser view of scheduled time.

MONOCHRONIC AND POLYCHRONIC TEMPORAL CONCEPTION

The two attitudes described in the preceding section are by no means limited to the United States and Saudi Arabia. In fact, most societies can be characterized as following one of these two patterns, with the Saudi pattern somewhat more predominant. The two culturally derived concepts of time are called *monochronic* and *polychronic*. Table 8.1 delineates the salient features of both types of temporal conception. In our example, the U.S. approach to scheduled time is exemplary of the monochronic temporal conception. The Saudi pattern, in turn, illustrates the polychronic temporal conception.

Monochronic Business Cultures

In monochronic business cultures, members are taught to hold a monochronic temporal conception at least in the work environment. Monochronic business cultures, generally speaking, dominate the con-

Table 8.1 MONOCHRONIC AND POLYCHRONIC CHARACTERISTICS

	Monochronic U.S.	Polychronic
Interpersonal relations	Interpersonal relations are subordinate to preset schedule	Preset schedule is subordinate to interpersonal relations
Activity coordination	Schedule coordinates activity; appointment time is rigid	Interpersonal relations coordinate activity; appointment time is flexible
Task handling	One task handled at a time	Many tasks are handled simultaneously
Breaks and personal time	Breaks and personal time are sacrosanct regardless of personal ties	Breaks and personal time subordinate to personal ties
Temporal structure	Time is inflexible; time is tangible	Time is flexible; time is fluid
Work/personal time separability	Work time is clearly separable from personal time	Work time is not clearly separable from personal time
Organizational perception	Activities are isolated from organization as a whole; tasks are measured by output in time (activity per hour or minute)	Activities are integrated into organization as a whole; tasks are measured as part of overall organizational goal

ception of time in United States, anglophone Canada, Great Britain, Australia, New Zealand, Afrikaaner and British South Africa, Sweden, Norway, Denmark, Iceland, Germany, Luxembourg, Austria, the Netherlands, and the German portion of Switzerland. While fewer people are culturally patterned to hold a monochronic conception of time than a polychronic conception, the economic power of the monochronic cultures over the last two centuries makes the importance of monochronic temporal conception to business communication far greater than the collective population of these countries.

The word *monochronic* comes from the Greek and means "single time." Edward Hall, who coined the term, notes that in monochronic culture, "scheduling is used as a classification system that orders life" (1983, p. 48). In a monochronic conception, individuals handle tasks one at a time, according to preset schedules. In monochronic cultures, time—through scheduling—is seen as a coordinator of activity. Because it allows individuals to focus their attention on one concern at a time, they tend to view time as tangible—as being squandered, spent, lost, made up, or saved. In monochronic cultures, time has become such a key factor in day-to-day existence that most members of those cultures have difficulty seeing time in any other way. 'Monochronic time is arbitrary and imposed, that is, learned," Hall writes. "Because it is so thoroughly learned and so thoroughly integrated into our [monochronic] culture, it is treated as though it were the only natural and logical way of organizing life" (1983, pp. 48–49).

Monochronic conception often presents a stumbling block to those from polychronic cultures. Eva Kras, explaining the monochronic approach to time to a Mexican readership, warns that, in the United States,

> "time is money" and since money is what business is all about, every decision, every activity, every commitment—whether at work or at home—is controlled by the clock. The executive is under constant pressure in order to meet time commitments, and much of his personal life is thereby sacrificed. Lack of punctuality is considered almost a disgrace, and excuses are seldom accepted. Verbal commitments are considered as binding as written ones. Life moves by the clock, and any disrespect for time has serious repercussions. Everyday work life is often referred to as a treadmill: to succeed you must stay on it; if you step off, you are lost. (1988, p. 61)

Similarly, Gary Althen, writing for foreigners coming to the United States, notes:

> One of the more difficult things many foreign businessmen and students must adjust to in the States is the notion that time must be saved whenever possible and used wisely every day.
>
> In their efforts to use time wisely, Americans are sometimes seen by foreign visitors as automatons, unhuman creatures who are so tied to their clocks and their schedules that they cannot participate in or enjoy the human interactions that are the truly important things in life. "They are like little machines running around," one foreign visitor said. (1988, p. 14)

While Kras and Althen specifically deal with the United States, their observations are applicable to the Netherlands, Great Britain, Germany, or any other monochronic culture.

Althen's example in particular indicates that monochronic behavior may seem machinelike to those unaccustomed to it. This generalization can be broken down into several behavioral manifestations that more specifically show how monochronic conception affects business communication.

First, monochronic time emphasizes the schedule as a major (perhaps the prime) determinant of human behavior. People in monochronic cultures tend—particularly in the workplace—to adhere to preset appointments at the expense of personal relationships. The most easily seen manifestation of the primacy of schedules is the stress on punctuality. The protocol expert Sandra Snowden (1986), for example, warns that "the first rule for U.S. meetings is, *Be punctual!* Most executives operate on a tight schedule. If you arrive late, you may not have as much time as you would like" (p. 394) and that "schedules are carefully observed in Britain, and being five minutes late is frowned upon" (p. 169).

The monochronic adherence to schedule is also evident in the workplace in several more subtle ways. In a monochronic society, personal time and work time are separate precisely because they can be scheduled as such. Consequently, a clearer distinction between work and personal relationships is possible in strictly monochronic societies than in other cultures. Because relationships at work tend to be defined more by position than by friendship, personal feelings do not interfere with the adherence to schedule. It is difficult to tell a close friend to leave your office— even though she has not completed the business at hand—simply because her scheduled appointment time has elapsed. For this reason, close friendships are not encouraged in the workplace.

Second, a person whose job is appraised by the clock is regimented. The employee is expected to function without a break during scheduled work periods. Significantly, however, the worker's break time is sacrosanct. For instance, the typical British or U.S. manager—regardless of rank—knows not to insist that work on a project continue during a scheduled break. If workers agree to forfeit their break, the manager knows that they deserve praise and is likely to view their sacrifice as a personal favor.

Finally, because time is compartmentalized, members of monochronic cultures tend to view their functions as isolated from those of the rest of the organization. As Edward Hall has observed, they "are less likely to see their activities in context as part of the larger whole . . . [because] the job itself or even the goals of the organization are seldom seen as a whole" (1983, p. 51). Instead, a job is thought of as an accomplishment in time: bottles processed on a conveyer belt over an hour, widgets sold in a month, or profits reported to shareholders over a quarter of a year.

Polychronic Business Cultures

Despite the economic importance of the monochronic minority, most cultures are polychronic. Moreover, many (e.g., Italy, Portugal, France, Spain, Greece, Brazil, Mexico, Turkey, Egypt, and India, to name just a few) are trading powers whose importance is equal to or greater than that of many monochronic cultures. Generally speaking, most of Latin America, the Arabic-speaking nations, Africa (with the exception of British and Afrikaaner South Africa), southern and western Asia, the Caribbean, and southern Europe are polychronic.

The word *polychronic,* coined by Edward Hall from the Greek, means "many or multiple time." In polychronic cultures, several tasks are handled simultaneously rather than in scheduled succession (as in monochronic cultures). In our example of the U.S. and Saudi speeches, the Saudi lecturer's behavior reflected a polychronic approach.

In cultures characterized by polychronic conception, time is less tangible than in monochronic societies. This does *not* mean that polychronic cultures lack a conception of scheduling or time (a common misunderstanding on the part of members of monochronic cultures). Instead, they tend to view time as flexible, as Hall explains:

> For polychronic people, time is seldom experienced as "wasted," and is apt to be considered a point rather than a ribbon or a road, but that point is often sacred. An Arab will say, "I will see you before one hour," or "I will see you after two days." What he means in the first instance is that it will not be longer than an hour before he sees you and at least two days in the second instance. These commitments are taken quite seriously as long as one remains in the P-time [polychronic] pattern. (1984, p. 46)

Polychronic conception places greater emphasis on personal interaction than on schedules. For example, in polychronic cultures, a task is usually completed even if it is necessary to go beyond the time scheduled for doing so. The delay, in turn, forces the next task off schedule. Still, the people who have the next appointment are not expected to be offended or irritated by the delay, because they know that, in its time, their project will also be handled completely. Scheduling is approximate rather than specific. An appointment guarantees that an individual will be seen; it does not guarantee when.

The polychronic concept of scheduling has a parallel in one profession even in most monochronic cultures: medicine. The physician's office even in as monochronic a society as the United States is generally run on polychronic time. Patients generally expect to sit in the physician's waiting room beyond the time scheduled for the appointment. The understanding is that it is impossible to estimate accurately how much time each patient's treatment will take. Moreover, the waiting patients know that emergencies take priority over relatively routine care.

In polychronic cultures all workplace interactions—not just the doctor's office–run on polychronic time. Individuals expect their concerns to be handled fully by the person with whom they hold the appointment. The polychronic businessperson is likely to consider ridiculous the notion of refusing to see someone with an emergency simply because that person has no appointment (as is not uncommon in a Dutch or British company).

Polychronic concepts of scheduling often create conflicts in international dealings with members of monochronic cultures:

> Particularly distressing to Americans is the way in which appointments are handled by polychronic people. Being on time simply doesn't mean the same thing as it does in the United States. Matters in a polychronic culture seem in a constant state of flux. Nothing is solid or firm, particularly plans for the future; even important plans may be changed right up to the minute of execution. (Hall, 1984, p. 47)

While the concept of lateness exists, what constitutes lateness is considerably more flexible than in monochronic cultures. A polychronic person would be less likely to view time as something one can waste than would a monochronic individual.

Some polychronic cultures allow for greater delays than others. Arguably the most extreme example occurs in African nations. "In Nigeria," as one scholar has noted, "it may take several days to wait one's turn at a government office, so professional 'waiters' do it for you" (Argyle, 1982, p. 68).

More typical is the way in which businesspeople accommodate the 20- to 40-minute scheduling delays common in southern Europe and Latin America. Indeed, punctuality may actually prove to be disruptive. For instance, as Phyllis Harrison has observed in writing about Brazil, "one businessman arriving precisely on time might find the other not yet ready" (Harrison, 1983, p. 733). While *attempting* to show up at the appointed time is not necessarily out of the ordinary, both being *expected* to do so and *insisting on being seen* on schedule is not. Businesspeople generally build flexibility into their day to allow for delays, sometimes by arranging to work while waiting. Again, the Brazilian approach is typical:

> The Brazilian method of dealing with this unpredictability is to schedule appointments in one's office, so one can work while waiting, or agree to meet in the other's office, where he must appear sooner or later and where the secretary can acknowledge that the other kept the appointment. Even if the appointment is scheduled over lunch or cocktails, it is wise to arrange to meet in one or the other's office rather than in a restaurant or bar. (Harrison, 1983, p. 73)

Polychronic attitudes toward scheduling affect considerably more than appointments — including the performance of services or the delivery of goods according to preset schedules. Eva Kras describes what may happen in Mexico:

> A firm may say, "Yes, your shipment will be ready on Tuesday." You arrive on Tuesday to pick it up but find it is not ready. No one is upset or

embarrassed; they politely explain that the paper work has not yet been processed, or they give some similar explanation.

Time commitments are considered desirable objectives but not binding promises. Little concern is felt for the time wasted by the client in waiting or for the inconvenience of making several trips to accomplish a single task. (1988, p. 60)

Margaret Nydell, advising U.S. and British business people on how to trade with Arab cultures, warns:

Frequently, an Arab shopkeeper or someone in a service trade fails to have something done by a promised time. Be flexible; everyone expects delays. You will appear unreasonably impatient and demanding if you insist on having things finished at a precise time. This pertains to public services (such as getting a telephone connected), personal services, bus and train departures, customer services (where standing in long lines can be expected) and bureaucratic procedures. (1987, p. 60)

The fact that polychronic time deemphasizes the schedule as the prime determinant of behavior in the workplace does not support the stereotype among some monochronic cultures that polychronic societies consider delays as something desirable. Rather, delays do not have the negative associations that they have in monochronic cultures. As John Condon (1985) says about Mexico, "it is not so much that putting things off until *mañana* is valued, as some Mexican stereotypes would have it, but that human activities are not expected to proceed like clock-work" (p. 66). Time, in polychronic cultures, simply exists; it conveys virtually none of the unspoken messages and value judgments that dominate business communication in monochronic cultures.

Instead, interpersonal relationships supersede preset schedules. People in polychronic cultures — whether in the workplace or in social life — place greater importance on personal relationships than on scheduled commitments.

The diminished importance of schedules has several far-reaching consequences in the workplace. In a polychronic society, personal time and work time are not necessarily separate, precisely because they can never fully be scheduled as such. Thus, in many polychronic societies, no clear distinction exists between work and personal relationships, and the emphasis on personal ties in the workplace encourages a blurring of social and work relationships. Relationships at work tend, in fact, to be defined more by friendships than by positions.

Considerable time is spent in establishing a foundation for personal relationships before individuals enter into serious business negotiation. Hours or even days and weeks may be spent in discussing common friends, background, or experiences before one person feels adequate trust in another to conduct business with him or her. Generally, the beginning of a meeting or even an entire first meeting will focus on the establishment of rapport. Sondra Snowden's description of a meeting in Italy is typical of most polychronic cultures: "The first part of the meeting will be devoted to getting acquainted. It will please your hosts if you compliment their country and city, and express your general desire to establish an ongoing business relationship. Questions about local artistic and cultural events will be welcome" (1986, p. 195). Questions regarding who one might know or an invitation to enjoy food at the host's favorite luncheon spot is neither small talk nor an opening to discuss business, as may be the case in monochronic cultures. It is an offering for the two parties to develop enough of a personal relationship *to conduct* business. Business, in short, is preferably *not* conducted between total strangers. This type of approach is, as we have seen, exactly the opposite pattern of work behavior cultivated in monochronic societies. Indeed, a German or Briton is likely to see such introductory sessions as at best overly leisurely and at worst an irritating waste of time. The German or Briton should realize, however, that in polychronic cultures a business enterprise may be cut off if the establishment of personal relationships does not precede it.

Such relationships, moreover, have ramifications for the way business is conducted over the long term. Friendships and personal relationships must be nurtured and require frequent face-to-face communication. For instance, Almaney and Alwan have observed business in the Gulf nation of Oman:

> Omanis attach a high degree of importance to personal relationships. Business, therefore, is conducted almost entirely with companies which have a local presence; and frequent visits by the foreign firm's home representatives are virtually prerequisite for market penetration even after local representation is established. (1982, p. 249)

Indeed, even the *opportunity* to know about business possibilities may occur only if one is an insider (that is, part of a web of personal relationships) or, at the very least, if one has access to information *from* an insider. Again, the case of conducting business in Oman is illustrative: "Opportunities for consultants, architects, engineers, or contractors are not always published; information can best be obtained by a competent local representative" (Almaney and Alwan, 1982, p. 249). Because a polychronic conception encourages personal relationships to flourish in the workplace, loyalty to one's business counterparts tends to be stronger than in most monochronic cultures. In both cultures, people feel a greater sense of commitment to close personal friends and family than to strangers or casual acquaintances. In personal relationships, a degree of loyalty is established as well as an unwritten balance sheet of favors provided and repaid. In the polychronic workplace, however, those with whom one works *are* those to whom one has personal ties. Suppliers become the friends of their primary customers, an accountant acts as a client's confidante, and a boss is a sort of parental figure. As a result, personal time is not easily separable from work time.

As we discussed earlier, in a U.S. or British company, a subordinate's break time is sacrosanct, and managers understand that they cannot expect employees to give up their break to keep a project on schedule. The distinction is much less clear in a polychronic culture. In Nigeria, for example, a manager may well ask subordinates to work through a personal break, and the employees would be much less likely to feel resentment than their U.S. or British counterparts. While the workers are aware that such a request represents a favor to the manager, it also provides an opportunity to repay past favors or to establish debts for future favors. Moreover, because Nigerian managers are probably more aware, than a U.S. or British supervisor, of the personal life of any individual employee, they would infringe on the employees' personal time only if truly necessary and if various factors in the employee's personal life made it appropriate to do so.

Because people do not strictly adhere to schedules in polychronic cultures, tasks do not usually present themselves in an orderly, one-by-one succession. Indeed, as the term *polychronic* indicates, many tasks are handled simultaneously. Meetings are often interrupted.

Finally, because time is not compartmentalized, employees are more likely to have a wholistic view of their role within an organization. As Edward Hall has observed, a polychronic conception of work "even though technical by its very nature, keeps reminding the subordinate that his job is not only a system, but part of a larger system" (1983, p. 50–51).

TIME BUDGETING AND THE RANGE OF TEMPORAL PERSPECTIVE

Quite apart from differences in monochronic and polychronic orientations toward time, another variance in temporal perception may affect business communication. Cultures appear to vary in the way they budget time, and the range of temporal perspective held by their members. *Time budget* has been defined as the "record of a person's use of time over a given period" (Anderson, 1971, p. 353).

The British analysts Shapcott and Steadman (1978) have established, in their culturally transmitted theory of temporal conception, that time budgets are socially learned and hence a result of one's cultural milieu. Members of certain cultures may be more likely than others to view aspects of work more in the long run or more in the short run.

The importance to international business communication of cultural differences in time budget is marked. In the United States and some other countries, short-term goals are generally emphasized over long-term goals. This manifests itself in business communication geared toward positive accomplishments that managers can report in quarterly plans, and the consequent need for relatively quick responses to initiatives. By contrast, Japanese, Soviet and other cultures with a longer perspective allow more time for carefully considered responses to initiatives. While such mulling sacrifices speed, it may gain in foreseeing difficulties. As Charles Valentine, director of the Trade Advisory Service of the U.S. accounting firm Arthur Young, has observed that

> executives in the United States have tended to stress short-term return on investment, with a consequent emphasis on the quarterly period as the unit of planning. Many U.S. companies consider long-term planning to mean planning ahead a year or two — at most, three to five years. European and Asian firms, by contrast, stress a long-term orientation, generally perceived as planning ahead at least ten years. (Grand strategies can extend to fifteen or twenty years or even longer.)
>
> Admittedly, these differences in time sense are partly a matter of opinion. They are a cultural variable. (1988, pp. 70–71)

Again it should be emphasized that neither system is inherently superior to the other, just different.

ACCOMMODATING INTERCULTURAL DIFFERENCES IN TEMPORAL CONCEPTION

Several suggestions may prove useful in accommodating intercultural differences in temporal conception. In each case, flexibility is central. This is easier to suggest than to practice, since cultural conception of time is so deeply ingrained and pervades so many aspects of business communication.

First, determine to which type of temporal orientation the culture with which you are conducting business belongs. Signs of polychronic or monochronic orientation are often evident in initial topics of conversation and interaction. It is generally advisable, therefore, to follow the lead of a counterpart. Individuals from another culture who seem intent on conducting business more quickly than you are accustomed to are probably more monochronic than you in other ways as well, while people who discuss nonbusiness topics longer than your usual sense of prebusiness small talk permits are likely to be more polychronic than you.

The extremes of polychronic and monochronic behavior are relatively easy to assess. Thus you can predict with rough accuracy that Arab businesses are likely to be highly polychronic and that U.S. and northern Europeans are more monochronic than most other cultures. Predicting middle-range cultures may prove more problematic. French business, for example, can be characterized by both (monochronic) punctuality and a need to develop personal (polychronic) relationships in the workplace. French meetings, therefore, are likely to begin with discussions of a less businesslike subject matter, and to be scheduled to last longer than in completely monochronic cultures; at the same time, French schedules are adhered to more strictly than in more completely polychronic cultures.

Some cultures defy readily classifiable behavior as either polychronic or monochronic and may display different temporal orientation according to the setting. While adherence to schedule is likely to provide the best clue to a culture's general temporal orientation, the astute business person should remain wary of exceptions. For example, Japanese business culture is essentially monochronic in scheduling. At the same time, Japan has traditionally been more polychronic in orientation. Because the resultant emphasis on strong personal relationships is difficult to maintain in the office setting, after-hours business gatherings in social settings such as clubs or bars play an important role in Japanese business life. Such unofficial gatherings enable people to develop polychronic relationships of strong personal ties outside the formalized monochronic scheduling pattern of the workplace. Unlike other monochronic cultures, going out after work with business associates in Japan is virtually mandatory.

You should also stay alert to clues of regional differences in temporal orientation within a country. Thus, while Italy is, in general terms, polychronic, businesses in the south — in Calabria, Sicily, and Sardinia — are likely to be more polychronic than those in Tuscany, Lombardy, or Venice. Similarly, although Germany is basically monochronic, firms in Swabia tend to be more monochronically oriented than those in Bavaria.

Try to determine if the corporate culture or even professional culture of the people with whom you deal are typical of the temporal orientation of the society as a whole. In this chapter, for instance, we indicated that, despite the monochronic orientation of the United States, most medical doctors use a more polychronically oriented conception in their practice.

It is useful in conducting business with people of a different temporal conception from your own to recognize the logic in the different system. The logic may be foreign, but it is not absent. Thus, a businessperson from Germany may find a polychronic approach taken in Oman to be irrational, which is simply not the case. The Omani may delay getting down to business for what seems to the German an unreasonable time, engaging in personal details and small talk. The delay, however, will be worth the investment in time for the German once a personal relationship is developed, both in the profitability of the business and in the depth of commitment and loyalty the Omani is — once business is finally undertaken — likely to show.

Similarly, an Omani may find the Germans to be impulsive and aggressive. This behavior, however, does not necessarily indicate that the Germans are arrogant or unfriendly and therefore not to be fully trusted. The Germans may or may not be trustworthy on other grounds, but their rush to do business is a product of their culturally learned temporal orientation. The Omani, in fact, may find it worthwhile to provide early signs of probable — if not binding — business commitment, simply to enable the Germans to send information back to their home office of progress, which will allow them to continue discussing business long enough (in Omani terms) to create a lasting business relationship.

A vital piece of advice for dealing with people from cultures with a different temporal conception is to brief your superiors thoroughly on the implications of such cross-cultural differences. The most important means to accommodate differences in temporal orientation only indirectly involves the individuals actually conducting the business face to face. Effective business communicators can probably shift from one communication strategy to another to meet the demands of a particular goal or the needs of a given audience. What is *likely* to sabotage even the best business communicator's ability to shift strategy is external pressure.

External pressure manifests itself in two ways, depending on the temporal orientation of the culture. Businesspeople from monochronic cultures attempting to deal with businesses in polychronic cultures may be pressured to speed up negotiations or at least provide signs of progress. Sensitive businesspeople will probably recognize when speeding up negotiations or demanding adherence to arbitrary schedules will jeopardize potentially fruitful business relationships. Yet these communicators may be unable to devote the time necessary to such a project or provide the face-to-face interaction needed to cultivate the business relationship precisely because such policy issues as time allotted to negotiations and travel expenses are determined at a higher level in the corporation.

On the other hand, the superiors of businesspeople from a polychronic culture frequently criticize their subordinates for acting impulsively or even appearing too anxious for business when trading with those from monochronic cultures. Moreover, demands made too early for upper-level indications of commitment — even if not binding — are likely to be misunderstood, since such assurances would be unnecessary in situations where people had established the adequate personal relationships and the trust on which polychronic business is built. The person actually conducting business may understand and respect the need for strict scheduling and commitments, but his or her ability to act accordingly is constrained from above.

Those who set the policies governing the international businessperson's actions should be made aware of the effects of culturally divergent temporal orientation on the progress and nature of business. If those executives understand the implications of culturally variant temporal conception, they can decide whether such a negotiation is worth the added costs in time (if dealing with more polychronic cultures) or risk (if dealing with more monochronic cultures). Only then will the people with authority to bend the rules be able to do so in a manner that allows accommodation of such cultural differences.

Chapter
9

Conclusion

*T*he nuances of international business—defined as any business conducted across national borders—are different from those of solely domestic business. The fundamental principles of domestic business apply abroad but with added complexities. Just as business communication takes on new dimensions in international settings, complicating factors take place in matters involving accounting, taxation, financial market analysis, law, marketing, product design, production, and corporate organization and control in the global business environment. Success in international negotiations rests on ability in all fields of business, of which international communication is just one important element.

Traditionally, the study of the technical elements of business have been emphasized at the expense of international behavioral and communication aspects. This has particularly been the case in countries such as the United States, which have emphasized their own large domestic market over foreign markets. Henry Lane and Joseph DiStefano have noted:

> The human element in managing effectively across cultures is just as important and, sometimes, more important than the technical or business elements. However, the "people" skills are likely to be less developed than are the technical or business skills. This is not to mean that on some absolute scale people skills are more important than technical or business skills, and that the ability to work with people alone will lead to success. A package of skills is needed to be successful—business, technical and people skills. People chosen to work in other countries, or to work in the international side of business, generally will have developed a basic set of business and technical skills. The skills of relating to and working with people from other cultures are needed to

complement those basic skills. If a person does not have these skills, he or she may never get the opportunity to use their business or technical skills. (1988, pp. 6–7)

It is unlikely that, armed only with international business skills, an individual will succeed in international business. Still, it is probably better to have mediocre technical skills and excellent international business communication skills than to have excellent technical skills and poor international business communication skills.

To this end, this book has emphasized those factors most needed to detect the key elements as well as the nuances of international business communication. We have seen how international business communication is affected by the culturally linked variables of language, environment and technological considerations, social organization, contexting, authority conception, nonverbal communication, and temporal conception.

Ultimately, you are only as effective as your ability to communicate what you know. The international businessperson with poor communication skills will communicate poorly what he or she knows. The excellent international business communicator, by contrast, will convey what he or she knows clearly and fully. In such a case, even if your knowledge is limited, at least you will be able to convey a full understanding of that limited knowledge. To this end, we hope that this book has provided a method to supplement the reader's other international and domestic technical and business skills with a means for developing effective international business communication skills.

Bibliography

Addington, D. W. "The Relationship of Selected Vocal Characteristics to Personality-Perceptions." *Speech Monographs,* vol. 35, 1968, pp. 492–503.

Adler, N. J. *International Dimensions of Organizational Behavior.* Boston: Kent, 1986.

Agar, M. *Independents Declared: The Dilemma of Independent Trucking.* Washington, D.C.: Smithsonian Institution, 1985.

Ajami, F. *The Arab Predicament: Arab Political Thought and Practice Since 1967.* Cambridge: Cambridge University Press, 1981.

Almaney, A. J., and Alwan, A. J. *Communicating with the Arabs: A Handbook for the Business Executive.* Prospect Heights, Ill.: Waveland Press, 1982.

Althen, G. *American Ways: A Guide for Foreigners in the United States.* Yarmouth, Me.: Intercultural Press, 1988.

"American Attitudes Toward Europe: A New Gallup Poll." *Europe.* March 1988, pp. 22–24.

Anderson, J. "Space-Time Budgets and Activity Studies in Urban Geography and Planning." *Environment and Planning.* 1971, 3:53–368.

Ardagh, J. *France Today.* Harmondsworth, Middlesex: Penguin Books, 1987.

Ardagh, J., *Germany and the Germans: An Anatomy of Society Today.* New York: Harper & Row, 1987.

Argyle, M. "Inter-cultural Communication." *Cultures in Contact: Studies in Cross-Cultural Interaction* (Stephen Bochner: ed.). Oxford: Pergamon Press, 1982, pp. 61–79.

Barnlund, D. C. "Public and Private Self in Communicating with Japan." *Business Horizons.* March–April 1989, pp. 32–40.

Barnlund, D. C. *Public and Private Self in Japan and the United States: Communicative Styles of Two Cultures.* Tokyo: Simul Press, 1975.

Barthes, R. *Système de la Mode.* Paris: Seuil, 1967.

Bartlett, C. A., and Ghosal, S. "Tap Your Subsidiaries for Global Reach." *Harvard Business Review*. November–December 1986, pp. 87–94.

Bartova, E. "Images of the Woman and the Family." *Images of the World in the Year 2000: A Comparative Ten-Nation Study* (H. Ornauer, H. Wiberg, A. Sicinski, and J. Galtung: eds.). The Hague, Netherlands: Mouton, 1976, pp. 255–278.

Bass, B. M., and Burger, P. C. *Assessment of Managers: An International Comparison*. New York: The Free Press, 1979.

Basso, K. H. "'To Give Up on Words': Silence in Western Apache Culture." *Language and Social Context* (Pier Paolo Giglioli: ed.). Harmondsworth, Middlesex: Penguin Books, 1972, pp. 67–86.

Beamer, L. "Intercultural Business Communication: Modelling the Learning Process." Paper presented at the *Association for Business Communication International Convention*, San Antonio, Texas, November 8, 1990.

Beebe, S. "Eye Contact: A Nonverbal Determinant of Speaker Credibility." *Speech Teacher*. 1974, 23:21–25.

Beier, E. G., and Zautra, A. J. "Identification of Vocal Communication of Emotions Across Cultures." *Journal of Consulting and Clinical Psychology*, 34, 1972, p. 166.

Berger, C., and Calabrese, R. "Some Explorations in Initial Interactions and Beyond: Toward a Developmental Theory of Interpersonal Communication." *Human Communication Research*. 1975, 1:99–112.

Berlitz, C. *Native Tongues*. New York: Perigee Books, 1982.

Bharati, A. "The Self in Hindu Thought and Action." *Culture and Self: Asian and Western Perspectives* (Anthony J. Marsella, George DeVos, and Francis L. K. Hsu: eds.). New York: Tavistock, 1985, pp. 185–230.

Birdwhistell, R. L. *Kinesics and Context: Essays on Body Motion Communication*. Philadelphia: University of Pennsylvania Press, 1970.

Birks, J. S., and Sinclair, C. A. "Economic and Social Implications of Current Developments in the Arab Gulf: The Oriental Connection." *Social and Economic Development in the Arab Gulf* (Tim Niblock: ed.). New York: St. Martin's Press, 1980, pp. 135–150.

Blainey, G. *The Minerals of Broken Hill* (1982), cited in *The Global Marketplace*, by Milton Moskowitz, 1987, p. 111.

Blaxall, M., and Reagan, B. (eds.). *Women and the Workplace: The Implications of Occupational Segregation*. Chicago: University of Chicago Press, 1976.

Bliss, M. *Northern Enterprise: Five Centuries Of Canadian Business*. Toronto: McClelland and Stewart, 1987.

Boas, F. "Introduction to *The Handbook of American Indian Language*." *Language, Culture and Society: A Book of Readings* (Ben G. Blount: ed.). Cambridge, Mass.: Winthrop, 1974, pp. 12–31.

Bonavia, D. *The Chinese*. New York: Lippincott & Crowell, 1980.

Bond, M. H., Leung, K., and Wan, K. C. "How Does Cultural Collectivism Operate? The Impact of Task and Maintenance Contributions on Reward Distribution." *Journal of Cross-Cultural Psychology*, vol. 13, no. 2, June 1982, pp. 186–200.

Borisoff, D., and Merrill, L. A. *The Power to Communicate: Gender Differences as Barriers.* Prospect Heights, Ill.: Waveland Press, 1985.

Borisoff, D., and Merrill, L. "Teaching the College Course on Gender Differences as Barriers to Conflict Resolution." *Advances in Gender and Communication Research* (L. B. Nadler, M. K. Nadler, and W. R. Todd-Mancillas: eds.) Lanaham, MD: University Press of America, 1987, pp. 351–363.

Borisoff, D., and Victor, D. A. *Conflict Management: A Communication Skills Approach.* Englewood Cliffs, N. J.: Prentice Hall, 1989.

Boserup, E. *Woman's Role in Economic Development.* London: Allen & Unwin, 1970.

Boucher, J. D., and Carlson, G. E., "Recognition of Facial Expression in Three Cultures," *Journal of Cross-Cultural Psychology,* 11, 1980, pp. 263–80.

Brandt, V. S. R. "Stratification, Integration, and Challenges to Authority in Contemporary South Korea." Washington, D. C.: Department of State External Research Document, August 331, 1983.

Brown, R. L., and Herndl, C. G. "An Ethnographic Study of Corporate Writing: Job Status as Reflected in Written Text." *Functional Approaches to Writing: Research Perspectives* (Barbara Couture: ed.). Norwood, N.J.: Ablex, 1986.

Bruner, J. S. "On the Perception of Incongruity: A Paradigm." *Jerome S. Bruner —Beyond the Information Given: Studies in the Psychology of Knowing* (Jeremy M. Anglin: ed.). New York: Norton, 1973, pp. 68–83.

Bullock, N., Dickens, P., Shapcott, M., and Steadman, P. "Time Budgets and Model of Urban Activity Patterns." *Social Trends.* 1974, 5:45–63.

Burgoon, J. K., and Saine, T. *The Unspoken Dialogue.* Boston: Houghton Mifflin, 1978.

Calder, N. *Technopolis: Social Control of the Uses of Science.* New York: Clarion/ Simon & Schuster, 1969.

Campbell, D. "On the Conflicts Between Biological and Social Evolution Between Psychology and Moral Tradition." *American Psychologist,* vol. 30, no. 12, 1975, pp. 1103–1126.

Campbell, R. W., *Soviet Economic Power: Its Organization, Growth and Challenge.* 2nd ed. Boston: Houghton Mifflin, 1966.

Careless, J. M. S. *Canada—A Story of Challenge.* Toronto: Macmillan, 1965.

Carroll, R. *Cultural Misunderstandings: The French–American Experience* (Carol Volk: trans.). Chicago: University of Chicago Press, 1988.

Cash, T. F., Gillen, B., and Burns, D. S. "Sexism and 'Beautyism' in Personnel Consultant Decision Making." *Journal of Applied Psychology.* 1977, 62:301–310.

Charlesworth, W. R., and Kreutzer, M. A. "Facial Expressions of Infants and Children." *Darwin and Facial Expression* (Paul Ekman: ed.). New York: Academic Press, 1973.

Chesanow, N. *The World Class Executive.* New York: Rawson, 1985.

Cheskin, L. *How to Predict What People Will Buy.* New York: Liveright, 1957.

Childs, M. *Sweden: The Middle Way on Trial.* New Haven: Yale University Press, 1980.

Christopher, R. C. *Second to None: American Companies in Japan*. New York: Fawcett Columbine, 1986.

Clark, R. *The Japanese Company*. New Haven: Yale University Press, 1979.

Clatterbuck, G. W. "Attributional Confidence and Uncertainty in Initial Interactions." *Human Communication Research*. 1979, 5:147–157.

Cleveland, J. N., and Landy, F. J. "The Effects of Person and Job Stereotypes on Two Personnel Decisions." *Journal of Applied Psychology*. 1983, 68: 609–619.

Clifford, J. "Introduction: Partial Truths." *Writing Culture: The Poetics and Politics of Ethnography* (James Clifford and George E. Marcus: eds.). Berkeley: University of California Press, 1986, pp. 1–26.

Clifford, J. *The Predicament of Culture*. Cambridge, Mass.: Harvard University Press, 1988.

Condon, J. C. *Good Neighbors: Communicating with the Mexicans*. Yarmouth, Me: Intercultural Press, 1985.

Condon, J. C. *With Respect to the Japanese: A Guide for Americans*. Yarmouth, Me: Intercultural Press, 1984.

Condon, J., and Yousef, F. *An Introduction to Intercultural Communication*. New York: Macmillan, 1985.

Conner, W. "The Impact of Homelands upon Diasporas." *Modern Diasporas in International Politics* (Gabriel Sheffer: ed.). New York: St. Martins Press, 1986.

Copeland, L., and Griggs, L. *Going International: How to Make Friends and Deal Effectively in the Global Marketplace*. New York: Random House, 1985.

Crabbs, R. A. "Work Motivation in the Culturally Complex Panama Canal Company." *Academy of Management Proceedings*. 1973, pp. 119–126.

Crooks, L. A. *An Investigation of Sources of Bias in the Prediction of Job Performance: A Six-Year Study*. Princeton, N.J.: Educational Testing Service, 1972.

Dahl, R. *Who Governs?* New Haven: Yale University Press, 1961.

Dandridge, T. C. "The Life Stages of a Symbol: When Symbols Work and When They Can't." *Organizational Culture* (Peter J. Frost, Larry F. Moore, Meryl Reis Louis, Craig C. Lundberg, and Joanne Martin: eds.). Beverly Hills: Sage, 1985, pp. 141–153.

Davitz, J. R. *The Communication of Emotional Meaning*. New York: McGraw-Hill, 1964.

De Benedetti, C. "How to Make Europe More Competitive." *Wall Street Journal*. March 30, 1988, p. 19.

Decker, J. S. "Marija Dixon: Building Bridges Between East and West." *Detroit Marketplace*. December, 1990, pp. 20–26.

De Grazia, S. *Of Time, Work, and Leisure*. New York: Doubleday Anchor Books, 1964.

DeMente, B. *Chinese Etiquette and Ethics in Business*. Lincolnwood, Ill.: NTC Business Books, 1989.

DeMente B. *Korean Etiquette and Ethics in Business*. Lincolnwood, Ill.: NTC Business Books, 1988.

DeMente, B. *The Japanese Way of Doing Business: The Psychology of Management in Japan*. Englewood Cliffs, N.J.: Prentice-Hall, 1981.

DeMente, B. *Made in Japan*. Lincolnwood, Ill.: Passport Books, 1987.

De Meuse, K. P. "A Review of the Effects of Non-Verbal Cues on the Performance Appraisal Process." *Journal of Occupational Psychology*. 1987, 67:207–226.

Denmark, F. L., and Waters, J. A. "Male and Female in Children's Readers: A Cross-Cultural Analysis." *Basic Problems in Cross-Cultural Psychology* (Y. H. Poortinga: ed.). Amsterdam: Swets and Zeitlinger, 1977.

Deręgowski, J. B. "Effect of Cultural Value of Time upon Recall." *British Journal of Social and Clinical Psychology*. 1970, 9:37–41.

Deręgowski, J. B. "Perception." *Handbook of Cross-Cultural Psychology: Basic Processes* (Harry C. Triandis and Walter Lonner: eds.). Boston: Allyn & Bacon, 1980, 3:21–116.

DeVos, G., Marsella, A. J., and Hsu, F. L. K. "Introduction: Approaches to Culture and Self." *Culture and Self: Asian and Western Perspectives* (Anthony J. Marsella, George DeVos, and Francis L. K. Hsu: eds.). New York: Tavistock, 1985, pp. 2–23.

Dicks, B. *The Israelis: How They Live and Work*. New York: Praeger/Holt, Rinehart and Winston, 1977.

Dodd, C. H. *Dynamics of Intercultural Communications*. Dubuque, Iowa: William C. Brown, 1982.

Doob, L. W. *Patterning of Time*. New Haven: Yale University Press, 1971.

Douglas, M. "Do Dogs Laugh? A Cross-Cultural Approach to Body Symbolism." *Journal of Psychosomatic Research*. 1971, 15:387–390.

Douglas, M. *How Institutions Think*. Syracuse, N.Y.: Syracuse University Press, 1986.

Douglas, M. *Natural Symbols: Explorations in Cosmology*. Harmondsworth, Middlesex: Penguin Books, 1973.

Douglas, M. *Purity and Danger: An Analysis of Concepts of Pollution and Taboo*. Harmondsworth, Middlesex: Penguin Books, 1970.

Doyle, J. "Cultures Can Be Bridged." Birmingham *Observer and Eccentric*. October 26, 1989, p. 17.

Doz, Y. L., and Prahalad, C. K. "Headquarters Influence and Strategic Control in MNC's." *Sloan Management Review*. Fall 1981, pp. 15–29.

Drucker, P. F. *The Frontiers of Management*. New York: Harper & Row, 1986.

Drucker, P. F. *Technology, Management and Society*. New York: Harper & Row, 1970.

Duncker, K. "The Influence of Past Experience upon Perceptual Properties." *American Journal of Psychology*, 1939, 52:255–265.

Edwards, H. *Sociology of Sport*. Homewood, Ill.: Dorsey Press, 1973.

Eiler, M., and Victor, D. A. "Genre and Function in the Italian and U.S. Business Letter." Paper presented at *The Sixth Annual Conference on Languages and Communications for World Business and the Professions*, Ann Arbor, Mich., April 6–9, 1988.

Ekman, P., and Friesen, W. V. "Hand Movement." *Journal of Communication.* 1972, 22:353–354.

Ekman, P., and Friesen, W. V. "Nonverbal Behavior and Psychotherapy." *The Psychology of Depression: Contemporary Theory of Research* (R. J. Friedman and M. M. Katz: eds.). Washington, D.C.: Winston, 1974.

Ekman, P., and Friesen, W. V. "The Repertoire of Nonverbal Behavior: Categories, Origins, Usage and Coding." *Semiotica.* 1969, 1:49–98.

Ekman, P., Friesen, W. V., et al. "Universal and Cultural Differences in the Judgments of Facial Expressions and Emotion." *Journal of Personality and Social Psychology.* 1987, 53:4:712–717.

Ekman, P., Friesen, W. V., and Ellsworth, P. *Emotion in the Human Face: Guidelines for Research and an Integration of Findings.* Elmsford, N.Y.: Pergamon Press, 1972.

Ekman, P., Sorenson, E. R., and Friesen, W. V. "Pan-Cultural Elements in Facial Displays of Emotion." *Science.* 1969, 164:3875:86–88.

Ellegard, A., Hägerstrand, T., and Lenntorp, B. "Activity Organization and the Generation of Daily Travel: Two Further Alternatives." *Economic Geography,* 1977, 53:126–152.

Ellsworth, P., and Ludwig, L. "Visual Behavior in Social Interaction. *Journal of Communication.* 1972, 22:353–354.

Ellul, J. *The Technological Society.* New York: Vintage, 1964.

Elon, A. *The Israelis.* London: Sphere Books, 1972.

Engbersen, R. and Engbersen, G. "The Death of Dutch?" *The World and I,* vol. 6, no. 4, April 1991, pp. 638–645.

Etzioni, A. *A Comparative Analysis of Complex Organizations: On Power, Involvement, and Their Correlates.* New York: Free Press, 1975.

Ewing, J. S. "Review of 'The Lessons to Be Learned—American Industry in Developing Countries.'" *Columbia Journal of World Business.* November–December 1969, pp. 83–84.

Exline, R. V. "Exploration in the Process of Person Perception: Visual Interaction in Relation to Competition, Sex, and the Need for Affiliation." *Journal of Personality.* 1963, 31:1–10.

Falk, J. S. "Social Dialects." *Language: Introductory Readings.* 3rd ed. (Virginia P. Clark, Paul A. Eschholz, and Alfred F. Rosa: eds.). New York: St. Martin's Press, 1981, pp. 508–511.

Fast, J. *Body Language.* New York: M. Evans & Co., 1970.

Feldman, S. P. "Culture, Charisma, and the CEO: An Essay on the Meaning of High Office." *Human Relations.* 1986, 39:3:211–228.

Ferguson, G. *Signs and Symbols in Christian Art.* Oxford: Oxford University Press, 1954. Rev. ed. 1976.

Fidler, J. *The British Business Elite.* London: Routledge & Kegan Paul, 1981.

Fieg, J. P. *Thais and North Americans.* Yarmouth, Me.: Intercultural Press, 1980.

Fields, G. *From Bonsai to Levis, When West Meets East: An Insider's Surprising Account of How the Japanese Live.* New York: New American Library, 1983.

Fisher, G. *Mindsets: The Role of Culture and Perception in International Relations.* Yarmouth, Me.: Intercultural Press, 1988.

Foucault, M. *Power/Knowledge.* New York: Pantheon, 1980.

Fox, S. *The Mirror Makers: A History of American Advertising and Its Creators.* New York: Vintage Books, 1985.

Fraser, J. T. *Time: The Familiar Stranger.* Amherst: University of Massachusetts Press, 1987.

Furnham, A., and Bochner, S. *Culture Shock: Psychological Reactions to Unfamiliar Environments.* London: Methuen, 1986.

Gallimore, R., Boggs, J. W., and Jordan, C. *Culture, Behavior and Education: A Study of Hawaiian-Americans.* Beverly Hills, Calif.: Sage, 1974.

Garland, J., and Farmer, R. N. *International Dimensions of Business Policy and Strategy.* Boston: Kent, 1986.

Garvey, C. *Children's Talk.* Cambridge, Mass.: Harvard University Press, 1984.

Garvin, G. "International English: Some Strings Attached." *Communications at Work: Proceedings of the 1985 Combined Eastern/Canadian ABCA/Canadian STC Meeting* (Herb Smith: ed.). Toronto, 1985, pp. 53–63.

Gates, D. "Reed to New York: Drop Dead." *Newsweek.* January 30, 1989, p. 68.

George, C. S. *Supervision in Action: The Art of Managing Others.* 3rd ed. Reston, Va.: Reston, 1982.

Gibbons, K. "Communication Aspects of Women's Clothes and Their Relation to Fashionability." *British Journal of Social and Clinical Psychology.* 1969, 8:301–312.

Goldman, M. *Gorbachev's Challenge: Economic Reform in the Age of High Technology.* New York: Norton, 1987.

Gorbachev. M. *Perestroika: New Thinking for Our Country and the World.* New York: Harper & Row, 1987.

Gorden, R. L. *Living in Latin America: A Case Study in Cross-Cultural Communication.* Lincolnwood, Ill.: National Textbook, 1974.

Gordon, G., and McGoon, C. "The British Are Coming!" *Communication World.* December 1986, pp. 20–27.

Gregory-Smith, D. "Science and Technology in East Asia." *Philosophy East and West.* 1979, 29:221–236.

Gudykunst, W. B. "Uncertainty Reduction and Predictability of Behavior in Low and High Context Cultures: An Exploratory Study. *Communication Quarterly.* Winter 1983, 31:1:49–55.

Gudykunst, W. B., and Ting-Toomey, S. "Culture and Affective Communication." *American Behavioral Scientist.* January–February 1988, 31:3:384–400.

Gupta, N., Beehr, T. A., and Jenkins, G. D. "The Relationship Between Employee, Gender, and Supervisor-Subordinate Cross-Ratings." *Academy of Management.* 1980, 40:396–400.

Habermas, J. *Theorie des kommunikativen Handelns. Band I, Handlungsrationalität und gesellschaftliche Rationalisierung.* (English trans.: Thomas McCarthy). Boston: Beacon Press, 1984.

Hägerstrand, T. "Tartorsgrupper som Regionsamhållen, in Regioner att Leva I." *Rapport från ERU.* Stockholm: Allmänna Förlaget, 1972, pp. 141–173.

Hägerstrand, T. "What About People in Regional Science?" *Papers of the Regional Science Association.* 1970, 24:7–21.

Haglund, E. "Japan: Cultural Considerations." *International Journal of Intercultural Relations.* 1984, 8:61–76.

Haire, M., Ghiselli, E. E., and Porter, L. W. *Managerial Thinking: An International Study.* New York: Wiley, 1966.

Haitani, K. *Comparative Economic Systems: Organizational and Managerial Perspectives.* Englewood Cliffs, N.J.: Prentice-Hall, 1986.

Halberstam, D. *The Reckoning.* New York: Morrow, 1986.

Hall, E. T. *Beyond Culture.* New York: Doubleday Anchor Books, 1976.

Hall, E. T. *The Dance of Life: The Other Dimensions of Time.* Garden City, N.Y.: Anchor Press/Doubleday, 1983.

Hall, E. T. *The Hidden Dimension.* New York: Doubleday, 1966.

Hall, E. T. *The Silent Language.* New York: Doubleday, 1959.

Hall, E. T., and Hall, M. R. *Hidden Differences: Doing Business with the Japanese.* Garden City, N.Y.: Doubleday Anchor Books, 1987.

Hall, J. *Nonverbal Sex Differences: Communication, Accuracy and Expressive Style.* Baltimore: John Hopkins University Press, 1984.

Hardesty, D. L. "Introduction: Ecological Anthropology." *Perspectives in Cultural Anthropology* (H. Applebaum: ed.). Albany: State University of New York Press, 1987, pp. 270–278.

Harrison, P. A. *Behaving Brazilian: A Comparison of Brazilian and North American Social Behavior.* Cambridge, Mass.: Newberry House, 1983.

Harrison, R. P. *Beyond Words: An Introduction to Nonverbal Communication.* Englewood Cliffs, N.J.: Prentice-Hall, 1974.

Hawkings, S. W. *A Brief History of Time: From the Big Bang to Black Holes.* New York: Bantam Books, 1988.

Hayakawa, S. I. *Through the Communication Barrier: On Speaking, Listening, and Understanding.* New York: Harper & Row, 1979.

Hayden, S. L., and Koepplin, L. W. "International Business, Foreign Languages and International Studies: Analysis of Relationships and Recommendations." *President's Commission on Foreign Languages and International Studies: Background Papers and Studies.* Washington, D.C.: Government Printing Office, 1979.

Heider, G. "New Studies in Transparency, Form and Color." *Psychologische Forschung.* 1932, 17:13–55.

Heller, T. "Changing Authority Patterns: A Cultural Perspective." *Academy of Management Review.* 1985, 10:3:488–495.

Henley, N. M. *Body Politics: Power, Sex, and Nonverbal Communication.* Englewood Cliffs, N.J.: Prentice-Hall, 1977.

Herzberg, F., Mausner, B., and Snyderman, B. B. *The Motivation to Work.* New York: Wiley, 1959.

Heslin, R. "Steps Toward a Taxonomy of Touching." Paper presented to the Midwestern Psychological Association, Chicago, May 1974, cited in M. L. Knapp, *Essentials of Nonverbal Behavior.* New York: Holt, Rinehart & Winston, 1980.

Hildebrandt, H. W. "Communication Barriers Between German Subsidiaries and Parent American Companies." *Michigan Business Review.* July 1973, p. 677.

Hines, G. H. "Achievement, Motivation, Occupations, and Labor Turnover in New Zealand." *Journal of Applied Psychology.* 1973, 58:3:313–317.

Hobsbawm, E. J. *Industry and Empire.* London: Weidenfeld and Nicolson, 1968.

Hofstede, G. *Culture's Consequences: International Differences in Work-Related Values.* Beverly Hills, Calif.: Sage, 1984.

Hofstede, G. "Motivation, Leadership and Organization: Do American Theories Apply Abroad?" *Organizational Dynamics.* Summer, 1990, pp. 42–63.

Holly, B. P. "The Problem of Scale in Time-Space Research." *Time and Regional Dynamics* (T. Carlstein, D. N. Parkes, and N. J. Thrift: eds.). London: Arnold, 1978, pp. 5–18.

Horovitz, J. H. *Top Management Control in Europe.* New York: St. Martin's Press, 1980.

Huck, J. R., and Bray, D. W. "Management Assessment Center Evaluations and Subsequent Job Performance of White and Black Females." *Personnel Psychology.* 1976, 29:13–30.

Huizinga, J. H. *Dutch Civilization in the Seventeenth Century.* New York: Doubleday, 1968.

Hulbert, J. M., and Brandt, W. K. *Managing the Multinational Subsidiary.* New York: Holt, Rinehart and Winston, 1980.

Illich, I. *Toward a History of Needs.* New York: Pantheon, 1977.

Ivens, M. "Behind the Organization Man." *Twentieth Century.* Spring 1965, 17:3:21–22.

Izard, C. E. "Cross-Cultural Perspectives on Emotion and Emotion Communication." *Handbook of Cross-Cultural Psychology* (Harry Triandis and Walter Lonner: eds.). Vol. 3. Boston: Allyn & Bacon, 1980, pp. 185–221.

Izard, C. E. *The Face of Emotion.* New York: Appleton-Century-Crofts, 1971.

Jaggi, B. "Need Importance of Indian Managers." *Management International Review.* 1979, 19:1:107–113.

"Japanese Women as Hidden Resource." *Wall Street Journal.* June 17, 1988, p. 17.

Jaspers, J. M. F., and Frazer, C. "Attitudes and Social Representations." *Social Representations* (S. Moscovici and R. Farr; eds.). Cambridge; Cambridge University Press, 1981.

Jensen, J. V. "Perspectives on Nonverbal Intercultural Communication." *Intercultural Communication: A Reader.* (L. A. Samovar and R. E. Porter; eds.). Belmont, Calif.: Wadsworth, 1982, pp. 260–276.

Johnson, F. "The Western Concept of Self." *Culture and Self: Asian and Western Perspectives* (Anthony J. Marsella, George DeVos, and Francis L. K. Hsu: eds.). New York: Tavistock, 1985, pp. 91–138.

Joseph, M. *Sociology for Business.* Oxford: Polity Press, 1989.

Kamarck, A. M. *The Tropics and Economic Development.* Washington, D.C.: World Bank, 1976.

Kamioka, K. *Japanese Business Pioneers.* Union City, Ca.: Heian International, 1988.

Kaplan, D., and Manners, R. A. *Culture Theory.* Englewood Cliffs, N.J.: Prentice-Hall, 1972.

Kennedy, G. *Doing Business Abroad.* New York: Simon & Schuster, 1985.

Ketcham, H. *Color Planning for Business and Industry.* New York: Harper, 1958.

Kim, C., and Lawson, C. M. "The Law of the Subtle Mind: The Traditional Japanese Conception of Law," 28, *The International & Comparative Law Quarterly,* 1979, pp. 491–513.

Klar, H. "Reintegration Difficulties for Europeans After Their Return from Developing Countries." *Medico,* no. 10. Mannheim: Boehringer, 1968.

Kluckhohn, C. *Mirror for Man: A Survey of Human Behavior and Social Attitudes.* Greenwich, Conn.: Fawcett, 1964.

Knapp, M. L. *Essentials of Nonverbal Communication.* New York: Holt, Rinehart and Winston, 1980.

Kohls, L. R. *Developing Intercultural Awareness.* Washington, D.C.: SIETAR, 1981.

Kolde, E. S. *The Multinational Company.* Lexington, Mass.: Heath, 1974.

Konishi, A., Kondo, T., and Ogata, S. "Behind the Screen: Three Prominent Japanese Candidly Discuss the Future of Their Country and Its Changing Relations with the United States." *The World and I.* November 1990, 5:11:44–51.

Koren, L. *283 Useful Ideas from Japan for Entrepreneurs and Everyone Else.* San Francisco: Chronicle Books, 1988.

Kotkin, J., and Kishimoto, Y. "Theory F." *Inc.* April 1986, pp. 53–60.

Kramer, E. "The Judgment of Personal Characteristics and Emotions from Nonverbal Properties of Speech." *Psychological Bulletin.* 1963, 60:408–420.

Kras, E. S. *Management in Two Cultures: Bridging the Gap Between U.S. and Mexican Managers.* Yarmouth, Me.: Intercultural Press, 1988.

Kroeber, A. L. *Anthropology.* New York: Harcourt Brace Jovanovich, 1948.

Kroeber, A. L., and Kluckhohn, C. *Culture: A Critical Review of Concepts and Definitions.* New York: Random House, 1954.

"Labor Letter." *Wall Street Journal.* December 29, 1987, p. 1.

Landy, D., and Sigall, H. "Beauty Is Talent: Task Evaluation as a Function of the Performer's Physical Attractiveness." *Journal of Personality and Social Psychology.* 1974, 29:299–304.

Lane, H., and DiStefano, J. *International Behavior: From Policy to Practice.* Scarborough, Ont.: Nelson Canada, 1988.

Lansing, P., and Wechselblatt, M. "Doing Business in Japan: The Importance of the Unwritten Law." *International Lawyer.* 1983, 17:4:647–666.

Lasswell, H. D., and Kaplan. A. *Power and Society.* New Haven: Yale University Press, 1950.

Latour, B., and Woolgar, S. *Laboratory Life: The Social Construction of Scientific Facts.* Beverly Hills, Calif.: Sage, 1979.

Laurent, A. "The Cross-Cultural Puzzle of International Human Resource Management." *Human Resource Management.* 1986, 25:1:91–102.

Laurent, A. "The Cultural Diversity of Western Conceptions of Management." *International Studies of Management and Organizations.* 1983, 13:1–2:79–96.

Leach, E. "Culture and Social Cohesion: An Anthropologist's View." *Science and Culture* (Gerald Horton: ed.). Boston: Beacon Press, 1965.

Leathers, D. G. *Nonverbal Communication Systems.* Boston: Allyn & Bacon, 1976.

Lennon, D. "English Is Everywhere." *Europe.* May 1989, pp. 5–7.

Leonard, W. M. II. *A Sociological Perspective of Sport.* 2nd ed. Minneapolis: Burgess, 1984.

Lévi-Strauss, C. *Structural Anthropology.* Garden City, N.Y.: Doubleday Anchor, 1967.

Lim, L. Y. C. "Capitalism, Imperialism, and Patriarchy: The Dilemma of Third-World Women Workers in Multinational Factories. *Women, Men and the International Division of Labor* (June Nashand and Maria P. Fernandez-Kelly: eds.). Albany: State University of New York Press, 1983, pp. 70–91.

Lindsay, C. P., and Dempsey, B. L. "Experiences in Training Chinese Business People to Use U.S. Management Techniques." *Journal of Applied Behavioral Science.* 1985, 21:1:65–78.

Livingstone, J. M. *The International Enterprise.* New York: Wiley, 1975.

Lorénzen, L. *Of Swedish Ways.* New York: Harper & Row/Barnes & Noble Books, 1964.

Lüscher, M. *Lüscher-Test Anleitung und Farbtafeln: Klinischer Test zur psychosamatischen Persönlichkeitsdiagnostik.* Basel: Test-Verlag, 1948.

Lüscher, M. "Die Farbwahl als psychosomatischer Test." *Deutsches Medizinisches Journal.* 1961, 12:11:406ff.

Lüscher, M. *Psychologie der Farben.* Basel: Test-Verlag, 1949.

Lüscher, M. *Psychologie und Psychotherapie als Kultur.* Basel: Test-Verlag, 1955.

Lüscher, M. *Verständis und Mißverständnis in der Psychologie der Farben.* Basel: Test-Verlag, 1959.

Lyon, M. *Belgium.* New York: Walker, 1971.

Mackey, S. *The Saudis: Inside the Desert Kingdom.* Boston: Houghton Mifflin, 1987.

Malcolm, A. H. *The Canadians.* Toronto: Bantam Books, 1986.

Mandelbaum, D. G. (ed.) *Selected Writings of Edward Sapir.* Berkeley: University of California Press, 1949.

March, R. M. *The Japanese Negotiator: Subtlety and Strategy Beyond Western Logic.* Tokyo: Kodansha International, 1988.

Marcus, G. E. "Contemporary Problems of Ethnography in the Modern World System." *Writing Culture: The Poetics and Politics of Ethnography* (J. Clifford and G. E. Marcus: eds.) Berkeley: University of California Press, 1986, pp. 155–193.

Martin, J. N., and Hammer, M. R. "Behavioral Categories of Intercultural Communication Competence: Everyday Communicators' Perceptions." *International Journal of Intercultural Relations.* 1989, 13:3:303–332.

Maslow, A. H. *Motivation and Personality.* New York: Harper & Row, 1954.

Matsumoto, M. *The Unspoken Way: Harage—Silence in Japanese Business and Society.* Tokyo: Kodansha International, 1988.

Maxwell, R. J. "Anthropological Perspectives." *The Future of Time: Man's Temporal Environment* (H. Yaker, H. Osmond, and F. Cheek: eds.). London: Hogarth Press, 1972.

Mazrui, A. "The Robes of Rebellion: Sex, Dress and Politics in Africa." *The Body Reader: Social Aspects of the Human Body* (T. Polhemus: ed.). New York: Pantheon Books, 1978, pp. 196–217.

McCaffery, J. A. "Independent Effectiveness: A Reconsideration of Cross-Cultural Orientation and Training." *International Journal of Intercultural Relations.* 1986, 10:2:159–177.

McCaffrey, J. A., and Hafner, C. R. "When Two Cultures Collide: Doing Business Overseas." *Training and Development Journal.* October, 1985, pp. 26–31.

McClelland, D. C. *The Achieving Society.* Princeton, N.J.: Van Nostrand Reinhold, 1961.

McCrum, R., Cran, W., and MacNeil, R. *The Story of English.* New York: Viking, 1986.

McGregor, D. *The Human Side of Enterprise.* New York: McGraw-Hill, 1960.

Mead, G. H. "Mind." *Mind, Self and Society* (C. W. Morris: ed.). Chicago: University of Chicago Press, 1934.

Meade, R. D., and Singh, L. "Motivation and Progress Effects on Psychological Time in Sub-cultures of India." *Journal of Social Psychology.* 1970, 80:3–10.

Melikian, L. "Acculturation, Time Perspective and Feeling Tone: A Cross-Cultural Study of Perception of the Days." *Journal of Social Psychology.* 1969, 79:273–298.

Mendenhall, M., and Oddou, G. "The Dimensions of Expatriate Acculturation: A Review." *Academy of Management Review.* 1985, 10:1:39–47.

Merriam, C. E. *Political Power: Its Composition and Incidence.* New York: McGraw-Hill, 1934.

Mesthene, E. G. "Symposium: The Role of Technology in Society—Some General Implications of the Research of the Harvard University Program on Technology with Society." *Technology and Culture.* 1969, 10:4, cited in Terpstra and David, 1985.

Michaels, J. "Why Heinz Went Sour in Brazil." *Advertising Age.* December 5, 1988, pp. 61, 67.

Miller, J. D., Drayton, J., and Lyon, T. *USA–Hispanic South America Culture Capsules.* Rowley, Mass.: Newbury House, 1979.

Miller, S. "Understanding Europeans." *Management Review.* 1987, 76:11:56–58.

Molloy, J. T. *Dress for Success.* New York: Warner Books, 1975.

Molloy, J. T. *The Woman's Dress for Success Book.* New York: Warner Books, 1977.

Morain, G. G. "Kinesics and Cross-Cultural Understanding." *Toward Internationalism: Readings on Cross-Cultural Communication.* 2nd ed. (L. F. Luce and E. C. Smith: eds.). Cambridge, Mass.: Newbury House, 1987, pp. 117–142.

Moreira, M. "As the World Turns." *Advertising Age.* April 2, 1990, pp. 16–17, 35.

Morita, A. *Made in Japan: Akio Morita and SONY.* New York: New American Library, 1986.

Morris, D., Collett, P., Marsh, P., and O'Shaughnessy, M. *Gestures: Their Origins and Distribution.* Briarcliff Manor, N.Y.: Stein and Day, 1979.

Moskowitz, M. *The Global Marketplace: 102 of the Most Influential Companies Outside America.* New York: Macmillan, 1987.

Moskowitz, M. Levering, R., and Katz, M. *Everybody's Business: A Field Guide to the 400 Leading Companies in America.* New York: Currency/Doubleday, 1990.

Muller, S. "Universities Are Turning Out Highly Skilled Barbarians." *U.S. News & World Report.* November 10, 1980, pp. 30–31.

Negandhi, A. R. *International Management.* Newton, Mass.: Allyn & Bacon, 1987.

Nierenberg, G. I., and Calero, H. H. *How to Read a Person Like a Book.* New York: Pocket Books, 1971.

Nydell, M. *Understanding Arabs: A Guide for Westerners.* Yarmouth, Me. Intercultural Press, 1987.

Oh, T. K. "Theory Y in the People's Republic of China." *California Management Review.* 1976, 19:2:77–84.

Ohmae, K. *Beyond National Borders: Reflections on Japan and the World.* Homewood, Ill.: Dow-Jones, Irwin, 1987.

Ohmae, K. *Triad Power: The Coming Shape of Global Competition.* New York: Free Press, 1985.

Packard, V. *The Hidden Persuaders.* New York: McKay, 1957.

Park, F. "Class Stratification in Socialist Societies." *British Journal of Sociology.* 1969, 20:4.

Parkes, D. N., and Thrift, N. J. *Times, Spaces, and Places: A Chronogeographic Perspective.* New York: Wiley, 1980.

Pascale, R. T., and Athos, A. G. *The Art of Japanese Management: Applications for American Executives.* New York: Warner Books, 1981.

Pascarella, P., DiBianca, V., and Gioja, L. "The Power of Being Responsible." *Industry Week.* December 5, 1988, pp. 41–50.

Peirce, C. S. *Collected Papers.* (Charles Hartshorne and Paul Weiss: eds.). 8 vols. Cambridge: Cambridge University Press, 1931–1966.

Peters, T. "Symbols, Patterns, and Settings: An Optimistic Case for Getting Things Done." *Organizational Dynamics.* 1978, 7:3–23.

Pfeffer, J. "Management as Symbolic Action: The Creation and Maintenance of Organizational Paradigms." *Research in Organizational Behavior* (Larry L. Cummings and Barry M. Staw: eds.). Greenwich, Conn.: JAI Press, 1981, 3:1–52.

Phatak, A. *International Dimensions of Management.* 2nd ed. Boston: Kent Publishing, 1989.

Prosser, M. H. *The Cultural Dialogue.* Washington, D. C.: SIETAR, 1985.

Pye, L. W. *Asian Power and Politics: The Cultural Dimensions of Authority.* Cambridge, Mass.: Belknap Press, 1985.

Radcliffe-Brown, A. R. "On Social Structure." *Perspectives in Cultural Anthropology* (Herbert Applebaum: ed.). Albany: State University of New York Press, 1987, pp. 121–146.

Reddy, K. P. "Impact of Culture on Organizational Design." *Vikalpa.* April 1984, 9:143–153.

Reitz, J., and Graf, G. *Similarities and Differences Among Mexican Workers in Attitudes to Worker Motivation.* Bloomington: Indiana University Press, 1973.

Rheingold, H. *They Have a Word for It.* Los Angeles: Tarcher, 1988.

Ricks, D. A. *Big Business Blunders: Mistakes in Multinational Marketing.* Homewood, Ill.: Dow-Jones Irwin, 1983.

Ricks, D. A., and Czinkota, M. R. "International Business: An Examination of the Corporate Viewpoint." *Journal of International Business Studies.* Fall 1979, 10:97–100.

Ricks, D. A., Fu, M. Y. C., and Arpan, J. S. *International Business Blunders.* 2nd ed. Columbus, Ohio: GRID, 1974.

Rigby, J. M. "The Challenge of Multinational Team Development." *Journal of Management Development.* 1987, 6:3:65–72.

Robson, K. S. "The Role of Eye to Eye Contact in Maternal-Infant Attachment." *Journal of Child Psychology.* 1967, 8:13–25.

Rogers, P. S. "The Impact of Context on Managerial Writing: Managers Choose Narrative for Dealer Contact Reports." *1988 Proceedings of the 53rd National and 15th International Convention of the Association for Business Communication — Global Implications for Business Communications: Theory, Technology and Practice* (Sam J. Bruno: ed.). Houston, 1988, pp. 23–39.

Rosch, M., and Segler, K. "Communication with Japanese." *Management International Review.* 1987, 27:4:56–67.

Rose, C. "Reflections on the Nation of Time Incorporated in Hägerstrand's Time-Geographic Model of Society." *Tidjschrift voor Economische en Sociale Geografie,* 68:48–50.

Rosen, B., and Jerdee, T. H. "The Influence of Sex Role Stereotypes on Personnel Decisions." *Journal of Applied Psychology.* 1973, 59:44–48.

Rosenfeld, L. B., and Plax, T. G. "Clothing as Communication." *Journal of Communication.* 1977, 27:24–31.

Rosenthal, R., et al. "Assessing Sensitivity to Nonverbal Communication: The PONS Test." *Division 8 Newsletter.* Division of Personality and Social Psychology of the American Psychological Association, January, 1974, pp. 1–3.

Rosenthal, R., and DePaulo, B. M. "Sex Differences in Eavesdropping on Nonverbal Cues." *Journal of Personality and Social Psychology.* 1979, 37:273–285.

Rosenthal, R., Hall, J., DiMatteo, M., Rogers, P., and Archer, D. *Sensitivity of Nonverbal Communication: The PONS Test.* Baltimore: John Hopkins University Press, 1979.

Ross, M. "Football Red and Baseball Green." *The Study of Sociology* (Peter I. Rose: ed.). New York: Random House, 1977, 111–119.

Rossman, M. L. *The International Businesswoman: A Guide to Success in the Global Marketplace.* New York: Praeger, 1986.

Rowland, D. *Japanese Business Etiquette: A Practical Guide to Success with the Japanese.* New York: Warner Books, 1985.

Rubin, L. B. *Worlds of Pain: Life in the Working-Class Family.* New York: Basic Books, 1976.

Russell, B. *Powers: A New Social Analysis.* New York: Norton, 1938.

Rybczynski, W. *Taming the Tiger: The Struggle to Control Technology.* New York: Viking Penguin, 1983.

Sampson, A. *The Changing Anatomy of Britain.* London: Hodden and Stoughton, 1982.

Sathe, V. *Culture and Related Corporate Realities.* Homewood, Ill.: Irwin, 1985.

Saussure, F. *Course in General Linguistics* (Charles Bally and Albert Sechehage: eds.; Roy Harris: trans.). London: Duckworth, 1915, 1983.

Schiller, H. I. *Communication and Cultural Domination.* White Plains, N.Y.: Sharpe, 1976.

Schiller, Z., and Kapstein, J. "On the Verge of a World War in White Goods: Heated Battles Lie Ahead as Big Appliance Makers Go Global." *Business Week.* November 2, 1987, pp. 91–98.

Schlesinger, R. B. *Comparative Law: Cases, Tests, Materials.* 3rd ed. Mineola, N.Y.: Foundation Press, Inc./University Casebooks Series, 1970.

Schloßstein, S. *Trade War: Greed, Power, and Industrial Policy on Opposite Sides of the Pacific.* New York: Congdon and Weed, 1984.

Schmitt, N., and Hill, T. E. "Sex and Race Compositions of Assessment Center Groups as a Determinant of Peer and Assessor Ratings." *Journal of Applied Psychology.* 1977, 62:428–435.

Schmitt, N., and Lappin, M. "Race and Sex as Determinants of the Mean and Variance of Performance Ratings." *Journal of Applied Psychology,* 65, 1980, pp. 428–435.

Schneider, D. J. "Implicit Personality Theory: A Review." *Psychological Bulletin.* 1973, 79:294–309.

Schneier, C. E., and Beusse, W. E. "The Impact of Sex and Time in Grade on Management Rating in the Public Sector: Prospects for the Civil Service Reform Act." *Proceedings of the Academy of Management.* 1980, 40:329–333.

Schwab, D. P., and Heneman, H. G. "Age Stereotyping in Performance Appraisal." *Journal of Applied Psychology.* 1978, 63:573–578.

Schwitzgebel, R. "The Performance of Dutch and Zulu Adults on Selected Perceptual Tests." *Journal of Social Psychology.* 1962, 57:73–77.

Seelye, H. N. *Teaching Culture: Strategies for Intercultural Communication.* Lincolnwood, Ill.: National Textbook, 1984.

Seligman, S. D. *Dealing with the Chinese: A Practical Guide to Business Etiquette in the People's Republic Today.* New York: Warner Books, 1989.

Settle, R. B., and Alreck, P. L. *Why They Buy: American Consumers Inside and Out.* New York: Wiley, 1986.

Shapcott, M., and Steadman, P. "Rhythms of Urban Activity." *Human Activity and Time Geography.* (T. Carlstein, D. N. Parkes, and N. J. Thrift: eds.). Vol. 2. London: Arnold, 1978, pp. 49–74.

Shaver, P., Schwartz, J., Kirson, D., and O'Connor, C. "Emotion Knowledge: Further Explorations of a Prototype Approach." *Journal of Personality and Social Psychology.* 1987, 52:1061–1086.

Shils, E. "Center and Periphery." *The Logic of Personal Knowledge.* Glencoe, Ill.: Free Press, 1961, pp. 117–130.

Shirk, S. L. *Competitive Comrades.* Berkeley: University of California Press, 1982.

Shrout, P. E., and Fiske, D. W. "Nonverbal Behaviors and Social Evaluation." *Journal of Personality.* 1981, 49:115–128.

Shuter, R. "Proxemics and Tactility in Latin America." *Journal of Communication.* 1976, 23:46–52.

Shuy, R. W. "Dialects: How They Differ." *Language: Introductory Readings.* 3rd ed. (Virginia P. Clark, Paul A. Eschholz, and Alfred F. Rosa: eds.). New York: St. Martin's Press, 1981, pp. 485–507.

Simon, B. "Canada Expands Its Third World Exports." *Financial Times.* April 27, 1984, p. 8.

Singer, M. R. *Intercultural Communication: A Perceptual Approach.* Englewood Cliffs, N.J.: Prentice-Hall, 1987.

Smith, H. *The Russians.* New York: Quadrangle, 1976.

Smolowe, J. "A Mountain Moves." *Time.* August 7, 1989, pp. 24–26.

Snowdon, S. *The Global Edge: How Your Company Can Win in the International Marketplace.* New York: Simon & Schuster, 1986.

Solo, S. "Japan Discovers Woman Power." *Fortune.* June 19, 1989, pp. 153–158.

Solomon, J. *The Signs of Our Time. Semiotics: The Hidden Messages of Environments, Objects, and Cultural Images.* Los Angeles: Tarcher, 1988.

Sorokin, P. A., and Merton, R. K. "Social Time: A Methodological and Functional Analysis." *American Journal of Sociology.* 1937, 42:615–629.

Steiner, G. *After Babel: Aspects of Language and Translation.* London: Oxford University Press, 1975.

Stephens, D., Kedia, B., and Ezell, D. "Managerial Need Structures in U.S. and Peruvian Industries." *Management International Review.* 1979, 19:27–39.

Stern, D. *The First Relationship: Infant and Mother.* Cambridge, Mass.: Harvard University Press, 1977.

Terpstra, V., and David, K. *The Cultural Environment of International Business.* 2nd ed. Cincinnati: South-Western, 1985.

Ting-Toomey, S. "Toward a Theory of Conflict and Culture." *Comunication, Culture, and Organizational Processes* (William B. Gudykunst, Lea P. Stewart, and Stella Ting-Toomey: eds.). Beverly Hills, Calif.: Sage, 1985, pp. 71–86.

Tirkkonen-Condit, S. "Argumentation in English and Finnish Editorials." *Across the Lines of Discipline* (Frans Van Eemeren, Rob Grootendorst, J. Anthony Blair, and Charles A. Willard: eds.). Dordrecht, Netherlands: Foris, 1987, pp. 374–378.

Tirkkonen-Condit, S. "Explicitness vs. Implicitness of Argumentation: An Intercultural Comparison." Paper presented at the Colloquium on the Role of Argument in the Creation of Community, Venice, August 7–11, 1988.

Trager, G. L. "Paralanguage: A First Approximation." *Studies in Linguistics.* 1958, 13:1–12.

Train, J. *Famous Financial Fiascos.* New York: Potter/Crown, 1985.

Trasker, P. *The Japanese: A Major Exploration of Modern Japan.* New York: Talley Books/Dutton, 1987.

Tugendhat, C. *The Multinationals.* Harmondsworth, Middlesex: Penguin Books, 1971.

Valentine, C. F. *The Arthur Young International Business Guide.* New York: Wiley, 1988.

Van Fleet, D., and Al-Tuhaih, S. "A Cross-Cultural Analysis of Perceived Leader Behaviors." *Management International Review.* April 1979, 19:81–88.

Vargas, M. F. *Louder Than Words: An Introduction to Nonverbal Communication.* Ames: Iowa State University Press, 1986.

Varner, I. I. "A Comparison of American and French Business Communication." *Journal of Business Communication.* Fall 1988, 25:4:55–65.

Varner, I. I. "Communication Between Headquarters and Foreign Subsidiaries: A Review of the Literature." Paper presented at the Association for Business Communication International Convention, San Antonio, November 9, 1990.

Victor, D. A. "Franco-American Business Communication Practices: A Survey." *World Communication.* 1987, 16:2:157–175.

"Viewpoint: Letters." *Advertising Age.* June 29, 1987, p. 20.

Wardhaugh, R. *How Conversation Works.* Oxford: Blackwell, 1985.

Weber, M. *The Protestant Ethic and the Spirit of Capitalism* (Talcott Parsons: trans.). New York: Scribner, 1958.

Weeks, F. F. "Communication at Sea." *English for International Communication* (C. J. Brumfit: ed.). Oxford: Pergamon Press, 1982.

Weiner, M. "Labor Migrations as Incipient Diasporas." *Modern Diasporas in International Politics* (Gabriel Sheffer: ed). New York: St. Martin's Press, 1986, pp. 47–74.

Wendelken, D. J., and Inn, A. "Nonperformance Evaluation: A Laboratory Phenomenon?" *Journal of Applied Psychology.* 1981, 66:149–158.

"West Germany's Competitive Advantage." *Fortune.* June 19, 1989, p. 36.

Whorf, B. L. *Collected Papers on Metalinguistics.* Washington, D.C.: Department of State, Foreign Service Institute, 1952.

Williams, F. "The Psychological Correlates of Speech Characteristics: On Sounding Disadvantaged." *Journal of Speech and Hearing Research.* 1970, 13:472–488.

Williams, J. E., and Best, D. L. *Measuring Sex Stereotypes: A Thirty Nation Study.* Beverly Hills, Calif.: Sage, 1982.

Willis, D. K. *Klass: How Russians Really Live.* New York: Avon Books, 1985.

Willis, P. *Learning to Labour: How Working Class Kids Get Working Class Jobs.* New York: Columbia University Press, 1981.

Winston, G. C. *The Timing of Economic Activities: Firms, Households, and Markets in Time-Specific Analysis.* Cambridge: Cambridge University Press, 1982.

World Data Annual. Chicago: Encyclopaedia Britannica, 1991.

Wysocki, B., Jr. "In Japan, They Even Have Cram Schools for the Cram Schools." *Wall Street Journal.* January 13, 1988, pp. 1, 16.

"Young People, Nations Have Higher Mobility." *The Wall Street Journal,* May 2, 1991, p. B-1.

Zeldin, T. *The French.* New York: Vintage Books, 1984.

Zuckerman, M., Amidon, M. D., Bishop, S. E., and Pomerantz, S. D. "Face and Tone of Voice in the Communication of Deception." *Journal of Personality and Social Psychology.* 1982, 32:347–357.

Zurcher, L. and Meadow, A. "On Bullfights and Baseball: An Example of Social Institutions." *Sport: Readings from a Sociological Perspective* (Eric Dunning: ed.). Toronto: University of Toronto Press, 1972, pp. 111–119.

Acknowledgments

Page 6   Glen Fischer, *Mindsets: The Role and Perception in International Relations*. Yarmouth, Maine: Intercultural Press, 1988.

Page 10   Reprinted with permission from the April 2, 1990, Creativity supplement of *Advertising Age*. Copyright Crain Communications Inc., 1990.

Page 17   From *Native Tongues* by Charles Berlitz. Copyright 1982 by Charles Berlitz. Reprinted by permission of Grosset & Dunlap.

Page 34   Reprinted with permission from *Advertising Age*, June 29, 1987. Copyright Crain Communications Inc., 1987.

Page 36   David Lennon, "English is Everywhere," *Europe*, May 1989, pp. 5–7.

Page 60   *1991 Britannica World Data*, Chicago: Encyclopædia Britannica, Inc.

Page 66   J.S. Decker, "Marija Dixon: Building Bridges Between East and West." Detroit Marketplace, December 1990, pp. 20–26.

Page 79   John C. Condon, *Good Neighbors: Communications with The Mexicans*. Yarmouth, Maine: Intercultural Press, 1985.

Page 82   S. Mackey, *The Saudis: Inside the Desert Kingdom*. Boston: Houghton Mifflin Company, 1987.

Page 94   G. Gordon and C. McGoon, "The British Are Coming!" *Communication World*, December 1986, pp. 20–27.

Page 126   P. Lansing and M. Wechselblatt, "Doing Business in Japan: The Importance of the Unwritten Law," *International Lawyer*, 1983, 17:4, pp. 647–666. Reprinted by permission of the American Bar Association.

Page 143   M. Rosch, and K. Segler, "Communication with Japanese," *Management International Review*, 1987, 27:4:56–67.

Page 148   From *The Dance of Life* by Edward T. Hall. Copyright 1983 by Edward T. Hall. Used by permission of Doubleday, a division of Bantam Doubleday Dell Publishing Group, Inc.

Page 155   J.A. McCaffrey and C.R. Hafner, "When Two Cultures Collide: Doing Business Overseas," *Training and Development Journal*, October 1985, pp. 26–31.

Page 171   S.P. Feldman, "Culture, Charisma, and the CEO: An Essay on the Meaning of High Office," *Human Relations*, 1986, 39:3, pp. 211–228.

Page 175   Reprinted with permission from NTL Institute, "Experiences in Training Chinese Business People to Use U.S. Management Techniques," by

Cindy P. Lindsay & Bobby L. Dempsey, *Journal of Applied Behavioral Science*, Vol. 21, No. 1, pp. 65–78, copyright 1985.

Page 178   Geert Hofstede, *Culture's Consequences: International Differences in Work-Related Values*. Beverly Hills, California: SAGE Publications, 1984. Reprinted by permission of Sage Publications, Inc.

Page 195   Marjorie Fink Vargas, *Louder Than Words: An Introduction to Nonverbal Communication*. Ames, Iowa: Iowa State University Press, 1986.

Page 207   J. Doyle, "Cultures Can Be Bridged," *The Birmingham Observer and Eccentric*, October 26, 1989, p. 17.

Name Index

Culture and Nation Index

Afghanistan, 28
Africa, 7, 17, 36, 57, 78, 79, 83, 154,
    172, 204, 207, 226, 237, 238. *See also*
    individual countries or regions
'Aina Pumehana, 183–184
Albania, 27
Algeria, 28–29, 38, 69, 129
Apache, Western, 153–154
Arabs, 4, 25, 78, 80, 113, 130, 143,
    145–146, 152, 156, 160, 162–164,
    191, 198, 204, 207, 215, 220, 225,
    237, 239, 242. *See also individual*
    countries
Arab World. *See* Arabs; Middle East; North
    Africa; Persian Gulf
Argentina, 103, 178, 193
Asia, 7, 57, 71, 78, 87, 97, 107, 111, 145,
    162, 164, 172, 173, 175, 176, 181,
    188, 193, 206, 219, 220, 237, 238,
    239, 240, 231, 242. *See also individual*
    countries
Australia, 16, 17, 36, 48, 56, 60, 64–66,
    68, 69, 79, 100, 102, 103, 107, 128,
    172, 178, 218, 219, 221–222, 224,
    226, 230, 235
Austria, 8, 34, 36, 57, 99, 103, 177, 178,
    235

Bangladesh, 60, 223
Belgium, 8, 10, 13, 16, 28, 36, 41, 56, 60,
    103, 119, 178, 189, 198–199
Bolivia, 23, 28, 69
Botswana, 28
Brazil, 26, 36, 56, 59–60, 103, 178, 193,
    194, 237, 238
Britain. *See* United Kingdom
Bulgaria, 27, 195

Burma (Myanmar), 69, 219
Burundi, 28, 69

Cambodia, 206
Cameroon, 28
Canada, 11, 13, 16, 27–28, 36, 38, 54,
    59, 60, 66, 68, 69, 79, 92, 100,
    102–103, 113, 116, 126, 128, 172,
    178, 189–190, 195, 206, 209–211,
    212, 218, 219, 220, 223–224, 226,
    235. *See also* North America
Caribbean, the, 7, 237
Central America. *See* Latin America
Chad, 28, 69
Chile, 103, 178
China, People's Republic of, 36, 43, 48,
    59, 60, 73, 74, 79, 163, 164, 165,
    175, 176, 181, 194, 201, 219. *See also*
    Taiwan
Colombia, 69, 99, 103, 162, 178, 199,
    202–203, 212
Comoros, 28
Costa Rica, 212
Culture. *See also* Multiculturalism
    and communication, 6–7
    definition of, 2–3, 6–7, 12–13
    early acquisition of, 6, 193, 196, 226
    and group behavior, 6, 27–29,
        101–106, 114–115
    and historical influences on, 23, 24, 25
    and MNCs, 2, 8–9, 54, 56, 57
    and nation states, 12–13, 54, 56,
        123–124
    and subcultures, role of in, 27, 31,
        34–35, 114, 141–142, 183–184,
        207, 243

Subject Index